# Marriages

*of*

# Claiborne & Campbell

# Counties, Tennessee

# Marriages

*of*

# Claiborne County,

# Tennessee,

### 1838-1850

*&*

# Campbell County,

# Tennessee,

### 1838-1853

*Compiled by*
**EDYTHE RUCKER WHITLEY**

CLEARFIELD

Reprinted for
Clearfield Company, Inc. by
Genealogical Publishing Co., Inc.
Baltimore, Maryland
1996, 2002

Library of Congress Catalogue Card Number 83-81460
International Standard Book Number 0-8063-1041-3
Made in the United States of America

# Introduction

LAIBORNE COUNTY was erected in 1801 from parts of Grainger and Hawkins counties, and Campbell County from parts of Anderson and Claiborne five years later. Both counties, therefore, besides being among the oldest in the state, were situated in the direct path of the settlers moving westward from North Carolina and Virginia and of those who took the northern route through the Cumberland Gap. They were also in the path of the settlers who followed the Clinch River into Middle Tennessee or who sought homes in the border counties of southeastern Kentucky.

This book comprises the earliest surviving marriage records of both of these strategically-placed counties. The records date from 1838 when marriage registers came into official use in the state. Earlier records of marriage, loose bonds and licenses, for example, are no longer extant, and, in the case of Claiborne County at any rate, were almost certainly lost in a fire.

With regard to the marriage records the reader should be reminded that the first date given in each entry is the date of issue of either the marriage bond or license. The date following (in parentheses) is the date the marriage was performed. If no date of marriage is given, then the single date provided, usually accompanied by the reference "No Return," refers merely to the date of issue of the marriage bond or license and does not *prove* that a marriage actually took place.

*Edythe Rucker Whitley*
Nashville, Tennessee

Jesse L. Jones and Martha Welch, June 30, 1838. Thomas
L. Davis, J.P. (July 3, 1838).
Thos. J. Lanham and Eliza Green, July 25, 1838. Thomas
L. Davis, J.P. (July 25, 1838).
Matthew Bussel and Lurana Johnstan, May 24, 1838.
Thomas L. Davis, J.P. (May 24, 1838).
Isaac Carmac (Carmack) and Camfret Hail, Mar. 14, 1838.
Adam Yearry, J.P. (Mar. 27, 1838).
Pleasant Chadwell and Elizabeth Bowman, Mar. 13, 1838.
Adam Yearry, J.P. (Mar. 13, 1838).
Joseph Wadkins and Catharine Thomas, Jan. 9, 1838.
Archibald Bales, J.P. (Jan. 9, 1838).
John Berry and Harrett Kid, Dec. 27, 1837. Peter Neil,
J.P. (Dec. 29, 1837).
John Baker and Permdy Vancy, Feb. 21, 1838. John
McNeil, J.P. (Feb. 22, 1838).
Martin Cadle and Martha J. Bruster, Feb. 19, 1838.
Thos. L. Davis, J.P. (Feb. 19, 1838).
Briant Baker and Martha J. Locke, Feb. 9, 1838. Thomas
L. Davis, J.P. (Feb. 14, 1838).
Heram Hoskins and Kissah Locke, Jan. 3, 1838. Adam
Yearry, J.P. (Jan. 4, 1838).
Robert Quay and Sarah Carroll, Jan. 7, 1838. Archd.
Bales, J.P. (Jan. 7, 1838).
Elihugh Baker and Marcyann Read, Mar. 10, 1838. Thos.
L. Davis, J.P. (Apr. 7, 1838).
Harvy Powell and Sally McBee, May 3, 1838. Thomas L.
Davis, J.P. (May 6, 1838).
Joseph Butcher and Ruthy Jackson, May 19, 1838. T. L.
Davis, J.P.
James Braden and Sarah Maddy, Oct. 13, 1838. William
McBee, J.P.
Samuel Litrell and Ann Shumate, Dec. 30, 1838. J. P.
McDowell, J.P. (Dec. 31, 1838).
Jessee Hooper and Jane Pall, Feb. 15, 1838. Saml.
Wilson, J.P. (Feb. 15, 1838).
Wm. Lamare and Labitha Robinson, Feb. 24, 1838. Samuel
Wilson, J.P. (Feb. 27, 1838).
John Allen and Martha Gideans, Mar. 31, 1838. Marshall
Braver, J.P. (Apr. 1, 1838).
Stephen Allen and Mary Rhea, Apr. 5, 1838. Martial (?)
Braver, J.P. (Apr. 5, 1838).

Jas. Butcher and Ruth Jackson, May 19, 1838.  Thos. L.
 Davis, J.P.  (May 19, 1838).
Randolph Furry and Mary Welch, Apr. 6, 1838.  Thos. L.
 Davis, J.P.  (Apr. 7, 1838).
Andrew Mynett and Elizabeth Boset, Jan. 29, 1838.  Adam
 Yearry, J.P.  (Feb. 1, 1838).
Henry Sharp and Celia Freemon, July 5, 1838.  Wm.
 McBee, J.P.  (July 6, 1838).
Thomas McClane and Susan Crutchfield, Feb. 21, 1838.
 Saml. Wilson, J.P.  (Feb. 22, 1838).
Macknep Rowlett and Nancy Brooks, July 31, 1838.  Peter
 Neal, J.P.  (Aug. 1, 1838).
Greenberry Ford and Catharine Thompson, Jan. 14, 1838.
 William Lewis, J.P.  (Jan. 14, 1838).
Jno. Jennings and Mary Moore, July 23, 1838.  No return.
Andrew Phellps and Martha J. Gowin, Dec. 5, 1837.
 William Lewis, J.P.  (Dec. 5, 1837).
Jesse Collins and Cintha Smith, Aug. 17, 1838.  Samuel
 Wilson, J.P.  (Aug. 18, 1838).
W. B. Pheleps and Charity Owsley, Nov. 12, 1837.  Wm.
 Lewis, J.P.  (Nov. 12, 1837).
Abraham Jones and Sarah Furry, Sep. 1, 1838.  Thos. L.
 Davis, J.P.  (Sep. 1, 1838).
Wm. Dearnal and Elizabeth Roark, Aug. 20, 1838.  Thos.
 L. Davis, J.P.  (Aug. 21, 1838).
Pridmore and Nancy Ball, July 28, 1838.  Adam Yearry,
 J.P.  (July 29, 1838).
Isaac A. Grimes and Thursy England, Sep. 5, 1838.  Adam
 Yearry, J.P.  (Sep. 5, 1838).
John Lingar and Sarah Chumbly, Jan. 27, 1838.  Wm. McBee,
 J.P.  (Feb. 13, 1838).
William Green and Mary Jane Lanham, Aug. 14, 1838.
 Thomas L. Davis, J.P.  (Aug. 16, 1838).
Vardamon Minton and Nancy Locke, Aug. 25, 1838.  George
 Shults, J.P.  (Aug. 25, 1838).
Madison Hollensworth and Mahala Maddy, Sep. 12, 1838.
 William McBee, J.P.  (Sep. 18, 1838).
Peter Balloo and Rebecca Dowys (?), Sep. 10, 1838.
 George Hamblen, J.P.  (Sep. 15, 1838).
Elisha Nunn and Effy Huddleston (?), Aug. 1, 1838.
 George Hamblen, J.P.  (Aug. 1, 1838).
Robert Sutten and Lucy Muncy, Sep. 30, 1838.  Isaac
 Thomas, J.P.  (Sep. 30, 1838).
Nelson Taylor and Louisa Nunn, Sep. 10, 1838.  Geo.
 Hamblen, J.P.  (Sep. 10, 1838).
Ambrose Arthur and Susan Hail, Sep. 19, 1838).  Thomas
 L. David, J.P.  (Sep. 19, 1838).
Mark Cadle and Mary Covy, Aug. 6, 1838.  Thos. L. Davis,
 J.P.  (Aug. 9, 1838).
James H. Davis and Belenda Crumbly, Nov. 2, 1838.
 Archibald Bales, J.P.  (Nov. 4, 1838).
John L. Lane and Elizabeth Sowder, Oct. 4, 1838.
 Hezekiah Brock, J.P.  (Oct. 14, 1838).
Joshua Hamelton and Elzera Collensworth, Oct. 27, 1838.
 Hezekiah Brock, J.P.  (Oct. 29, 1838).

Jno. Conner and Elisa Zeck, Oct. 5, 1838. Hezekiah
   Brock, J.P. (Oct. 7, 1838).
C. B. Bullard and Rebecca Hodge, Nov. 10, 1838. No
   return.
Enoch Bush and Agga Vance, Nov. 19, 1838. T. L. Davis,
   J.P. (Nov. 20, 1838).
Charles Bussell and Surrena Meeler, Oct. 9, 1838. T.
   L. Davis, J.P.
Wm. Ramsey and Nancy Clause, Dec. 10, 1838. Archd
   Bales, J.P. (Dec. 11, 1838).
Jno. Braden and Respy Lynch, Dec. 11, 1838. No return.
Abner Nunn and Margaret Harrell, Dec. 15, 1838. No
   return.
Jno Sanders and Arrena (?) Bundren, Dec. 24, 1838.
   Joseph Davis, J.P. (Dec. 25, 1838).
Wm H. Candy and Louisa (?) Barnard, Dec. 25, 1838.
   No return.
William Rogers and Lucy Moor, Jan. 5, 1839. No return.
G. W. Smith and Matilda Lane, Jan. 7, 1839. Joseph
   Davis, J.P. (Jan. 13, 1839).
Wyley Laycock and Louisa Ray, Aug. 1, 1838. Marshal
   Brewer, J.P. (Aug. 12, 1838).
Jeremiah Singleton and Lotty Carpenter, Nov. 30, 1838.
   Marshal Brewer, J.P. (Dec. 2, 1838).
Jas. W. Taylor and Susan Chadwell, Jan. 9, 1839. Adam
   Yearry, J.P. (Jan. 10, 1839).
Jas. Stansberry and Catharine Barnard, Jan. 11, 1839.
   Joseph Davis, J.P. (Jan. 13, 1839).
John E. R. Gray and Rachael Williams, Jan. 13, 1839.
   No return.
Geo. Sumpter and Lucy Hoult, July 26, 1838. Archibald
   Bales, J.P.
Abejah (?) Bray and Polly Webb, Jan. 4, 1838. Joseph
   Davis, J.P. (Jan. 10, 1839).
E. Hutson and Mary Bowman, Dec. 21, 1838. Hezekiah
   Brock, J.P. (Dec. 25, 1838).
Charles Blankinship and Susanah Little, July 21, 1838.
   Archibald Bales, J.P. (July 22, 1838).
John Mcmakan and Nancy Cloud, Dec. 2, 1838. William
   Bullard, J.P. (Dec. 6, 1838).
Felix Pirkins and Nancy Mckchan (?), Jan. 17, 1839.
   No return.
Christian Henderson and Emelia Parton, Jan. 17, 1839.
   Geo. Hamblen, J.P. (Feb. 9, 1839).
Jno. Province and Susanah Baley, Jan. 19, 1839. T. L.
   'Davis, J.P. (Jan. 20, 1839).
Hugh Nighbert and Manirvy (?) Smith, Jan. 29, 1839.
   J. E. Bowman, J.P. (Jan. 30, 1839).
Jesse Fortner and Elizabeth Isaacks, Jan. 29, 1839.
   Benjanin Sewell, J.P. (Jan. 29, 1839).
Cornelius Braden and Susanah Ausmus, Jan. 22, 1839.
   Wm. Williams, M.G. (Jan. 29, 1839).
Coventan Collensworth and Jane Jones, Jan. 30, 1839.
   Adam Yearry, J.P. (Jan. 31, 1839).
James Belvin and Nancy Dobkins, Jan. 30, 1839. No return.

William Carroll and Polly Slatten (?), Feb. 8, 1839.
T. L. Davis, J.P. (Feb. 21, 1839).
David Ray and Betsy Maples, Feb. 9, 1839. No return.
Pearson Lee and Polly Bray, Feb. 14, 1839. Jas. Davis,
J.P. (Feb. 21, 1839).
George Givin and Sally Ferrell, Feb. 16, 1839. J. E.
Bowman, J.P. (Feb. 17, 1839).
Jessee F. Beeler and Polly Beeler, Feb. 18, 1839.
William Lewis, J.P. (Feb. 22, 1839).
Wm. McHenry and Sally Huffaker, Feb. 25, 1839. Thos.
L. Davis, J.P. (Feb. 28, 1839).
Larkin Webb and Peggy Lea, Feb. 26, 1839. Jas. Davis,
J.P. (Feb. 28, 1839).
Johnston Jones and Rhoda Burnt Vigger (?), Feb. 27,
1839. No return.
Simon (?) Peace (?) and Gincy Balloo, Oct. 1, 1838.
George Hamblen, J.P. (Oct. 10, 1838).
Benajah Peace (?) and Elizabeth Fusian, Oct. 1, 1839 (?).
George Hamblen, J.P. (Oct. 7, 1838).
F. Perkins and Nancy Mckehan, Jan. 17, 1839. George
Hamblen, J.P. (Feb. 9, 1839).
Alexe Dobkins and Mary Ann Neil, Mar. 18, 1839. Peter
Neil, J.P. (Apr. 2, 1839).
Wm Rogers and Lucy Moor, Jan. 5, 1839. Wm Bullard,
J.P. (Jan. 6, 1839).
Jno. D. Mathes and Mary Ann Mason, Mar. 26, 1839. No
return.
Wayman Lambert and Nancy Southern, Feb. 19, 1839.
Isaac Thomas, J.P. (Feb. 19, 1839).
Henry Sumpter and Ann Doolen, Apr. 12, 1839. Adam
Yearry, J.P. (Apr. 12, 1839).
Preston Morgan and Effy Field (?), Apr. 13, 1839. No
return.
Thos. J. Johnston and Eliza J. Graham, Apr. 17, 1839.
Benj. Sewell, J.P. (Apr. 17, 1839).
William Sexton and Jane Strifle (?), Apr. 20, 1839.
Benjamin Sewell, J.P. (Mar., 1838?).
Levi Brewer and Sally Johnston, Mar. 6, 1838. Benjamin
Sewell, J.P. (Mar. 6, 1838).
Ezekiel Dougherty and Mary Furry, Aug. 30, 1838. Thos.
L. Davis, J.P. (Sep. 4, 1838).
Wayman Lambert and Nancy Southern, Feb. 12, 1839. Isaac
Thomas, J.P. (Feb. 19, 1839).
Wm Hamelton and Nancy Hamelton, Apr. 26, 1839. Hezekiah
Brock, J.P. (Apr. 30, 1839).
Abejah Gilbert and Martha J. Gibson, Apr. 30, 1839.
(?) McDowell (?). (May 2, 1839).
Wm Wheelus and Polly Legeer (?), Apr. 1, 1839. Marshal
Brewer, J.P. (Apr. 11, 1839).
Austin Honeycut and Rebecca Robinson, May 14, 1839.
Wm William. (May 14, 1839).
Saml. Cloud and Peggy Bowyers, May 15, 1839. John
Hunter, J.P. (May 15, 1839).
Henry Keck and Elizabeth Edwards, May 17, 1839. Wm
Williams, M.G. (May 19, 1839).

4

William Guthry and Rebecca Lickliter, May 18, 1839.
Wm Williams, M.G. (May 19, 1839).
Jefferson Winter (?) and Susanah Beeler, Nov. 26, 1836
(?). Ja. E. Bowman, J.P.
Jeremiah Hopper and Abigail (?) Fulps, May 22, 1839.
William Lewis, J.P. (May 24, 1839).
John Brock and Melvina Nicely, June 1, 1839. William
Lewis, J.P. (June 3, 1839).
Joseph Thomas and Catharine Wirich, May 28, 1839.
Archibald Bales, J.P. (May 8, 1839 ?).
Green B. W. Ford and Nancy Lynch, June 15, 1839. C.
Stimp (?). (June, 1839).
Jesse Lynch and Lavina Ford, June 15, 1839. C. Stimp
(?). (June 18, 1839).
Obadiah Norris and Rebecca Brandsan, June 19, 1839.
William Lewis, J.P. (June 20, 1839).
Lazarus Dobson and Rebecca Freeman, June 21, 1839.
Thos. L. Davis, J.P. (June 29, 1839).
Adam Summermon and Jane Carpenter, June 29, 1839.
George Shults, J.P. (June 30, 1839).
Tennessee Bruden (?) and Elizabeth Day, July 4, 1839.
John McNeil, J.P. (July 4, 1839).
Ransam Cupp and Sarah Lynch, July 8, 1839. C. Stimp
(?), Rev. (July 14, 1839).
Danl. Keck and Cementha Whited (?), July 16, 1839.
Wm Williams. (July 18, 1839).
William Young and Jane Carpenter, July 15, 1839. No
return.
Samuel Moor and Polly Beeler, July 19, 1839. William
Lewis, J.P. (July 20, 1839).
Henry Walker and Lucenda Dougherty, July 20, 1839.
Henry Holt, M.G. (July 21, 1839).
Isaac Vanbebber and Sarah Hamelton, July 23, 1839.
C. Stimp, M.G. (July 30, 1839).
Jesse J. Geabolf (?) and Priscilla Evans, July 24,
1839. Thos. Whited, J.P. (July 28, 1839).
John Ritter and Syntha Hurst, July 24, 1839. No return.
Thos. L. Sawyers and Louisa Dobbs, July 30, 1839.
C. Mcnally E.M.E.G. (?). (July 30, 1839).
Josiah Russell and Elizabeth Gentry, Aug. 13, 1839.
Wm Williams. (Aug. 13, 1839).
William Welch and Luritta Ramsey, Apr. 16, 1839. Thos.
L. Davis, J.P. (Aug. 18, 1839).
William Latham and Phibi Dobkins, Aug. 24, 1839. No
return.
James Robinson and Elizabeth Honeycutt, Aug. 26, 1839.
Wm Williams. (Aug. 27, 1839).
Charles W. Runnyans and Jane Eastus, Aug. 27, 1839.
Peter Neil, J.P. (Aug. 27, 1839).
Jesse Rector and Susannah Rector, Sep. 2, 1839. Adam
Yearry, Esq. (Sep. 3, 1839).
Sampson Taylor and Polly Miller, July 27, 1839. Isaac
Thomas, J.P. (July 27, 1839).
Stephen Southern and Polly Lambert, Aug. 13, 1839.
Isaac Thomas, J.P. (Aug. 13, 1839).

Claborne Welbourn and Polly Gibert, Apr. 13, 1839.
    Isaac Thomas, J.P. (Apr. 14, 1839).
Martin Harris and Rhoda Dougherty, Aug. 20, 1839.
    Isaac Thomas, J.P. (Aug. 20, 1839).
Silas Glanden and Sarah Williams, Sep. 7, 1839. Saml.
    Day, J.P. (Sep. 8, 1839).
Wm. Robinson and Rebecca Rogers (?), Sep. 10, 1839).
    Wm Williams. (Sep. 17, 1839).
John Forgerson and Lavina Semmonds, Sep. 12, 1839.
    Thos. L. Davis, J.P. (Sep. 12, 1839).
Thomas J. Wheeler and Francis J. McHenry, Sep. 20, 1839.
    James Kennon, M.G. (Oct. 8, 1839).
John Robinson and Louisa Sharp, Sep. 21, 1839. Wm
    Williams. (Sep. 22, 1839).
Sturling Gowin and Mary Keck, Oct. 2, 1839. No return.
B. Brooks and M. S. E. Rowlett, Sep. 28, 1839. No
    return.
Adam Hatfield and Mary Davis, Oct. 7, 1839. Adam
    Yearry, J.P. (Oct. 13, 1839).
Nelson Gowin and Polly Putchard (?), Oct. 8, 1839.
    Thomas Whited, J.P. (Oct. 10, 1839).
Wiatt J. Robinson and Polly Williams, Oct. 12, 1839.
    No return.
William Romines and Polly Presly, Oct. 12, 1839.
    William Bullard, J.P. (Oct. 13, 1839).
David Huddleston and Peggy Seals, Oct. 16, 1839. Thomas
    Whited, J.P. (Oct. 17, 1839).
Jno. C. Dodson and Barthina Dobkins, Oct. 19, 1839.
    No return.
Royal Lebow and Rawsy (?) Sanders, Oct. 23, 1839.
    Joseph Davis, J.P. (Dec. 15, 1839).
William Carroll and Polly Hamelton, Oct. 24, 1839. Thos.
    L. Davis, J.P. (Oct. 31, 1839).
Williamson Laycock and Elizabeth Russell, Nov. 13,
    1839. Joseph Davis, J.P. (Dec. 13, 1839).
Granville (?) A. Cheek and Eliza Hurst, Nov. 20, 1839.
    John Mcneal, J.P. (Nov. 21, 1839).
George Powell and Loucinda Hopper, Nov. 22, 1839. N. G.
    (?) McDowell. (Nov. 23, 1839).
William Rutledge and Nancy Eastus, Nov. 23, 1839. No
    return.
Wm Wilson and Permila (?) Kincaid, Dec. 3, 1839. No
    return.
William Cox and Elizabeth Rector, Dec. 4, 1839. No
    return.
William McNeal and Nancy Gilbert, Dec. 6, 1839. John
    Mcneal, J.P. (Dec. 6, 1839).
William C. McBee and Permelia Greer, Dec. 10, 1839.
    Thomas Whited, J.P. (Dec. 15, 1839).
Edward Black and Franky Brownlow, Dec. 18, 1839.
    Marshal Brewer, J.P. (Dec. 22, 1839).
Azariah Hurst and Mary Ann Williams, Dec. 19, 1839.
    George Shults, J.P. (Dec. 19, 1839).
Samuel W. Pleming and Lavina Sanders, Dec. 19, 1839.
    John McNeil, J.P. (Dec. 19, 1839).

William Mills and Rhoda Lawson, Dec. 19, 1839. Adam
  Yearry, J.P. (Dec. 19 (?), 1839).
Isaac Gowin and Mary Vanoy, Dec. 19, 1839. Joseph
  Davis, J.P. (Dec. 22, 1839).
Abadiah Collins and Polly Smith, Dec. 20, 1839. George
  Shults, J.P. (Dec. 20, 1839).
James H. Ellis and Margaret Furry, Dec. 21, 1839. No
  return.
James Mills and Sarah Lawson, Dec. 21, 1839. No return.
Hugh Cane (?) and Orlina (?) Ritter (?). Dec. 24, 1839.
  George Shults, J.P. (Dec. 24, 1839).
Aaron Hurst and Elmira Ritter, Jan. 27, 1840. Saml.
  Day, J.P. (Jan. 27, 1840).
James Vanbebber and Elizabeth Snuffer, Dec. 30, 1839.
  Wm McBee, J.P. (Feb. 14, 1841 (?)).
William Cox and Luhany Thompson, Dec. 31, 1839. Adam
  Yearry, J.P. (Jan. 1, 1840).
A. A. McAmis and Matilda (?) Weir, Jan. 8, 1840.
  Nathanl. Hood, M.G. (Jan. 9, 1840).
Washington Rowe and Margaret Smith, Jan. 9, 1840.
  George Shults, J.P. (Jan. 10, 1840).
Pleasant Miller and Winney Runnalds, Jan. 14, 1840.
  Wm Williams. (Jan. 23, 1840).
Thomas Cox and Barthena Hill, Jan. 10, 1840. Thos. L.
  Davis, J.P. (Jan. 12, 1840).
Levi Sharp and Elizabeth Graves, Jan. 18, 1840. Thomas
  Whited, J.P. (June 30, 1840).
William Lastly (?) and Elizabeth Crabtree, Dec. 25,
  1839. Isaac Thomas, J.P. (Dec. 25, 1839).
Oliven Tackett and Nancy Hall, Dec. 12, 1839. Isaac
  Thomas, J.P. (Dec. 12, 1839).
George Forber and Loucy Southern, Nov. 15, 1839.
  Isaac Thomas, J.P. (Nov. 15, 1839).
Stephen Hopkins and Maniak, Nov. 15, 1839. Isaac
  Thomas, J.P. (Nov. 15, 1839).
Richard Singleton and Rachael Cumber (?), Oct. 20, 1839.
  Isaac Thomas, J.P. (Oct. 20, 1839).
John Clouse and Sally Fletcher, Oct. 17, 1839. Isaac
  Thomas, J.P. (Oct. 17, 1839).
John H. Welch and Susanah Brooks, Jan. 30, 1840.
  Adam Yearry. (Jan. 30, 1840).
Thos. Epison and Elizabeth Rowe, Jan. 31, 1840. Elan
  (?) John Day. (Feb. 6, 1840).
Jas. Dosset and Phebe Lynch, Feb. 11, 1840. No return.
William Neil and Margaret E. Graham, Feb. 11, 1840.
  J. Kennon, M.G. (Feb. 11, 1840).
John R. Cassle and Judy Ann Wright, Feb. 15, 1840. D.
  F. Rogers, J.P. (Feb. 18, 1840).
Richd. Sowder and Sidney Lin (?), Feb. 17, 1840.
  Hezekiah Brock. (May 17, 1840).
Robt. B. Lane (?) and Martha Jane McNew, Feb. 20, 1840.
  W. C. Reynolds, L.E. (?) M.G. (Feb. 27, 1840).
Lynch Hatfield and Jane Dodson, Feb. 24, 1840. Martial
  Brewer, J.P. (Feb. 27, 1840).
Claiborne McBee and Sementha Hurst, Feb. 25, 1840. No
  return.

Wm M. Rogers and Susan Paul (?), Feb. 26, 1840. No
   return.
Sinclar Cade and Elly Baker, Feb. 18, 1840. Thos. L.
   Davis, J.P. (Feb. 22, 1840).
J. H. Ellis and Margaret Furry, Feb. 21, 1840. Thos.
   L. Davis, J.P. (Dec. 23, 1839 (?)).
Silas D. Woods and Emily Ferrile, Mar. 3, 1840.
   No return.
Russell Miller (?) and Polly Smith, Mar. 10, 1840.
   No return.
Iredele Webb and Dicy Lee, May 19, 1840. Marshal
   Brewer, J.P. (Feb. (?) 19, 1840).
Squire C. Hurst and Neely Sharp, Feb. 24, 1840. Wm
   Williams. (Feb. 27, 1840).
James R. Jennings and Louisa Campbell, Feb. 20, 1840.
   No return.
Jacob Sharp and Elizabeth Nash, Mar. 13, 1840. No
   return.
Timothy Roarks and Polly Williams, Mar. 12. 1840.
   No return.
A. McConnel and Sarah Graves, Mar. 19, 1840. Wm C.
   Reynolds, M.G. (Mar. 13 (?), 1840).
Barnet (?) Campbell and Jane Kesterson, Mar. 26, 1840.
   Benjm Sewell, J.P. (Mar. 26, 1840).
Jno. McNew and Louisas Hurst, Apr. 11, 1840. No return.
Adam Groseclose (?) and Sophia Snavely, Apr. 6, 1840.
   Thos. L. Davis, J.P. (Apr. 8, 1840).
Adam Clouse and Temperance Eastridge (?), Apr. 18, 1840.
   W. C. Reynolds, M.G. (Apr. 25, 1840).
Michael Maser and Sally Graves, Apr. 18, 1840. Thomas
   Whitehead. (May 3, 1840).
Henry P. Luster (?) and Mary Ann Cadle, Apr. 30, 1840.
   Thos. L. Davis. (May 1, 1840).
Elihu Jones and Elmirah Powell, May 2, 1840. Thos
   Whitehead (?). (Apr. 26 (?), 1840).
Henry A. Brown and Catharin Cheek, May 6, 1840. No
   return.
George W. Miller and Lucy King, May 9, 1840. No return.
Allen Burnet and Viney Martain, May 9, 1840. No return.
Chesley West and Sally Barnard, May 12, 1840. No return.
Alexr. Collins and Margaret Collins, May 13, 1840.
   No return.
John Graves and Lucindy Hurst, May 23, 1840. No return.
Wm L Overton and Rachel Fugate, June (?) 8, 1840.
   No return.
Jno J. Baker and Rosannah Standerfe (?), June 11, 1840.
   No return.
Wm N Moyers and H. (?) Moyers, May 14, 1840. No return.
Jo Hiram (?) Pridmore and Esther (?) Hoskins, June
   11, 1840. No return.
James Ritchie and Barbary Parkey, July 7, 1840. No
   return.
Preston Fostnez and Rachael Johnson. T. L. Davis, J.P.
   (Aug. 16, 1841).

CLAIBORNE COUNTY MARRIAGES

Gideon Brooks and Winney Hurst. Solomon Dobkins,
J.P. (Aug. 19, 1841).
David Redman and Mary Ann Carmack. T. L. Davis, J.P.
(Sep. 5, 1841).
Wm Maples and Betsy Hammock, Sep. 25, 1841. Thomas
Whiteted (?), J.P. (Sep. 30, 1841).
Benjamin D. Miles (?) and Harreet Grantham, Sep. 25,
1841. Isaac Thomas, J.P. (Sep. 26, 1841).
James Grimes and Matilda Leford, Sep. 29, 1841. Adam
Yearry, J.P. (Sep. 30, 1841).
Richard Carder and Polly Grimes (?), Oct. 4, 1841.
John Hunter, J.P. (Dec. 22, 1841).
John Province and Margaret Bishop, Oct. 4, 1841. T.
L. Davis, J.P. (Oct. 10, 1841).
Charles Baley and Mary Balls, Oct. 5, 1841. Thomas
L. Davis, J.P. (Nov. 7, 1841).
Pleasant C. Mundy and Elizabet (?) Williams, Oct. 9,
1841. Mark Hurst, M.G. (Oct. 17, 1841).
Wm Rutherford and Rachael Smith, Oct. 9, 1841. Solom
Dobkins, J.P. (Oct. 10, 1841).
Wm Houston (?) and Elizabeth Honeycutt, Oct. 11, 1841.
John Hunter, J.P. (Oct. 14, 1841).
George Washington Wallace and Molinda Hendrix, Oct. 16,
1841. Thos L. Davis, J.P. (Oct. 17, 1841).
Spencer (?) Edwards and Antamasa (?), Oct. 28, 1841.
No return.
Henry Hatfield and Emily Davis, Nov. 13, 1841. James
Bishop. (Nov. 21, 1841).
David Miller (?) and Ann Runolds (?), Nov. 13, 1841.
Thomas Whiteted (?), J.P. (Nov. 28, 1841).
Alexander Carter and Rachael Lussey, Nov. 16, 1841.
Archibald Bales, J.P. (Nov. 21, 1841).
William Kirkpatrick (?) and Louisa Evans, Nov. 18, 1841.
Landy James, M.G. (Nov. 18, 1841).
Janathan C. (?) and Nancy Mattox, Nov. 18, 1841. Isaac
Thomas, J.P. (Nov. 19, 1841).
Greenberry Right and Sarah (?) Jane Hopper, Nov. 23,
1841. John Hunter (?), J.P. (Nov. 25, 1841).
Russel Nunn and Flurrender Nunn, Nov. 24, 1841. J. B.
S. Leforce, J.P. (Nov. 25, 1841).
Anderson Collins and Letty (?) Bray, Nov. 27, 1841.
Joseph H. Davis, J.P. (Nov. 28, 1841).
Chastin (?) S. Moore and Nancy W Jones, Nov. 27, 1841.
No return.
Timothy Whitaker and Sarah Southern, Nov. 30, 1841.
Reuben Mason, J.P. (Dec. 1, 1841).
Ambrous Johnson and Mary Southern, Dec. 1, 1841.
Mark Hurst, M.G. (Dec. 2, 1841).
George W. Cup and Catharin Wilson, Dec. 7, 1841. No
return.
James Hunter and Nancy Brooks, Dec. 8, 1841. Thos.
L. Davis, J.P. (Dec. 8, 1841).
Andrew J. Brock and Sarah Day, Dec. 13, 1841. Haram
(?) Hurst. (Dec. 16, 1841).

# CLAIBORNE COUNTY MARRIAGES

James True (?) and Nancy Pitman, Dec. 15, 1841.
George Shults, J.P. (Dec. 17, 1841).
Wm White and Sarah Masan, Dec. 15, 1841. Jas. H.
Davis, J.P. (Dec. 26, 1841).
Samuel D. Code and Sarah Code, Dec. 21, 1841.
Benjamin Sewell, J.P. (Dec. 21, 1841).
Thomas Mathes and Susannah Davis, Dec. 27, 1841.
Martial Brewer, J.P. (Dec. 29, 1841).
William King and Nancy Braver (?), Dec. 28, 1841.
Martial Brewer, J.P. (Dec. 29, 1841).
Isaac Eastrage and Noomy (?) Powers, Dec. 29, 1841.
Reuben Mason, J.P. (Dec. 29, 1841).
John Burch and Mary Willis, Dec. 30, 1841. George
Shults, J.P. (Jan. 2, 1842).
Moses Retter and Rhoda Carr, Jan. 5, 1842. Wm McBee,
J.P. (Jan. 6, 1842).
Lewis Day and Polly Evans, Jan. 11, 1842. Haram
Hurst. (Jan. 23, 1842).
Isaac Bolinger and Elizabeth Right, Jan. 13, 1842.
Wm Williams. (Jan. 22, 1842).
John Barns (?) and Rosamial (?) Grace, Jan. 14, 1842.
No return.
Eli Fugate and Lelitha Woolven, Jan. 31, 1842. Archi-
bald Bales, J.P. (Feb. 1, 1842).
Thomas Robinson and Nancy Hunter, Jan. 18, 1842. John
Hunter, J.P. (Jan. 23, 1842).
Alexander Woodard and Martha Bobit, Jan. 18, 1842.
John Hunter, J.P. (Apr. 4, 1842).
James McCarty and Margaret Mcfarlin, Jan. 20, 1842.
Isaac Thomas, J.P. (Jan. 21, 1842).
William C. Willis (?) and Elixna (?) King, Jan. 20,
1842. Geo. Shultz, J.P. (Jan. 21, 1842).
Jerrice (?) D. Mays and Carolina Treese (?), Jan. 21,
1842. Solomon Phelp, J.P. (Jan. 30, 1842).
James McAnelly and Manila Mitchel, Jan. 22, 1842. W.
Williams, Local Deacan. (Jan. 26, 1842).
John (?) and Fereby Crabtree, Jan. 22, 1842. No return.
William Arber and Juicy Taylor, Jan. 22, 1842. Archi-
bald Bales, J.P. (Jan. 23, 1842).
William Hurst and Sarah Cemore, Jan. 27, 1842. Samuel
Day, J.P. (Jan. 27, 1842).
Hamelton McAnelly and Winny Simmons, Feb. 5, 1842.
Samuel Day, J.P. (Feb. 6, 1842).
James P. Edwards and Malenda McNeil, Feb. 10, 1842.
John McNeil, J.P. (Feb. 10, 1842).
George Campbell and Nancy Eastrage, Feb. 10, 1842.
Reuben Mason, J.P. (Feb. 10, 1842).
Nathaniel Presnell and Eliza Jones (?), Feb. 10, 1842.
H. Brock, J.P. (Feb. 11, 1842).
George Cole and Martha Baker, Feb. 14, 1842. H.
Holt. (Feb. 14, 1842).
Moses Huneycutt and Hannah Beeler, Feb. 15, 1842.
John Hunter, J.P. (Feb. 20, 1842).
Jefferson Trece and Cristiniy (?) Wilson, Feb. 19, 1842.
No return.

Calvin Partan and Milly Bray, Feb. 20, 1842.  J. B. S.
Leford (?), J.P.  (Feb. 26, 1842).
James M. Monk and Manila Bray, Feb. 21, 1842.  Solomon
Dobkins, J.P.  (Feb. 22, 1842).
William J. Canter and Eliza Robinson, Feb. 28, 1842.
Archibald Bales, J.P.  (Feb. 28, 1842).
William Johnson and 'Sarah Fortner, Feb. 28, 1842.  Wm
Bullard, J.P.  (Mar. 1, 1842).
Esaw Sharp and Tabitha (?) L. Toliver, Mar. 1, 1842.
E. K. Hutsell.  (Mar. 6, 1842).
Franklin M. Smith and Elizabeth Alexander, Mar. 5, 1842.
Wm McBee, J.P.  (Mar. 8, 1842).
John Alexander and Olive Root, Mar. 5, 1842.  Wm McBee,
J.P.  (Mar. 10, 1842).
Obediah Cardwell and Martha L. (?) Thompson, Mar. 8,
1842.  E. K. Hutsell.  (Mar. 8, 1842).
David B. Capps and Nancy Hurst, Mar. 17, 1842.  Hiram
Hurst, M.G.  (Mar. 17, 1842).
Vincent Moyer and Jane Fulp, Mar. 19, 1842.  Jacob
Cloud, J.P.  (Apr. 14, 1842).
Stephen Drummond and Polly Cupp, Mar. 24, 1842.  Levi
(?) Goin, J.P.  (Mar. 24, 1842).
William Gilbert (?) and Mary Ann Jackson, Mar. 26,
1842.  No return.
James M. Martain and Susannah Gibert (?), Mar. 27, 1842.
Archibald Bales, J.P.  (Mar. 30, 1842).
Landax (?) C. Minter (?) and Mary Montgomery, Apr. 4,
1842.  John Ritchie, J.P.  (Apr. 5, 1842).
Larkan Vandevarter (?) and Ony (?) Slaven (?), Apr. 5,
1842.  William L. Thomas, J.P.  (Apr. 7, 1842).
Arthur Speer (?) and Mary Margraves, Apr. 13, 1842.
R. H. Harripan, J.P.  (Apr. 14, 1842).
Joel Southerland and Martha Hamelton, Apr. 14, 1842.
R. H. Harripan, J.P.  (Apr. 14, 1842).
Enas (?) Day and Mary Parker, Apr. 22, 1842.  No return.
Jeptha (?) Edwards and Sarah Matilda Goforth, Apr. 23,
1842.  John Burch, J.P.  (May 16, 1842).
Martain Burchfield and Susan Bullard, Apr. 27, 1842.
R. H. Harripan, J.P.  (Apr. 27, 1842).
Allen Robertson and Elizabeth Bolinger, Apr. 30, 1842.
No return.
Moab (?) Hammons and Elizabeth Seal, May 5, 1842.
Martial Brewer, J.P.  (July 10, 1842).
William Strevle and Nancy Lane (?), May 11, 1842.
Thomas Whiteted (?), J.P.  (May 15, 1842).
Joseph Farris (?) and Catharin J. Hopkins, May 16,
1842.  John Farmer, J.P.  (May 17, 1842).
Benjamin Jackson and Mary Ayers, Mar. 12, 1842.  Isaac
Thomas, J.P.  (Mar. 13, 1842).
John Marlow and Venila Late (?), May 16, 1842.  Prior
J. Parrett, J.P.  (May 25, 1842).
Jesse Bruice (?) and Deborah Crank (?), May 21, 1842.
William McNeil, J.P.  (May 22, 1842).
Stokely R. Lanham and Carolein Henderson, June 2, 1842.
John Hurst, J.P.  (June 2, 1842).

11

Bird Bussle (?) and Susan Baltrip, June 3, 1842.  James
    Cheek, J.P.  (June (?) 8, 1842).
Bezeet (?) Burch and Mary Tucker (?), June 11, 1842.
    James F. Hooper, J.P.  (June 16, 1842).
Thomas C. Killion and Mary Rossan (?), June 11, 1842.
    L. L. (?) Herral, J.P.  (June 12, 1842).
Wilson Taff (?) and Margaret Worley, June 14, 1842.
    Wm McNeil, J.P.  (June 15, 1842).
Lee (?) White and Margaret McNielin (?), June 16, 1842.
    James F. Hooper, J.P.  (June 16, 1842).
William Johnson and Sarah Fortiner, Mar. 1, 1841.
    Isaac Bullard, J.P.  (Mar. 1, 1841).
Wm Whiteted (?) and Frances Cyraus, June 17, 1842.
    Thomas Whiteted, J.P.  (June 21, 1842).
James K. Rogers and Eliza Lajasce (?), June 18, 1842.
    No return.
James S. (?) Rice and Bartheny Nunn, June 20, 1842.
    Samuel Day, J.P.  (June 20, 1842).
Philip Veatch and Vineny Nunn, Mar. 20, 1842.  Samuel
    Day, J.P.  (June 20, 1842).
James M. Hurst and Polly Cookard (?), June 22, 1842.
    Hiram Hurst, M.G.  (June 22, 1842).
Jackson Landers and Mary E. Williams, June 27, 1842.
    Jos H. Davis, J.P.  (June 30, 1842).
Samuel T. (?) Lemar (?) and Rebecco Montgomery, July 5,
    1842.  John Ritchie, J.P.  (July 5, 1842).
Greenberry Short and Catharin Ferrel, July 13, 1842.
    James Cheek, J.P.  (July 14, 1842).
Henry Baker and Anny Harris (?), July 16, 1842.  E. K.
    Hutsell.  (July 19, 1842).
Benjamin Cloud and Mariah (?) Barnard, July 19, 1842.
    Jos. H. Davis, J.P.  (July 21, 1842).
Joseph Bunch and Wilmirth Harral, July 28, 1842.  John
    Ritchie, J.P.  (July 28, 1842).
George M. Billingly and Eliza Shumate, Aug. 9, 1842.
    Wm McNeel (?), J.P.  (Aug. 9, 1842).
Hiram Furry and Levisa (?) Maurae, Aug. 17, 1842.
    E. K. Hutsell.  (Aug. 17, 1842).
Calvin C. Woodward and Nancy Williams, Aug. 18, 1842.
    R. J. Russel (?), J.P.  (Aug. 20, 1842).
Jefferson Rose and Sarah Brock, Aug. 23, 1842.  Wm
    McNeel (?), J.P.  (Aug. 24, 1842).
William Meotor (?) and Ally Slotton, Aug. 24, 1842.
    William McNeil, J.P.  (Oct. 25, 1842).
William Legeor (?) and Vina Hurley (?), Aug. 27, 1842.
    Martial Brewer (?), J.P.  (Aug. 28, 1842).
Eldridge Campbell and Sarah Walker, Aug. 31, 1842.
    John Ritchie, J.P.  (Sep. 1, 1842).
George B. Needham and Martha Jane Mays, Sep. 3, 1842.
    Jacob Cloud, J.P.  (Sep. 11, 1842).
James Drake and Rachel Totten (?), Sep. 4, 1842.  John
    Farmer, J.P.  (Sep. 4, 1842).
Thomas B. Walker and Elizabeth Nash, Sep. 15, 1842.
    No return.

CLAIBORNE COUNTY MARRIAGES

James Goforth and Sarah Jane Jones, Sep. 15, 1842.
Levi Goin, J.P. (Sep. 15, 1842).
Ezekiel Gooden and Tempy (?) A. Cain, Sep. 18, 1842.
Thos. L. Davis, J.P. (Sep. 18, 1842).
Joseph B. Moyers and Livisa (?) Ausmus, Sep. 22, 1842.
R. J. Russel (?), J.P. (Sep. 27, 1842).
Benjamin Campbell and Louisa Eastridge, Sep. 28, 1842.
(Sep. 29, 1842).
Robert Hurst and Sarah Neil, Sep. 29, 1842. John
Hurst, J.P. (Sep. 29, 1842).
John Wyatt and Elizabeth Doty, Sep. 30, 1842. Thos.
L. Davis, J.P. (Sep. 30, 1842).
John M. (?) Leach (?) and Trifany (?) Bruce, Sep. 30,
1842. Prior J. Parrott, J.P. (Oct. 2, 1842).
John F. Thompson and Meeley (?) Harris, Oct. 7, 1842.
John Hurst, J.P. (Oct. 8, 1842).
William Blankenship and Belenda Burgin, Oct. 7, 1842.
Isaac Vanbebber, J.P. (Oct. 7, 1842).
Abner C. Hansard and Mary A. H. Marcum, Oct. 11, 1842.
No return.
John A. Buchanan and Sarah Calar (?), Oct. 18, 1842.
William McNeel (?), J.P. (Oct. 23, 1842).
John Sulivan and Lucindy Davis, Oct. 19, 1842. Joseph
H. Davis, J.P. (Oct. 20, 1842).
James Burk and Nancy Mays (?), Oct. 22, 1842. No return.
Collin (?) Bailey (?) and Mary A. Smith, Nov. 1, 1842.
James Cheek, J.P. (Nov. 2, 1842).
John Nuckels and Jane Bray, Nov. 11, 1842. William
Smith, J.P. (Nov. 15, 1842).
Lewis (?) Rhea (?) and Margarett Latan (?), Nov. 14,
1842. James Cheek, J.P. (Nov. 22, 1842).
Spencer Chaden (?) and Polly Weir, Nov. 17, 1842.
James Cheek, J.P. (Nov. 20, 1842).
Thomas Clarrick (?) and Susannah Doolin, Nov. 26, 1842.
John Hurst, J.P. (Nov. 26, 1842).
Hubbard Bralock (Blalock) and Catharin Graceclose,
Dec. 10, 1842. Thos. L. Davis, J.P. (Dec. 12, 1842).
Creed Rowland and Emaline Smith, Dec. 17, 1842. Wm
McNeel (?), J.P. (Dec. 22, 1842).
Wm H. Litrell and Rachel Pridemoor (Pridemore), Dec. 19,
1842. J. Cheek, J.P. (Dec. 25, 1842).
Walter Davis and Catharin Pearson, Dec. 20, 1842. Joseph
H. Davis, J.P. (Dec. 22, 1842).
William Warnicutt and Letty Ward, Dec. 21, 1842. Levi
Goin, J.P. (Dec. 23, 1842).
William Beaty and Catharine Minton (?), Dec. 26, 1842.
No return.
Preston C. Goforth and Louisa Brogain, Dec. 28, 1842.
Levi Goin, J.P. (Jan. 4, 1843).
Saviour (?) Gibson (?) and Milley Willis, Dec. 29,
1842. No return.
William (?) Waggoner (?) and Lucinda Braden, Jan. 7,
1843. Thomas Whiteted (?), J.P. (Feb. 19, 1843).
Martain Barlet (?) and Ann McNeil, Jan. 7, 1843. James
Gilbert (?). (Jan. 8, 1843).

13

Silas Williams and Levisa (?) Willis, Jan. 14, 1843.
No return.
Jesse Green Palmer and Sarah Sharp, Jan. 16, 1843.
Reuben Steele, M.G. (Jan., 1843).
James H. Lyngar (?) and Eliza Chumley, Jan. 18, 1843.
Wm McNeel (?), J.P. (Jan. 19, 1843).
Joseph Moore and Manervy Greer, Jan. 19, 1843. J. E.
Bowman, J.P. (Jan. 19, 1843).
Crispin Collins and Prudy (?) Collins, Jan. 19, 1843.
Wm Smith, J.P. (Jan. 22, 1843).
John Lambert and Marthat (?) E. England, Jan. 24, 1843.
James Cheek, J.P. (Jan. 25, 1843).
Samuel McCullough and Elizabeth Farchilds, Jan. 24,
1843. Martial Brewer, J.P. (Jan. 26, 1843).
William Wilbern and Manervy Seals, Jan. 24, 1843.
Martial Brewer, J.P. (Jan. 29, 1843).
Alson (?) Hetton and Caroline Helton, Jan. 25, 1843.
Wm. Smith, J.P. (Jan. 26, 1843).
Ralph Hatfield and Elizabeth Ann Worrick, Jan. 25,
1843. James Cheek, J.P. (Jan. 26, 1843).
James C. Herrall and Rachel Herrall (Bundran), Jan. 28,
1843. Wm Smith, J.P. (Jan. 29, 1843).
Moses J. Renfro and Mary Ann Danahoo, Jan. 28, 1843.
William McNeil, J.P. (Jan. 28, 1843).
Brison Collins and Eliza Camier (?), Feb. 2, 1843.
No return.
Traves (?) Brooks and Elizabeth Whitecar (?), Feb. 8,
1843. Sandy (?) James, M.G. (Feb. 8, 1843).
Henry Claxton and Nancy Mannon (?), Feb. 21, 1843. H.
Holt, M.G. (Feb. 21, 1843).
Henry F. Harry and Manervy J. Bartley, Feb. 21, 1843.
Henry Holt, M.G. (Feb. 28, 1843).
Nathaniel D. Cain and Mary Sharp, Feb. 25, 1843.
No return.
Royal Neil and Mary Hodges, Mar. 1, 1843. John Hurst,
J.P. (Mar. 1, 1843).
William E. Dean and Mary Moore, Mar. 7, 1843. W. L.
Turner, M.G. (Mar. 7, 1843).
Nathan Collins and Jemina Mays (?), Mar. 7, 1843. R.
J. Russell, J.P. (Mar. 7, 1843).
William R. Gibson and Mary Catterell (?), Mar. 18, 1843.
N. S. (?) McDowell, M.G. (Mar. 21, 1843).
John Vanderpool and Manervy Smith, Mar. 18, 1843. No
return.
Benjamin A. Yaden and Eve Hunter, Mar. 27, 1843.
William Williams. (Apr. 2, 1843).
William Welch and Clarkis Scivofield (?), Mar. (?) 29,
1843. No return.
John Jackson and Sarah Colson, Apr. 6, 1843. James
Cheek, J.P. (Apr. 15, 1843).
John M. Vanbebber and Manervia J. Kincaid, Apr. 12,
1843. Reuben Steele, M.G. (Apr., 1843).
Lisay (?) Hurst and Eliza James, Apr. 12, 1843. Mark
Hurst, M.G. (Apr. 12, 1843.
John Keck and Rebecco Yaden, Apr. 14, 1843. No return.

Henry A. Burchfield and Polly A. Phelips, Apr. 15, 1843.
Jacob Cloud, J.P. (Apr. 16, 1843).
Hendly (?) Fugate and Rebecca Parkey, Apr. 18, 1843.
Elder James Bushep (?), Pastor. (Apr. 20, 1843).
Jefferson Chick and Priscella Fulks, Apr. 19, 1843.
James Chick, J.P. (Apr. 20, 1843).
William Ayers and Jeminia (?) Hatfield, Apr. 22, 1843.
James Chick, J.P. (Apr. 23, 1843).
Isaac Hopkins and Nancy Ann Pew, Apr. 22, 1843. John
Farmer, J.P. (Apr. 30, 1843).
James N. Lifard (?) and Manervy Hatfield, Apr. 29, 1843.
S. Hobbs, M.G. (Apr. 30, 1843).
William Epps and Lucy Janes (?) Evans, May 2, 1843.
Robert Glenn, M.G. (May 2, 1843).
John Wallin and Elizabeth Billingsley (?), May 8, 1843.
No return.
John Ball and Rachel E. Lock, May 11, 1843. James
Cheek, J.P. (May 14, 1843).
Anderson Carpenter and Syntha A. Hopson, May 12, 1843.
George H. Cheek, J.P. (May 18, 1843).
Henry McGoingal and Agness Norris, May 15, 1843. Wm
Williams. (May 26, 1843).
Anneas Ely and Jane McCrary, May 27, 1843. Wm McBee,
J.P. (May 26, 1843).
B. F. Young and Ann Knuckles, June 3, 1843. No return.
Matthew Whiteaker and Sara Ann Estice, June 6, 1843.
John Hurst, J.P. (June 6, 1843).
Stuphin (?) Hopkins and Mary Ann Hopkins, June 7, 1843.
John Farmer, J.P. (June 7, 1843).
(?) Liford and Soperia (?) Grace, June 12, 1843. S.
Hobbs, M.G. (June 12, 1843).
Nelson Berry and Joannes (?) Pain, June 20, 1843. John
Hurst, J.P. (June 20, 1843).
William Hopson and Elizabeth Herral, July 5, 1843. Wm
Smith, J.P. (July 6, 1843).
John Minton and Sary Reed, July 11, 1843. No return.
John Cawood and Marlena Vanbebber, July 12, 1843. No
return.
Thos P. Bray and Lavesa Holt, July 22, 1843. John
Ritchie, J.P. (July 24, 1843).
(?) S. (?) White and Emily J. Wanocott, July 24, 1843.
James F. Hooper, J.P. (Aug. 3, 1843).
Andrew Hubbard and Sarah Stowers, July 14, 1843. Nathan
Buchanan, J.P. (July 18, 1843).
Jno. L. Going and Cass (?) Ann Going, July 27, 1843.
Lt L. (?) Herral, J.P. (July 30, 1843).
William Clarkson and Martha Clarkson, July 30, 1843.
No return.
Timothy Friar and Mary Whiteaker, Aug. 3, 1843. No
return.
John A. Davis and Sarah Buckhanan, Aug. 8, 1843. No
return.
James Campbell and Melvina Whiteaker, Aug. 14, 1843.
John Hurst, J.P. (Aug. 15, 1843).

William Gains and Elizabeth Bunch, Aug. 25, 1843.  Geo.
H. Cheek, J.P.  (Aug. 27, 1843).
Marcus Flemming (?) and Mary Owsley, Sep. 1, 1843.
Thomas Whiteted (?), J.P.  (Oct. 2, 1843).
George Powell and Mary Owens, Sep. 12, 1843.  Wm.
McBee, J.P.  (Sep., 1843).
Hugh L. W. Rogers and Barbara Caywood, Sep. 12, 1843.
Rev. P. Rogers (?).  (Oct. 5, 1843).
Owin Edwards and Fanny Smith, Sep. 12, 1843.  William
S. Thomas, J.P.  (Dec. 11, 1843).
Caleb W. Rutledge and Eliza Ann Berry, Sep. 20, 1843.
John Hurst, J.P.  (Sep. 20, 1843).
Daniel Roberson and Nancy Lemar, Sep. 20, 1843.
No return.
Morris P. (?) Rowatt (?) and Darkey Campbell, Sep. 26,
1843.  John Ritchie, J.P.  (Sep. 27, 1843).
Michael Sowder and Mandy Lea, Sep. 28, 1843.  No return.
William Dykes and Eliza Brasher, Oct. 2, 1843.  Levi
Goin, J.P.  (Oct. 2, 1843).
John Myers and Arminda Carpentur (?), Oct. 9, 1843.
Geo. H. Cheek, J.P.  (Oct. 19, 1843).
James J. Lambert and Polly Ann Rowark, Oct. 11, 1843.
John Hurst, J.P.  (Oct. 14, 1843).
William England and Lydia Ann Lambert, Oct. 11, 1843.
John Hurst, J.P.  (Oct. 14, 1843).
Wm Owens and Elizabeth Hays (?), Oct. 11, 1843.  Isaac
Vanbebber, J.P.  (Oct. 12, 1843).
John Lorton (?) and Elizabeth Ellis, Oct. 14, 1843.
James Chick, J.P.  (Oct. 17, 1843).
Elisha Estice and Mariah Jones, Oct. 17, 1843.  John
Hurst, J.P.  (Oct. 18, 1843).
David Fulks and Nancy Woattan (?), Oct. 17, 1843.
James F. Hooper, J.P.  (Oct. 18, 1843).
Edmand Napeer (Napier) and Matilda Ely, Oct. 21, 1843.
No return.
Benjamin S. (?) Carter and Nancy Carter, Oct. 22, 1843.
Samuel Day, J.P.  (Oct. 23, 1843).
Charles Baker and Elizabeth Brooks, Oct. 24, 1843.  No
return.
Sterling Hammock and Mary Jourden, Oct. 26, 1843.
Geo. H. Cheek, J.P.  (Oct. 26, 1843).
Flemman (?) Huddleston and Elizabeth White, Oct. 26,
1843.  J. F. Hopper, J.P.  (Oct. 26, 1843).
Robert Glenn and Margaret Weir, Oct. 26, 1843.  W. A.
Taytor (?), M.G.  (Oct. 26, 1843).
Henry A. Dunn and Elizabeth Anderson, Oct. 28, 1843.
R. J. Russell (?), J.P.  (Nov. 23, 1843).
John Mays and Lucinda Johnson, Oct. 30, 1843.  James
Seals, J.P.  (Nov. 7, 1843).
Joshua Adams and Timpa (?) Smith, Oct. 30, 1843.  Elder
James Bishop.  (Nov. 2, 1843).
James Lea and Catharine Howerton, Nov. 4, 1843.  George
H. Cheek, J.P.  (Nov. 9, 1843).
Isaac Southern and Sarah Chadwell, Nov. 7, 1843.  James
Chick, J.P.  (Oct. (?) 8, 1843).

Calvin Brooks and Judah E. L. (?) Estice, Nov. 7, 1843.
John Hurst, J.P. (Nov. 8, 1843).
Andrew J. Harmon and Benny Branscomb, Nov. 13, 1843.
Wm McBee, J.P. (Nov. 16, 1843).
Charles Bussle (?) and Sidney Ann Jones, Nov. 16,
1843. J. Chick, J.P. (Nov. 17, 1843).
Phelin Minks and Anna Brewer, Nov. 11, 1843. Nicholas
Speake. (Nov. 18, 1843).
John Sproles and Sarah Bales, Nov. 18, 1843. S. Hobbs,
M.G. (Nov. 23, 1843).
John C. Colson and Catharin Smith, Nov. 20, 1843.
S. Hobbs, M.G. (Dec. 25, 1843).
Joab January and Amanda M. L. Ward, Nov. 23, 1843.
Geo. H. Cheek, J.P. (Nov. 23, 1844 (?)).
Matthias (?) Hinshilder (?) and Nancy Marcum, Nov. 23,
1843. W. L. Turner. (June 10, 1844(?)).
Ransam (?) Day and Catharine Bowman, Nov. 25, 1843.
George H. Cheek, J.P. (Nov. 28, 1843).
Elisha Butcher and Jane Calestane (?), Nov. 28, 1843.
James Chick (?), J.P. (Dec. 1, 1843).
James D. Green and Lucy Ann Lanham, Dec. 2, 1843. Mark
Hurst, M.G. (Dec. 3, 1843).
David Winegar (?) and Mary Yearry, Dec. 4, 1843. S.
Hobbs, M.G. (Dec. 7, 1843).
James Waller and Livisa (?) Liford, Dec. 5, 1843.
James Chick, J.P. (Dec. 10, 1843).
James M. Hopkins and Rebecca Baker, Dec. 8, 1843. John
Farmer, J.P. (Dec. 9, 1843).
Charley M. Day and Hannah Guthery, Dec. 15, 1843.
Wm McBee, J.P. (Dec. 17, 1843).
John Molana (?) and Bilenda (?) Hopkins, Dec. 16,
1843. John Farmer, J.P. (Dec. 17, 1843).
William Cunningham and Martha Hicks, Dec. 18, 1843.
John Ritchie, J.P. (Dec. 22, 1843).
Elijah Hudson and Rebecco J. Norvell, Dec. 19, 1843.
Wm McBee, J.P. (Dec. 19, 1843).
John Lunday and Rachel Snavely, Dec. 20, 1843. James
Chick, J.P. (Dec. 21, 1843).
Jonathan T. (?) Walker and Amanda J. Tussey (?), Dec.
23, 1843. John Ritchie, J.P. (Dec. 25, 1843).
Jirriael (?) Smith and Mary Ann Fletcher, Dec. 25,
1843. N. Speake. (Dec. 27, 1843).
David Lynch and Nancy Lynch, Dec. 28, 1843. Jacob
Cloud, J.P. (Dec. 28, 1843).
Isom Gibson and Elizabeth J. Burch, Jan. 1, 1844.
Geo. H. Cheek, J.P. (Jan. 2, 1844).
David Estice and Mary Householder, Jan. 2, 1844.
W. L. Turner (Jan. 2, 1844).
Thompson Sherman and Elizabeth England, Jan. 8, 1844.
John M. Burch, J.P. (Jan. 9, 1844).
Joshua Rossan (?) and Elizabeth Large, Jan. 17, 1844.
L. L. (?) Herrel, J.P. (Jan. 18, 1844).
John Green and Susannah Shelby, Jan. 17, 1844. R. J.
Russel, J.P. (Jan. 18, 1844).
William Marteal and Malinda Hooper, Jan. 20, 1844.
James F. Hooper, J.P. (Jan. 21, 1844).

Robert Sanders and Mary England, Jan. 20, 1844. Geo.
  H. Cheek, J.P. (Jan. 21, 1844).
James F. Fernay (?) and Perlina (?) Cain, Jan. 21,
  1844. Samuel Gibson, J.P. (Jan. 21, 1844).
Wm Eldridge and Ruthy Owin, Jan. 23, 1844. S. Hobbs,
  M.G. (Jan. 25, 1844).
John Lankford and Ruthy S. Rowland, Jan. 25, 1844.
  Levi Goin, J.P. (Jan. 26, 1844).
George Evans and Eliza Day, Jan. 30, 1844. Geo. H.
  Cheek, J.P. (Feb. 1, 1844).
John Malone and Sarah Sharp, Feb. 1, 1844. Rev.
  Pleasant Rogers. (Feb. 8, 1844).
John Ray and Emily Davis, Feb. 1, 1844. Samuel Gibson,
  J.P. (Feb. 3, 1844).
William Bailey and Elizabeth Hoskins, Feb. 1, 1844.
  No return.
Hiram C. Wereman (?) and Hannah Province, Feb. 1, 1844.
  J. Cheek, J.P. (Feb. 22, 1844).
Joshua H. Chapman and Margarett Ellis, Feb. 8, 1844.
  Wm L. Turner. (Feb. 6, 1844).
Anderson Malicoat (?) and Elizabeth Bundren, Feb. 9,
  1844. No return.
Elijah Jones (?) and Sally Lea, Feb. 9, 1844. No return.
James T. (?) McCard (?) and Mary Ann Collins, Feb. 18,
  1844. No return.
James Parten and Jane Jackson, Feb. 21, 1844. James
  Cheek, J.P. (Feb. 22, 1844).
Paschal (?) Tucker and Rhoda Dees, Feb. 24, 1844.
  William Williams. (Feb. 29, 1844).
George W. Jennings and Ellender Waller, Mar. 2, 1844.
  G. H. Cheek, J.P. (Mar. 3, 1844).
Leftrage Clark and Mary Shoemaker, Mar. 12, 1844. George
  Ford, M.G. (Mar. 12, 1844).
Jacob Smiley and Susanah Wilburn (?), Mar. 27, 1844.
  No return.
Esom Loves (?) and Anny Grocecloce (?), Mar. 29, 1844.
  Samuel Gibson, J.P. (Mar. 29, 1844).
William F. Gibson and Elizabeth Dutton, Apr. 1, 1844.
  Samuel Gibson, J.P. (Apr. 1, 1844).
William Lock and Sarah Carroll, Apr. 5, 1844. No return.
Greenberry Lawson and Lavina Carter, Apr. 12, 1844.
  Henry Holt, M.G. (Apr. 16, 1844).
James M. Carr and Jane Hodge, Apr. 12, 1844. John M.
  Burch, J.P. (Apr. 14, 1844).
P. P. Duygns (?) and Emily Wilson, Apr. 13, 1844.
  J. F. Hoops (?), J.P. (Apr. 13, 1844).
N. McCrary and Norciss Willson, Apr. 29, 1844. Wm
  McBee, J.P. (Apr. 30, 1844).
D. W. Jones and Elizabeth Davis (?), May 4, 1844.
  John Farmer, J.P. (May 5, 1844).
Arthor (?) Hopkins and Nancy Jones, May 9, 1844.
  Wm. S. (?) Thomas, J.P. (May 11, 1844).
Roblins (?) Jones and Charity Snuffer, May 18, 1844.
  Wm McBee, J.P. (May 20, 1844).

CLAIBORNE COUNTY MARRIAGES

Joseph McWilliams and Moholey (?) Chumbley, May 28,
  1944. Samuel Gibson, J.P. (May 29, 1844).
Arnold (?) Hellon (?) and Nancy (?) Turnbull, June 3,
  1844. G. H. Cheek, J.P. (June 20, 1844).
Nathan Lawson and Elvisy (?) Mason, June 8, 1844.
  Georg H. Cheek, J.P. (June 9, 1844).
Hiram Hoskins and Polly Henderson, June 8, 1844.
  Samuel Gibson, J.P. (June 10, 1844).
Prior Cuningham and M. A. Dobkins, June 29, 1844. John
  Hurst, J.P. (June 29, 1844).
Eli Hawkins and Sarah Burns, July 1, 1844. P. J.
  Parrott (?), J.P. (July 1, 1844).
Joseph Dosier (?) and Barthena Barnet, July 1, 1844.
  P. J. Parrot (?), J.P. (July 20, 1844).
William Hornis (?) and Mary Cane (?), July 11, 1844.
  Georg (?) H. Cheek, J.P. (July 11, 1844).
Nathan H. Moore and Sarah Ann Thompson, July 25, 1844.
  John M. Burch, J.P. (July 25, 1844).
William Dulin and Elender Fields, July 25, 1844. John
  Hurst, J.P. (July 25, 1844).
John H. Carr and Mary Briant, July 27, 1844. Wm.
  McBee, J.P. (July 28, 1844).
A. I. Mulhos and Mary McConkuy (?), July 27, 1844.
  James Seals, J.P. (Aug. 1, 1844).
John Hicks and Jane Prisley (?), Aug. 3, 1844. Samuel
  Gibson, J.P. (Aug. 5, 1844).
A. I. Pridemore and Malinda Eastrage, Aug. 5, 1844.
  James Cheek, J.P. (Aug. 18, 1844).
William Owens and Sarah Vane, Aug. 5, 1844. G. H.
  Cheek, J.P. (Aug. 6, 1844).
Wm Gibbs and Barbery Suttun, Aug. 10, 1844. Samuel
  Gibson, J.P. (Aug. 12, 1844).
Vincen Roley and Tempy (?) Davis, Aug. 21, 1844. No
  return.
James Fordy (?) and Emily C. Evans, Aug. 22, 1844. No
  return.
Presley Cottral and Elisabeth (?) Owens, Aug. 24, 1844.
  S. Hoobbs (?), M.G. (Aug. 25, 1844).
Archable Owens and Tabitha Eldrage, Aug. 24, 1844.
  S. Hoobs (?), M.G. (Aug. 29, 1844).
John Owsley and Polla (?) Powell, Aug. 29, 1844. Thos.
  Whited (?), J.P. (Sep. 22, 1844).
Anderson Carpentr (?) and Polla Burton, Sep. 3, 1844.
  G. H. Cheek, J.P. (Sep. 3, 1844).
Wesley Parrott and Catharine Jennings, Sep. 7, 1844.
  G. H. Cheek, J.P. (Sep. 8, 1844).
J. M. Lowe and Delila Morris, Sep. 9, 1844. No return.
Elijah Taylor and Nancy Write, Sep. 10, 1844. No return.
Lewis Garland (?) and Rebecker (?) Lockoral (?), Sep.
  16, 1844. No return.
John Sufrage and Salla Calline, Sep. 19, 1844. L.
  Goins, J.P. (Sep. 19, 1844).
Wm H. Wallis and Mary Ann Mitchel, Sep. 19, 1844.
  J. H. Davis, J.P. (Sep. 22, 1844).

19

Thos. Brewer and Anna White, Sep. 20, 1844. Jacob
Cloud, J.P. (Sep. 21, 1844).
Edward N. Hill and Julia A. Brown, Sep. 24, 1844. Geo.
H. Cheek, J.P. (Sep. 20 (?), 1844).
Harvy Smith and Drueiller Goinbral, Sep. 23, 1844.
James F. Hooper, J.P. (Sep. 23, 1844).
A. J. Housholder and M. C. Marcum, Sep. 24, 1844.
Geo. H. Cheek, J.P. (Sep. 24, 1844).
Stokley Alton and Susanah Carpenter, Oct. 7, 1844. G.
H. Cheek. (Oct. 8, 1844).
William Jones and Mariah Cadel, Oct. 5, 1844. James
Cheek, J.P. (Oct. 6, 1844).
William Burton and Malisa Carpenter, Oct. 3, 1844.
G. H. Cheek, J.P. (Oct. 3, 1844).
Wm Parrat (?) and M. E. Bales, Oct. 7, 1844. James
Bishop. (Oct. 10, 1844).
Wm Hodge and Mariah Cloud, Oct. 9, 1844. G. H. Cheek.
(Oct. 10, 1844).
John Graves and (?) Willson, Oct. 7, 1844. Thos.
Whiteted (?), J.P. (Oct. 13, 1844).
Henry Renolds and Chaniy (?) Preday, Oct. 13, 1844.
J. M. Burch, J.P. (Oct. 13, 1844).
James Hopson and Martha Wills, Oct. 26, 1844. G. H.
Cheek, J.P. (Oct. 24 (?), 1844).
Zackariah Sutton and Lucy Ann Eastrage, Oct. 24, 1844.
James Chick, J.P. (Oct. 25, 1844).
John Shelby and Nancy Sheckels (?), Oct. 23, 1844.
Thos. Whiteted (?), J.P. (Oct. 27, 1844).
Reuben Cardwell and Luritta Sanders, Oct. 29, 1844.
G. H. Cheek, J.P. (Oct. 31, 1844).
James Grimes and Mary Pridemore, Oct. 31, 1844. James
Cheek, J.P. (Nov. 3, 1844).
A. Campbell and Levisa (?) Campbell, Oct. 2, 1844.
John Hurst, J.P. (Nov. 2, 1844).
Russel Brewor (?) and Polley Cloud (?), Nov. 4, 1844.
James Seals, J.P. (Nov. 7, 1844).
Henry Edwards and Sarah Williams, Nov. 8, 1844.
Wm Williams. (Nov. 10, 1844).
Jurdan (?) Hunter (?) and Jane Hicks, Nov. 15, 1844.
Wm Williams, M.G. (Nov. 18, 1844).
William Moyers and Susanah Bowman, Nov. 19, 1844.
No return.
A. F. Cromwell (?) and M. A. Scofield (?), Nov. 19,
1844. John Farmer, J.P. (Nov. 21, 1844).
Isaac Wallera (?) and Manirva Sumpter, Dec. 2, 1844.
No return.
Moses Mcafee and China Wallen, Nov. 22, 1844. N. L.
(?) McDowell, M.G. (Nov., 1844).
Wm B. Dunn and Nancy Sharp, Nov. 30, 1844. Wm Williams,
M.G. (Dec. 4, 1844).
Wm Shanon (?) and Milly (?) Rhey, Dec. 7, 1844. James
Chick, J.P. (Dec. 8, 1844).
Thomas Warrin (?) and Eleana (?) Smith, Dec. 9, 1844.
John E. Farmer, J.P. (Dec. 12, 1844).

John Sutton and Sarah Pridemore, Dec. 4, 1844. Samuel
    Gibson, J.P. (Dec. 16, 1844).
J. B. Millis and Elizabeth Johnson, Dec. 22, 1844.
    No return.
J. Cunningham and Nancy Cardwell, Dec. 23, 1844.
    Samuel Day, J.P. (Dec. 23, 1844).
James H. Osborn (?) and Elizabeth Jane Marcum (?), Dec.
    31, 1844. N. Speake. (Jan. 1, 1845).
A. S. Russel and Edney I. Neil, Jan. 11, 1845. Solemen
    Hobbs, M.G. (Jan. 16, 1845).
D. I. Gilbert and Nancy Ann Rice, Jan. 15, 1845. John
    Gilbert. (Jan. 17, 1845).
Bluford (?) Woodall and Nancy Toney (?), Jan. 11, 1845.
    Joseph H. Davis, J.P. (Jan. 12, 1845).
Elijah Marian (?) and Nancy Gilbert, Jan. 16, 1845.
    Wm S. Thomas, J.P. (Jan. 19, 1845).
William Grace and Drueiller (?) Cadle, Jan. 18, 1845.
    No return.
Jeel Venany (?) and F. Crumbley, Jan. 18, 1845.
    No return.
E. D. Willis and Orleany Lanham, Jan. 18, 1845.
    No return.
Philip M. Bully and Manervy Jennings, Jan. 22, 1845.
    H. F. Taylor, M.G. (Jan. 22, 1845).
Sterling (?) J. Barnard and Nancy Mason, Jan. 25, 1845.
    N. A. Evahs, J.P. (Jan. 27, 1845).
Samuel Hubbert and Mary Parton, Jan. 22, 1845. Nathan
    Buchanan, J.P. (Mar. 22, 1845).
Major Brewer and Mary Marler (?), Jan. 22, 1845. P. J.
    Parrtt, J.P. (Jan. 26, 1845).
Georg (?) Cartar and E. J. Harris, Jan. 28, 1845. No
    return.
Enas Day and Nancy Dougherty, Jan. 29, 1845. Wm McBee,
    J.P. (Jan. 30, 1845).
Joel Barker and Susan No (?), Feb. 14, 1845. No return.
Georg Cartar and Eliza Jane Carter, Jan. 28, 1845.
    S. Hobbs, M.G. (Jan. 29, 1845).
William Chick and Mary Cox, Feb. 5, 1845. James Chick,
    J.P. (Feb. 6, 1845).
Ryley Dykes and Lewrittey (?) Holton (?), Feb. 17, 1845.
    No return.
Kindruk (?) Holt and Polley (?) Sumpter, Feb. 15, 1845.
    John Ritchie, J.P. (Feb. 20, 1845).
Josiah Ramsey and Elizabeth Sims, Feb. 23, 1845.
    John Farmer, J.P. (Mar. 2, 1845).
Wm Owsley and Matilda (?) Herrel, Feb. 25, 1845. John
    M. Burch, J.P. (Feb. 25, 1845).
Stewart Collins and Catharine Collins, Mar. 8, 1845.
    Wm. Williams. (Mar. 9, 1845).
Ewing Yoakum and Martha Vanbebber, Mar. 15, 1845.
    Wm McBee, J.P. (Mar. 27, 1845).
Lazeros (?) Dotson and Elizabeth H. Carpentr (?),
    Mar. 20, 1845. John Hurst, J.P. (Mar. 21, 1845).
Isaac McNew and Mary Ann Arwine, Apr. 1, 1845. Samuel
    Day, J.P. (Apr. 1, 1845).

Shadrick Moor and Polley Ann Oneil, Apr. 7, 1845.
Soleman Pope. (Apr. 12, 1845).
Walter (?) Hatfield (?) and Polly Hurst, Apr. 10,
1845. S. Hobbs, M.G. (Apr. 10, 1845).
Jno. Grubb and Emiline (?) Sweet, Apr. 10, 1845. S. S.
(?) Herrell, J.P. (Apr. 10, 1845).
John Green and Mohaby (?) Goins, Apr. 14, 1845. Levi
Goin, J.P. (Apr. 4 (?), 1845).
Wm. H. Sharp and Elender (?) Oaks, Apr. 18, 1845.
Thomas Whiteted, J.P. (Apr. 20, 1845).
Tilmon D. Ball and Elizabeth Ball, Apr. 24, 1845.
No return.
Edmon Davis and Ackey (?) Jones, Apr. 15, 1845. Samuel
Day, J.P. (Apr. 15, 1845).
Wm. J. McNew and Caroline M. Rogers, Apr. 26, 1845.
W. Bruce. (May 1, 1845).
Nathaniel Dunn and Malinda Jennings, Apr. 26, 1845.
S. S. Herrll (?), J.P. (Apr. 27, 1845).
Peter Fips and Julia A. Lockwood, Apr. 29, 1845. N.
Speake. (Apr. 30, 1845).
Reubin Mills and S. Sutton, May 2, 1845. John Ritchie,
J.P. (May 4, 1845).
William Buck and Emaline Baltrip, May 4 (?), 1845.
S. Hobbs, M.G. (May 7, 1845).
John Chapman and Susanah Chadwell, May 29, 1845.
J. Chick (?), J.P. (June 8, 1845).
Jos. Ramsey and Margaret Baker, June 2, 1845. John
Farmer, J.P. (June 8, 1845).
D. Lawson and S. Hill, June 2, 1845. John Hurst, J.P.
(June 5, 1845).
John Grimes and E. Hatfield, June 4, 1845. John Hurst,
J.P. (June 5, 1845).
Wm. Buck and Emeline Baltrip, May 8, 1845. N. A. Evans,
J.P. (May 7, 1845).
Jos. Hazs and S. Mcanally (?), Feb. 15, 1845. No return.
John Brink (?) and Elejiceia (?) Spiers, June 7, 1845.
Samuel Gibson, J.P. (June 7, 1845).
B. Poor and M. E. Herell (?), June 14, 1845. No return.
Isaac Miller and Louisa Cloud, June 17, 1845. Geo. H.
Cheek, J.P. (June 17, 1845).
Cornelius Rogers and Manery (?) Bowman, June 19, 1845.
No return.
E. Campbell and Emaley Hazelwood (?), June 24, 1845.
J. Cloud, J.P. (June 4, 1845).
John Woods and Martha (?) C. Powers, June 26, 1845.
J. Chick (?), J.P. (June 25, 1845).
Richard Hopson and Hanner Ritter, July 15, 1845. Samuel
Day, J.P. (July 1 (?), 1845).
Reubin Burch and Phoeby Harrell, July 2, 1845. G. H.
Cheek, J.P. (July 3, 1845).
John W. Crisp and Mary (?) Havely (?), July 4, 1845.
H. F. Taylor, M.G. (July 8, 1845).
William Clouse and Rachel S. Wilson, July 9, 1845.
Henry Holt, M.G. (July 11, 1845).

Sterling G. Coleman and Elisabeth Jane Hobbs, July 10,
1845. James Bishop. (July 13, 1845).
James Snavely and Martha (?) Year (?), July 11, 1845.
S. Hobbs, M.G. (July 17, 1845).
Willis C. (?) and Nancy Angel, July 17, 1845. John
Easley, J.P. (July 17, 1845).
John Chany (?) and Margret Renolds, July 20, 1845.
John Easley, J.P. (July 20, 1845).
Preston C. Goforth and Malinda Hunnicutt, July 23,
1845. Thomas Whiteted, J.P. (July 24, 1845).
Wm. G. Payne and Roday (?) H. Marcum, July 23, 1845.
N. S. McDowell, M.G. (July, 1845).
Jesse Hopper (?) and Eliza Wells, Aug. 2, 1845. James
Gilbert. (Aug. 3, 1845).
William Williams and Sintha Roarks (?), July 2, 1845.
J. Chick (?), J.P. (July 3, 1845).
Simpson Parks and L. T. Nove (?), Aug. 20, 1845. John
Hurst, J.P. (Aug. 21, 1845).
Jacob Wolfingbargor and E. Rogers (?), Aug. 27, 1845.
John Farmer, J.P. (Aug. 28, 1845).
J. S. Cassel (?) and Nancy Hopper, Aug. 28, 1845.
No return.
Thos. Lawson and Hetty Moor, Aug. 7, 1845. John
Ritchie, J.P. (Aug. 7, 1845).
Reubin Kesterson and Adaline Henderson, Aug. 26, 1845.
N. A. Evans, J.P. (Aug. 26, 1845).
James McAffee (?) and Elizabeth Minton, Aug. 29, 1845.
J. Chick (?), J.P. (Aug. 30, 1845).
Reubin Norris and Nancy A. Moor, Sep. 1, 1845. No
return.
John Slatton and Malinda Chumbly, Sep. 6, 1845. No
return.
Jesse Lay and Sarah Shelby, Sep. 6, 1845. Wm. Williams,
M.G. (July 3, 1846).
Robert S. Bains (?) and Nancy L. Shomate (?), Sep. 6,
1845. J. Cloud, J.P. (Sep. 7, 1845).
James D. Burchett and Cinthy M. Johnson, Sep. 6, 1845.
John Gilbert. (Sep. 11, 1845).
Eldrage (?) H. Lanham and Perlina Henderson, Sep. 10,
1845. Mark Hurst, M.G. (Nov. 11, 1845).
William Price and Deby Large, Sep. 11, 1845. John
Easley, J.P. (Sep. 11, 1845).
William Dickinson and Margret Cauk (?), Sep. 16, 1845.
J. Chick (?), J.P. (Sep. 16, 1845).
J. R. Hopkins and Elisa (?) Hopkins, Sep. 27, 1845.
No return.
Robert Greer and Thursa Ann Evans, Oct. 18, 1845.
J. H. Cheek, J.P. (Oct. 12 (?), 1845).
Thos. B. Taff and N. I. Kellons (Kellogg), Oct. 4,
1845. N. A. Evans, J.P. (Oct. 5, 1845).
James Simmons and E. A. Thompson, Oct. 8, 1845. L. L.
(?) Harrell, J.P. (Oct. 9, 1845).
James Perkey and Dicey Wilborne, Oct. 17, 1845. James
Seals, J.P. (Nov. 10, 1845).

Jas. Carell and Elvira (?) M. Herrell, Oct. 27, 1845.
No return.
John Pullian and Sarah Carter (?), Oct. 30, 1845. S.
Hobbs, M.G. (Nov. 2, 1845).
Henry Fritts and Sarah Burchett, Nov. 3, 1845. James
Bishop. (Nov. 19, 1845).
William Janeway and Pricila Vance, Nov. 6, 1845. James
Long, M.G. (Nov. 9, 1845).
Alford Marcum (?) and Levina (?) R. Thomas, Nov. 7,
1845. S. Hobbs, M.G. (Nov. 9, 1845).
Nelson Evans and Elisabeth (?) Hurst, Nov. 7, 1845.
G. H. Cheek. (Nov. 9, 1845).
Elias Ely (?) and Jerusha (?) Billingsly (?), Nov. 7,
1845. W. L. Turner, M.G. (Nov. 9, 1845).
Silvester (?) Num (?) and Levisa Herrell, Nov. 12, 1845.
No return.
F. H. Rogers and Emaley (?) Beelor (Beelau), Nov. 14,
1845. No return.
Joel Turner and Mary Sharp, Nov. 14, 1845. Wm. Williams,
M.G. (Nov. 19, 1845).
S. McCankey (?) and M. Davis (?), Nov. 15, 1845. James
Seals, J.P. (Nov. 23, 1845).
A. Marion (?) and S. Hall, Nov. 18, 1845. John Farmer,
J.P. (Nov. 18, 1845).
Silvester Nunn and Levica Herrell, Nov. 12, 1845. C.
M. Cheek. (Nov. 13, 1845).
Nathaniel M. Scott and Elisabeth (?) Yauncy (Yancy),
Nov. 24, 1845. John Farmer, J.P. (Dec. 4, 1845).
C. Baker and Luckrisha (?) McGee, Nov. 24, 1845. Wm.
L. Thomas, J.P. (Nov. 27, 1845).
M. B. Nunn and Elisabeth (?) Forgerson, Nov. 26, 1845.
James Chick, J.P. (Nov. 28, 1845).
Ransam (?) Hose and Jane Freeman, Nov. 25, 1845. Joseph
H. Davis, J.P. (Nov. 25, 1845).
John B. Parker and M. B. Hawley (?), Sep. 21, 1845 (?).
Robert Southern, M.G. (Sep. 26, 1846(?)).
James Slone and E. Wolfenbarger, Dec. 29, 1845. Wm.
S. Thomas, J.P. (Nov. 30, 1845).
Heston Davis and Lucinda Lewis, Dec. 2, 1845. John
Burch, J.P. (Dec. 4, 1845).
G. W. Hamelton and Elisabeth (?) Lambert, Dec. 3, 1845.
No return.
Daniel Cupp and Nancy Parker, Dec. 4, 1845. Robert
Southern. (Dec. 6, 1845).
James Turnbull and Mary Raby, Dec. 4, 1845. No return.
Patrick Willis and Elizabeth Ann Pitman, Dec. 13, 1845.
G. H. (?) Cheek, J.P. (Dec. 14, 1845).
James L. Russel and Catharin L. Sharp, Dec. 20, 1845.
W. L. Turner, M.G. (Dec. 25, 1845).
Carroll Gibbs and Martha Owens, Dec. 21, 1845. Wm.
McBee, J.P. (Dec. 23, 1845).
Benjamin Burchett and Elisabeth (?) Ann Ray (?), Dec.
26, 1845. John Gilbert. (Dec. 30, 1845).
Linneius (?) Billingsley and Polly Hunter, Dec. 26,
1845. Wm. Williams. (Jan. 4, 1846).

B. F. Cloud and Elisabeth M. Shultz, Dec. 29, 1845.
John Easley, J.P. (Dec. 29, 1845).
Noah Eastrage (?) and Millay Pridemore, Dec. 30,
1845. J. Chick (?), J.P. (Jan. 4, 1846).
William Strevels (?) and Lidaey (?) Lane, Jan. 3,
1846. Thomas Whiteted, J.P. (Jan. 3, 1845(?)).
Jonathan Sharp and Margret Elviny (?) Lynch, Jan. 5,
1846. R. J. Russell, J.P. (Jan. 8, 1846).
Franklin Redmon and Anna (?) Murry, Jan. 7, 1846.
W. L. Turner, M.G. (Jan. 15, 1846).
John Purkey and Patsy Seals, Jan. 10, 1846. No return.
Abel Lanham and Ann Killion, Feb. 15, 1846. No return.
Andrew Killion and Samiramiss (?) Lanham, Feb. 15,
1846. No return.
William Parkey and Martha Ann Martin, Feb. 15, 1846.
No return.
M. Overton and C. Riley, Jan. 27, 1846. John Ritchie,
J.P. (Jan. 28, 1846).
Jos. M. Johnson and Rebeckey Hix, Jan. 10, 1846. No
return.
Drury Lawson and Mary Ann Lewis, Jan. 19, 1846. S.
Hobbs, M.G. (Jan. 20, 1846).
James Williams and Polly Ann Bullard, Jan. 20, 1846.
John M. Burch, J.P. (Jan. 20, 1846).
Ekils (?) Burchitt and Leor (?) Anderson, Jan. 23, 1846.
John Farmer, J.P. (Jan. 25, 1846).
Michel (?) Powers and Leeby (?) Ann (?) Murphy, Jan.
26, 1846. John Easley, J.P. (Feb. 6, 1846).
H. A. Johnson and Judy (?) Parratt, Dec. 18, 1846.
J. E. Bowman, J.P. (Dec. 18, 1845 (?)).
Thos. Lawson and Sarah Lawson, Jan. 27, 1846. John
Hurst, J.P. (Jan. 30, 1846).
Wm. P. Harris and E. J. Camin (?), Jan. 27, 1846.
James Chick, J.P. (Jan. 28, 1846).
Mathew Tucker and Mary Oaks, Jan. 27, 1846. Wm.
Williams. (Jan. 28, 1846).
M. Keck and E. Goin, Jan. 30, 1846. Thomas Whiteted,
J.P. (Jan. 31, 1846).
Abner Fields and Julia Morris, Jan. 31, 1846. John
(?), J.P. (Jan. 31, 1846).
Wm. Venable and Jane McNeil, Feb. 1, 1846. George
Ford, M.G. (Feb. 1, 1846).
George Marcum and Nancy Elizabeth Bales, Feb. 4, 1846.
Nicholas Speake. (Feb. 7, 1846).
E. King and E. Buice (?), Feb. 9, 1846. Mark Hurst,
M.G. (Feb. 12, 1846).
John Thomas and Pheby Large, Feb. 15, 1846. No return.
William Cox and Elisabeth Hoskins, Feb. 18, 1846. J.
Chick, J.P. (Mar. 5, 1846).
Wm. Provance and Serena Russell, Feb. 20, 1846. Samuel
Gibson, J.P. (Feb. 22, 1846).
Thos. Mays and E. Lawson, Feb. 21, 1846. Jas (?) H.
Davis, J.P. (Feb. 21, 1846).
Wm. Cox and E. Hoskins, Feb. 18, 1846. No return.

Johnathan Barnard and Clary Hill, Feb. 22, 1846. G. H.
(?) Cheek, J.P. (Feb. 22, 1846).
Henry Daiel and Nancy Croxdale (?), Feb. 24, 1846. Wm.
S. (?) Thomas, J.P. (Feb. 26, 1846).
John Roarks and K. Masingil (Massengale), Mar. 2, 1846.
J. Chick (?), J.P. (Mar. 5, 1846).
H. Hurst and S. Stone, Mar. 6, 1846. G. H. (?) Cheek,
J.P. (Mar. 8, 1846).
J. M. Welch and S. Welch, Mar. 7, 1846. Samuel Gibson,
J.P. (Mar. 8, 1846).
Wm. H. Blackomone (?) and E. Winn, Mar. 9, 1846. John
Farmer, J.P. (Mar. 18, 1846).
L. Hurst and S. Miller, Mar. 24, 1846. John Easley,
J.P. (Mar. 26, 1846).
Robert Ruha (?) and M. J. King, Mar. 24, 1846. Wm. S.
Thomas, J.P. (Apr. 1, 1846).
Jesse Seafield (?) and L. Callaham (?), Mar. 28, 1846.
John Farmer, J.P. (Apr. 4, 1846).
M. Jene (?) and E. Dorethy, Mar. 28, 1846. John Farmer,
J.P. (Apr. 4, 1846).
Wm. Kibert and Susan Arnel, Apr. 1, 1846. James Cheek
(?), J.P. (Apr. 5, 1846).
L. B. Shomate (?) and Louisa Hodges, Apr. 4, 1846.
L. L. Herrell, J.P. (Apr. 5, 1846).
Wm. Sowder and Sarah Brummit, Apr. 6, 1846. James
Parker. (Apr. 9, 1846).
Leroy Hamblin and Juda Hamblin, Apr. 21, 1845 (?).
Nathan Buchanan, J.P. (Apr. 23, 1846).
Isham Myres and Charlotta Ritter, Apr. 21, 1846. Jacob
Cloud, J.P. (Apr. 22, 1846).
John Ellis and Hanah Fauche (?), Apr. 12, 1846. John
Farmer, J.P. (Apr. 13, 1846).
Joseph Thomas and Sarah Ann Kirk, May 7, 1846. Nicholas
Speak. (May, 1846).
Jas. Louthr (?) and Mary Hatfield, May 9, 1846. Wm. S.
Thomas, J.P. (May 9, 1846).
Wm. Barnes and R. Grace, May 9, 1846. J. Chick, J.P.
(May 17, 1846).
Wm. Nash and Manda Nash, May 9, 1846. No return.
John W. Shomate and Beverley Billingsly, May 15, 1846.
Samuel Gibson, J.P. (May 15, 1846).
Jas. Woods and Sarah Mosby, May 16, 1846. Jos. H.
Davis, J.P. (May 17, 1846).
S. Bales and M. J. Lockmillor, May 16, 1846. S. (?)
Hobbs, M.G. (May 17, 1846).
Alexander Harrell and Liddy Prestly, May 20, 1846.
Jacob Cloud, J.P. (May 21, 1846).
John Nelson and Margret Shofny, May 26, 1846. John
Easley, J.P. (May 26, 1846).
John Killion and Matilda Lanham, May 29, 1846. No
return.
Mastin (?) H. West (?) and Malinda Jane Posey (?),
May 29, 1846. Daniel P. Mones. (May 31, 1846).
Lafayett Bingham and Rebeckah Baker, June 3, 1846.
Samuel Gibson, J.P. (June 3, 1846).

David Wetherford and Elisabt (?) Presby, June 8, 1846.
N. A. Evans, J.P. (June 8, 1846).

A. A. Kyle and M. A. Graham, June 11, 1846. H. F.
Taylor, M.G. (June 11, 1846).

David Cape (Cope) and Sally Hamons, June 15, 1846.
Samuel Gibson, J.P. (June 15, 1846).

Andrew Williams and Catharine Ritter, June 20, 1846.
James Ritter, J.P. (June 21, 1846).

Josiah (?) and Polly Hopkins, June 20, 1846. No return.

Jobies (?) Hopkins and Juda Bishop, June 25, 1846.
John Farmer, J.P. (June 28, 1846).

John Moor and Permealy (?) McMahan, June 26, 1846.
No return.

James M. Stout and Sarah Crage, June 28, 1846. Samuel
Gibson, J.P. (Nov. 29, 1846).

John Lynch and Mary Wamies (?), June 29, 1846. Thomas
Whiteted, J.P. (July 3, 1846).

Aquilliah (?) Farmer and Emoline Latham, June 29, 1846.
James Ritter, J.P. (June 29, 1846).

Owen Willson and Eliza Jane Moor, July 9, 1846. S. (?)
Hobbs, M.G. (July 9, 1846).

H. Burchfield and Jane Graham, July 2, 1846. John
Easley, J.P. (July 2, 1846).

Cany (?) Moyers and Sarah Smith, July 15, 1846. No
return.

Latan Rannins (?) and Becky Hammack, July 18, 1846.
Samuel Day, J.P. (July 19, 1846).

William A. Stahdsbery and Elisabeth (?) Carnard (?),
July 20, 1846. Robert Southern, M.G. (Aug. 21, 1846).

Fredrick Fults and Emaley Nunn (?), July 25, 1846. John
Easley, J.P. (July 25, 1846).

William Wilborne and Delpha Masan, July 29, 1846. No
return.

Eli D. Cane and Cleressey (?) Lamone (?), July 31,
1846. Aaron Lynch, J.P.

John L. Swann (?) and Elisabeth (?) E. Eve, July 23,
1846. H. F. Taylor, M.G. (Aug. 2, 1846).

John Hicks and Sally Large, Aug. 3, 1846. John Easley,
J.P. (Aug. 3, 1846).

Richard Crabtree and Mary Balls, Aug. 3, 1846. J.
Chick (?), J.P. (Aug. 4, 1846).

Charles H. Havely (?) and Louisa Parker (?), Aug. 11,
1846. Robert Southern, M.G. (Aug. 11, 1845).

Felix Brachett (?) and Neoma Howel (?), Aug. 13, 1846.
No return.

James Venable and Louisa McCrary, July 23, 1846. No
return.

David Farby (?) and Elizabeth Hopkins, Aug. 14, 1846.
John Farmer, J.P. (Aug. 16, 1846).

Thos. Eads and Sarah Weever (?), Aug. 17, 1846. R. J.
Russell, J.P. (Aug. 18, 1846).

William Nunn and Delpha Nunn, Aug. 25, 1846. Simpson
Hurst, J.P. (Aug. 27, 1846).

Noah Hopkins and Malinda Jones, Aug. 28, 1846. John
Farmer, J.P. (Aug. 29, 1846).

William A. A. (?) Mcanlush (?) and Emaley (?) Black,
Aug. 30, 1846. Samuel Gibson, J.P. (Mar. 30, 1846 (?)).
N. Hopkins and Malinda Jones, Aug. 28, 1846. No return.
William S. Frost and Vina J. Baker, Sep. 11, 1846. John
Farmer, J.P. (Sep. 13, 1846).
Uriah Gowins and Nancy Gowins, Sep. 26, 1846. Levi
Goins, J.P. (Sep. 27, 1846).
Wm. Bowman and Mary Ann King, Oct. 2, 1846. James
Parker. (Oct. 7, 1846).
John Eversal (?) and Nancy Ann Duff, Sep. 30, 1846.
No return.
Canada Rogers and Nancy Malinda Vanbedder, Oct. 2,
1846. No return.
William Chumley and Sarah Dotson, Oct. 6, 1846. Samuel
Gipson (?), J.P. (Sep. 5, 1846).
Calvin Ramsey and Polley Crumbley, Oct. 12, 1846. Wm.
S. Thomas, J.P. (Oct. 14, 1846).
John M. White and Charaty (?) Chadwich (?), Oct. 22,
1846. No return.
John Thomas and Milly Kirk, Oct. 22, 1846. Nicholas
Speake. (Oct. 24, 1846).
Elisha Clark and Pheba James, Oct. 29, 1846. John
Gilbert. (Nov. 1, 1846).
Jacob Pike and Barthene Jones, Oct. 29, 1846. Thomas
Whiteted, J.P. (Nov. 1, 1846).
James A. Smith and Nancey E. Ellison, Oct. 30, 1846.
Aaron Lynch, J.P.
George Fields and Polly Willis, Nov. 2, 1846. Thomas
Whiteted, J.P. (Dec. 20, 1846).
Milbern Overton and Elisabeth S. Parkey, Oct. 26,
1846. James Bishop. (Oct. 28, 1846).
Jeptha Lynch and Louisa Davis, Nov. 4, 1846. George
Ford, M.G. (Nov. 5, 1846).
A. I. (?) W. Parker and Mary Tony, Nov. 7, 1846.
James Ritter, J.P. (Nov. 8, 1846).
Jacob Walker and M. Davis, Nov. 9, 1846. Licence
returned.
Henry Beach and Mourning Parrott, Nov. 14, 1846. P. J.
Parrot, J.P. (Nov. 23, 1846).
M. M. Rogers and Mary White, Nov. 16, 1846. No return.
William Wyatt and Susan Grigery, Nov. 18, 1846. Samuel
Gibson, J.P. (Nov. 18, 1846).
M. A. Cook and D. L. Jones, Nov. 23, 1846. S. Hobbs,
M.G. (Nov. 23, 1846).
Samuel Arnel and Rachal Rolin, Nov. 24, 1846. Samuel
Gibson, J.P. (Nov. 25, 1846).
John F. Berry and Amanda Nash, Nov. 23, 1846. Wm.
Williams, M.G. (Nov. 24, 1846).
Jacob Walker and Louisa Lewis, Nov. 26, 1846. L. L.
Harrell, J.P. (Nov. 26, 1846).
Calvin McBee and Emeline McBee, Nov. 27, 1846. L. L.
Harrell, J.P. (Jan. 10, 1847).
William Ritter and Barbra Hollin, Nov. 27, 1846. Jacob
Clod (?), J.P. (Nov., 1846).

Baley Hernen (?) and Rodday Baley, Nov. 29, 1846. Samuel
Gibson, J.P. (Nov. 29, 1846).
Montgomery Herrell and Pertilly (?) Brooks, Dec. 3,
1846. John Hurst, J.P. (Dec. 3, 1846).
Mathew A. Herllon and Nancy Thacker, Nov. 18, 1846.
James Ritter, J.P. (Nov. 26, 1846).
John Owens and Orlena J. Fults, Dec. 4, 1846. John
Easley, J.P. (Dec. 4, 1846).
Samuel Reed and Sarah Lee, Dec. 7, 1846. Jas. H. Davis,
J.P. (Dec. 7, 1846).
James Caynard and Polly Ann Sharp, Dec. 9, 1846. No
return.
Mathew C. McDonel and Menervy J. Shomate, Dec. 9, 1846.
James Long, M.G. (Dec. 17, 1846).
John Doye and Polly Western, Dec. 18, 1846. James
Bishop. (Dec. 20, 1846).
John Cox and Neely Sharp, Dec. 21, 1846. Asbury
Brooks. (Dec. 22, 1846).
John Fletcher (?) and Ivey Ann Lanham, Dec. 21, 1846.
Mark Hurst, M.G. (Dec. 24, 1846).
Berrill (?) Smith and Faney (?), Dec. 22, 1846. J.
Chick (?), J.P. (Dec. 23, 1846).
John Houston and Nancy King, Dec. 23, 1846. P. J.
Parrott, J.P. (Dec. 27, 1846).
Mastin Gipson and Dosha Scott, Dec. 23, 1846. Simpson
Hurst, J.P. (Dec. 24, 1846).
E. V. Wallon and Jane Graham, Dec. 30, 1846. Samuel
Gibson, J.P. (Dec. 30, 1846).
Jacob Reed and Milly Webb, Dec. 31, 1846. Jas. H. Davis,
J.P. (Dec. 31, 1846).
Mark Jones and Sally Laffoon, Jan. 7, 1847. Simpson
Hurst, J.P. (Jan. 7, 1847).
Wiley Rowe and Emaley Person, Jan. 5, 1847. Jos. H.
Davis, J.P. (Jan. 6, 1847).
Mariel Hill and Louisa Day, Jan. 11, 1847. N. L. (?)
McDowell (?). (Jan., 1847).
William Daniel and Mary Liford, Jan. 11, 1847. L. (?)
Hobbs, M.G. (Jan. 12, 1847).
Richard Powel and Nancy Jones, Jan. 12, 1847. Thomas
Whiteted, J.P. (Jan. 12, 1847).
Josiah Chadwick and Temprance Presley, Jan. 13, 1847.
John Easley, J.P. (Jan. 14, 1847).
Joel Taylor and Sary Ann Ritter, Jan. 15, 1847. James
Ritchie, J.P. (Jan. 15, 1847).
Thos. Crafford and Mary Eada, Jan. 15, 1847. Samuel
Gibson, J.P. (Jan. 17, 1847).
Daniel F. Sowder and Nancy Willis, Jan. 16, 1847. William
H. Harper (?), M.G. (Feb. 21, 1847).
Sterling B. Carter and Margret Cole, Jan. 18, 1847.
James Ritter, J.P. (Jan. 19, 1847).
Rowen Elrod and Martha Davis, Jan. 18, 1847. Jos.
H. Davis, J.P. (? 21, 1847).
Eleane (?) Reed and Nancy Maden, Jan. 25, 1847. Jos.
H. Davis, J.P. (Jan. 26, 1847).

Drury D. Gibson and Claricey (?) Knight, Jan. 28, 1847.
John Easley, J.P. (Jan. 28, 1847).
Thos. Collins and Berthena Presley, Jan. 29, 1847. Levi
Goin, J.P. (Jan. 31, 1847).
Elnathan Cloud and Polly Ritter, Jan. 30, 1847. (Jan.,
1847).
Thos. Dum (?) and Elizabeth M. Brandscombe, Jan. 30,
1847. Aaron Lynch, J.P.
Henry Mills and Mahaley Hill, Feb. 1, 1847. No return.
William Burket and Lidia McMillion, Feb. 1, 1847. No
return.
C. F. (?) Rice and Dicey M. Rogers, Jan. 28, 1847. N.
(?) Bruce, J.P. (Jan. 1847).
Milton Hurst and Emaley Miller, Jan. 20, 1847. Mark
Hurst, M.G. (Jan. 21, 1847).
Constantin (?) Smith and Mary Moor, Feb. 6, 1847. S.
(?) Hobbs, M.G. (Feb. 11, 1847).
Johnson Davis and Emaley Lee, Feb. 9, 1847. No return.
John Powers and I. Thomas, Feb. 9, 1847. Nicholas
Speake. (Feb. 11, 1847).
Samuel Thomas and Nancy Snow, Feb. 9, 1847. Nicholas
Speak. (Feb. 11, 1847).
Mark Mannon and Mary A. Dulin, February 15, 1847. No
return.
James Hermen and Susan Vaughn, Feb. 17, 1847. S. (?)
Hobbs, M.G. (Feb. 18, 1847).
John Denny and Nancy Bullard, Feb. 20, 1847. William
Neil, J.P. (Feb. 21, 1847).
Alexander England and Susanah Mays, Feb. 22, 1847. Jacob
Cloud, J.P. (Mar. 4, 1847).
George Longworth and Mary A. Barker, Feb. 25, 1847.
John Easley, J.P. (Feb. 25, 1847).
William Standafer and Elizabeth Jones, Mar. 5, 1847.
John Ritchie, J.P. (Mar. 5, 1847).
James McCullum and Polly Gray, Mar. 15, 1847. Jos. H.
Davis, J.P. (Mar. 22, 1847).
Ellerlley (?) Neil and Caroline Mason, Apr. 18, 1847.
(Apr. 1 (?), 1847).
Eli Shelton and Mahaley Moser, Apr. 3, 1847. R. J.
Russell, J.P. (Apr. 4, 1847).
Harid (?) Hopson and Sarah A. Bunch, Apr. 7, 1847. James
Ritter, J.P. (Apr. 8, 1847).
Nicalis (?) Moner and Polly Strevels (?), Apr. 13,
1847. Thomas Whiteted, J.P. (Apr. 15, 1847).
Stokley Doyby and Ledia Woodard, Apr. 13, 1847. Thomas
Hobbs, M.G. (Apr. 15, 1847).
Isaac Edwards and Alby (?) Sebolt, Apr. 27, 1847.
John Ritchie, J.P. (Apr. 2 (?), 1847).
Isaac Shelvy (?) and Leor (?) Capps, Apr. 27, 1847.
Levi Goins, J.P. (Apr. 29, 1847).
Russel Brieding and Sarah Day, May 13, 1847. Simpson
Hurst, J.P. (May 14, 1847).
Andrew J. Breeding and Mary Pitman, May 19, 1847.
Simpson Hurst, J.P. (May 19, 1847).

CLAIBORNE COUNTY MARRIAGES

Andrew J. Dunkin (?) and Mary Venable, June 26, 1847.
  L. L. Harrell, J.P. (May 27 (?), 1847).
John J. Moncy (?) and Louisa Owens, May 29, 1847.
  No return.
George W. Eastes and Alice Pitman, June 5, 1847.
  Simpson Hurst, J.P. (June 6, 1847).
Henry Warick and Mary Burch, June 5, 1847. James
  Ritter, J.P. (June 6, 1847).
John L. Sensabagh (?) and Manila McAnalla, June 7, 1847.
  John Barringer, M.G. (June 9, 1847).
Christopher Deans and Eliza Toney, June 12, 1847.
  James Ritter, J.P. (June 16, 1847).
Preston Brooks and Lucy Ann Campbell, June 15, 1847.
  John Hurst, J.P. (June 15, 1847).
James Harlis and Susan Mabane (Mebane), June 15, 1847.
  Robert Sothers, M.G. (June 17, 1847).
Moses Hatfield and Sarah Grimes, June 17, 1847. S.
  Hobbs, M.G. (June 20, 1847).
Wiley Barnard and Malissa Lawson, June 19, 1847.
  No return.
Campbell Brummit and Mahaley Townsley, June 19, 1847.
  John Easley, J.P. (June 22, 1847).
Larkin D. Sharp and Nancy Janeway, June 19, 1847. John
  Easley, J.P. (June 20, 1847).
Alfred Evans and Sarah McNew, June 23, 1847. Simpson
  Hurst, J.P. (June 22, 1847).
Anderson W. Herrell and Eliza Cunningham, June 26,
  1847. John Hurst, J.P. (June 26, 1847).
Joseph White and Mary McHenry, June 28, 1847. John
  Barringer, M.G. (July 1, 1847).
James Spillers and E. J. Qualls, July 8, 1847. John
  Easley. (July 8, 1847).
John W. Grammer and Sarah E. Littral, July 22, 1847.
  J. Chick (?), J.P. (July 25, 1847).
John Y. Chadwich and Malvina White, July 28, 1847.
  John Easley, J.P. (July 29, 1847).
Anderson Barnard and Mary A. Singleton, July 9, 1847.
  Jas. Greenlee, G.M. (?). (July 10, 1847).
Calvin Dowel and Nancy Johnson, July 15, 1847.
  John Easley, J.P. (July 15, 1847).
Thos. Brooks and Catharine Brooks, July 15, 1847.
  John Hurst, J.P. (July 15, 1847).
Haisel (?) Hill and Permelia Sharp, Aug. 16, 1847.
  John Barringer. (Aug. 26, 1847).
William W. Lynch and Sarah Hunter, Aug. 17, 1847.
  Aaron Lynch, J.P.
William Barren and Nancy Jane Burns, Aug. 18, 1847. J.
  Chick (?), J.P. (Aug. 20, 1847).
Nelson Bowman and T. N. Wilson, Aug. 26, 1847. No
  return.
Andrew B. Smith and Ann Hobbs, Aug. 27, 1847. J.
  Click (?). (Aug. 29, 1847).
Daniel Jones and Ann Jane Cook, Sep. 1, 1847. No
  return.

William Mcfarland and Susannah Hopper, Sep. 2, 1847.
Levi Goin, J.P. (Sep. 2, 1847).
Enoch C. Simmons and Patey Davis, Sep. 4, 1847. N. S.
McDowell, M.G. (Sep. 5, 1847).
John M. Grimes and Emily Rose, Sep. 11, 1847. No return.
Granville McBee and Caroline Moore, Sep. 13, 1847. John
M. Burch, J.P. (Sep. 16, 1847).
James Minton and Elender Herrell, Sep. 30, 1847.
N. S. McDowell. (Oct., 1847).
William B. Alexander and Louisa Hodges, Oct. 2, 1847.
(Oct. 7, 1847).
Andrew C. Jones and Eliza Lee, Sep. 14, 1847.
Sterling C. Kincaid and Sarah Woodson, Sep. 15, 1847.
Not executed.
Levi Carmack and Mary Rollins, Sep. 15, 1847. J.
Click (?), J.P. (Sep. 20, 1847).
Alvis Brogan and Malinda Walker, Sep. 21, 1847. R. J.
Russell, J.P. (Sep. 23, 1847).
John W. Hall and Martha Roberts, Sep. 23, 1847. N. S.
McDowell, M.G. (Sep. 23, 1847).
William Carmack and Nancy Cocks, Sep. 23, 1847. James
Click (?), J.P. (Sep. 27, 1847).
Daniel Theirs and Kisicror (?) Kawin, Sep. 23, 1847.
J. Click, J.P. (Sep. 24, 1847).
James Gibson and Mary Province, Sep. 23, 1847. No
return.
Elisha Hall and Jane Goins, Sep. 29, 1847. John M.
Burch, J.P. (Sep. 29, 1847).
Albert Dougherty and Matilda Overton, Oct. 4, 1847.
John Ritchie, J.P. (Oct. 7, 1847).
George Devault and Margret Wircick, Oct. 6, 1847.
Simpson Hurst, J.P. (Oct. 6, 1847).
Abraham Mayers and Ama Gowin, Oct. 6, 1847. Levi
Goin, J.P. (Oct. 12, 1847).
James Shelly and Annice Seals, Oct. 23, 1847. Levi
Goin, J.P. (Nov. 4, 1847).
James M. Pridemore and Levina Lock, Oct. 30, 1847.
J. Click, J.P. (Oct. 31, 1847).
John Owens and Susan M. Hardy, Nov. 22, 1847. Wm
McBee, J.P. (Nov. 25, 1847).
Thos. Gilbert and Malvina Edwards, Nov. 24, 1847.
John Gilbert. (Nov. 24, 1847).
Tipton Baker and Susan Billingsly, Nov. 25, 1847.
Samuel Gibson, J.P. (Nov. 26, 1847).
William Graham and Polly Sweet, Dec. 4, 1847. Levi
Goin, J.P. (Dec. 5, 1847).
Henry M. Sowder and Rachel Ausmus, Dec. 6, 1847. Aaron
Lynch, J.P.
James Singleton and Caroline Barnard, Dec. 9, 1847.
James Ritter, J.P. (Dec. 11, 1847).
Hugh Graham and Rachel Hopper, Dec. 9, 1847. Levi
Goin, J.P. (Dec. 9, 1847).
Elvis Hill and Ann Hopper, Dec. 9, 1847. Wm. Williams,
M.G. (Dec. 14, 1847).

CLAIBORNE COUNTY MARRIAGES

William L. Vannoy and Levinda Venoy, Dec. 10, 1847.
   Samuel Gibson, J.P. (Dec. 10, 1847).
Nelson Cheek and Nancy Sutton, Dec. 12, 1847. J.
   Click (?), J.P. (Dec. 13, 1847).
John White and R. Hobbs, Dec. 14, 1847. No return.
Ambros Sharp and Elizabeth Shofner, Dec. 15, 1847.
   L. L. Harrell, J.P. (Dec. 16, 1847).
William B. Ford and (?) Smith, Dec. 16, 1847. L. Goin,
   J.P. (Dec. 19, 1847).
Elijah Hodges and Elisabeth Hodges, Dec. 16, 1847. Hiram
   Hurst, M.G. (Dec. 16, 1847).
John Robinson and Lerinda Hurst, Dec. 17, 1847. Robert
   Southern, M.G. (Dec. 23, 1847).
Nelson C. Bowman and Martha L. Rogers, Dec. 23, 1847.
   J. E. Bowman, J.P.
William Hopson and Chloe Bowers, Dec. 23, 1847. Samuel
   Day, J.P. (Dec. 26, 1847).
Harrod Hopson and Elisabeth M. Ritter, Dec. 23, 1847.
   James Ritter, J.P. (Dec. 23, 1847).
Fielding Hodges and Teney Shelton, Jan. 1, 1848.
   (Jan. 5, 1848).
Burton McBee and Mary A. Burk, Jan. 1, 1848. L. L.
   Harrell, J.P. (Jan. 3, 1848).
Washington Holden and Deaner Etten, Jan. 2, 1848. No
   return.
Joseph Anderson West and Susanah Posey, Jan. 6, 1848.
   Jas. Ritter, J.P. (Jan. 6, 1848).
E. J. Odell and Honer Williams, Jan. 8, 1848. Wm
   Williams. (Jan. 13, 1848).
James T. Ford and Margret K. Moody, Jan. 10, 1848.
   A. M. Goodykoontz. (Jan. 13, 1848).
John H. Brooks and Matilda Longworth, Jan. 11, 1848.
   No return.
William Deans and Patsy Bundren, Jan. 12, 1848. James
   Ritter, J.P. (Feb. 2, 1848).
Riley Stansbury and Elizabeth Webb, Jan. 15, 1848.
   No return.
Roman Owens and Abigal Frier, Jan. 17, 1848. Robert
   Southern, M.G. (Jan. 18, 1848).
Arthur Collins and Silvey Bruer (?), Jan. 17, 1848. No
   return.
Reuben M. Cook and Nancy N. Whitaker, Jan. 18, 1848.
   Mark Hurst, M.G. (Jan. 19, 1848).
Joseph Carter and Ellis George, Jan. 23, 1848. Solomon
   Holbs (?), M.G. (Jan. 27, 1848).
James W. Yeary and Susan Sutton, Jan. 25, 1848. No
   return.
Boyer Bullard and Mildred Lanham, Jan. 25, 1848. N. S.
   McDowell, M.G. (Jan., 1848).
James Laugh Miller and Mahaly I. (?) Stublefield, Jan.
   30, 1848. L. L. Harrell, J.P. (Feb. 10, 1848).
Thos. Friar and Martha J. Runnions, Feb. 3, 1848.
   John Hurst, J.P. (Feb. 4, 1848).
George R. Word and Ollely (?) Daey (?), Feb. 7, 1848.
   Hiram Hurst, M.G. (Feb. 7, 1848).

John F. Woodson and Eliza Fernell, Feb. 8, 1848.  W. L.
Turner, M.G.  (Feb. 9, 1848).

David Nicely and Polly Nance, Feb. 8, 1848.  Samuel
Day, J.P.  (Feb. 17, 1848).

Alexander Hill and Elisabeth Brooks, Feb. 15, 1848.
No return.

Fruatan Nunn and Elisabeth Ward, Feb. 17, 1848.  James
Ritter, J.P.  (Feb. 17, 1848).

John Meelor and Elizabeth Jane Woodson, Feb. 18, 1848.
W. L. Turner, M.G.  (Mar. 19, 1848).

A. Vanbebber and Louisa Lee, Feb. 25, 1848.  Wm. McBee,
J.P.  (Feb. 25, 1848).

Wiley Cazort and Nancy Hollon, Feb. 27, 1848.  John
Easley, J.P.  (Feb. 29, 1848).

Houston McBee and Lucinda Owens, Feb. 28, 1848.  Isaac
Vanbebber, J.P.  (Mar. 9, 1848).

William H. Norton and Martha A. Walker, Mar. 1, 1848.
Wm Williams.  (Mar. 5, 1848).

W. Holden and D. Etter, Feb. 2, 1848.  J. Chick (?),
J.P.  (Feb. 3, 1848).

Hiram Messer and Mary Doke, Mar. 4, 1848.  No return.

Newton A. Evans and Elizabeth J. Crockett, Mar. 7, 1848.
W. L. Turner, M.G.  (Mar. 7, 1848).

Isaac Walker and Alyra (?) Rice, Mar. 8, 1848.  John
Ritchie, J.P.  (Mar. 9, 1848).

Jacob Sowder and Matilda Ausmus, Mar. 13, 1848.
William H. Harpe, M.G.  (Mar. 16, 1848).

Anderson Drummonds and Susannah Ritter, Mar. 13, 1848.
Wm McBee, J.P.  (Mar. 19, 1848).

Joseph Edwards and Pheobe Sparks, Mar. 13, 1848.  George
Ford, M.G.  (Mar. 14, 1848).

Samuel Walker and Louisa Parks, Mar. 13, 1848.  John
Ritchie, J.P.  (Mar. 16, 1848).

Eldrege Mullens and Nancy O. (?) Carpenter, Mar. 17,
1848.  No return.

William Parker and Elisabeth Vermillion, Mar. 21, 1848.
Robt. Southern, M.G.  (Mar. 21, 1848).

Thos. Parkey and Polly Edwards, Mar. 24, 1848.  John
Easley, J.P.  (Mar. 24, 1848).

Ezekiel Goodin and Licha (?) Falkner, Mar. 26, 1848.
No return.

William Kinningham and Susan Baker, Mar. 27, 1848.
Samuel Gibson, J.P.  (Mar. 27, 1848).

Geo. W. Brooks and Cathrine Zicks, Apr. 3, 1848.  James
Ritter, J.P.  (Apr. 3, 1848).

Richard Harper and Milley McVay, Apr. 7, 1848.  Simpson
Hurst, J.P.  (Apr. 6 (?), 1848).

Benager Harpe and Elizabeth Sowder, Apr. 18, 1848.
William H. Harpe, M.G.  (Apr. 19, 1848).

Green B. Cadle and Elisabeth J. Moore, May 9, 1848.
R. E. Crockett, J.P.  (May 9, 1848).

James T. Shields and Mary A. Glenn, May 11, 1848.
Fielding Pope, M.G.  (May 11, 1848).

Rodden F. Owens and Amanda Ferrell, May 25, 1848.
Isaac Thomas, J.P.  (May 25, 1848).

Ambrose Sawyers and Elizabeth Jones, May 27, 1848. J.
  B. S. Leforce, J.P. (May 30, 1848).
John M. T. Shishen and Letta Warnacutt, May 31, 1848.
  John Easley, J.P. (May 31, 1848).
John Scott and Vina Brooks, June 10, 1848. John Brown,
  J.P. (June 11, 1848).
James W. Norton and T. Green, June 12, 1848. Jesse
  Rogers, J.P. (June 15, 1848).
George W. Lewis and Eliza A. Thompson, June 24, 1848.
  John M. Burch, J.P. (June 25, 1848).
Levi Brooks and Emily A. Campbell, July 1, 1848. John
  Brumn, J.P. (July 5, 1848).
David Williams and Ann Mayes, July 8, 1848. Wm. Williams.
  (July 13, 1848).
James Carr and Charlota J. Cloud, July 10, 1848. Wm
  Bullard, J.P. (July 13, 1848).
Franklin Chesnut and Cathrine Brigman, July 17, 1848.
  R. E. Crockett, J.P. (July 17, 1848).
John J. Carrol and Mary J. Sawyers, July 17, 1848. James
  Shoemaker, J.P. (July 19, 1848).
Joseph H. Bullard and Manery (?) Dobkins, July 20,
  1848. John Easley, J.P. (July 20, 1848).
Sylvester Harrell and Lugana Nunn, July 20, 1848. James
  Ritter, J.P. (July 20, 1848).
George Hamelton and Julia Ann Cadle, July 23, 1848.
  Samuel Gibson, J.P. (July 27, 1848).
George Barton and Matilda Jackson, July 25, 1848. John
  Easley, J.P. (July 25, 1848).
Zephaniah Dunn and Nancy Ragan (?), July 28, 1848.
  James Ritter, J.P. (Aug. 6, 1848).
Elijah Gregory and Nancy Ragan (?), Aug. 1, 1848. Samuel
  Gibson, J.P. (Aug. 18, 1848).
William Chittum and Malissa Munday, Aug. 5, 1848.
  William Turner, M.G. (Aug. 8, 1848).
Harry Nunn and Tabitha Bunch, Aug. 5, 1848. James
  Shoemaker, J.P. (Aug. 6, 1848).
William Cannon and Fanny McNeelence, Aug. 9, 1848.
  Robt. Glenn, M.G. (Aug. 9, 1848).
Caleb N. Thompson and Clementina N. Henderson, Aug. 10,
  1848. Robert Sothern (?), M.G. (Aug. 11, 1848).
William Whiteted and Mary Keck, Aug. 14, 1848. J. G.
  Palmer, J.P. (Aug. 16, 1848).
Andrew Brooks and Mary J. Brooks, Aug. 16, 1848. No
  return.
Alexander Tanny (?) and Elisabeth Clapp, Aug. 22, 1848.
  Simpson Hurst, J.P. (Aug. 22, 1848).
Hinam Messer and Mary Smith, Aug. 28, 1848. J. S. M.
  Dickinson, J.P. (Aug. 29, 1848).
James Chittan and Nancy Peck, Sep. 13, 1848. Jno.
  Easley, J.P. (Sep. 16, 1848).
Henderson Rogers and Anna Caywood, Sep. 13, 1848. Jesse
  Rogers, J.P. (Sep. 28, 1848).
James W. Plank and Mary Jane Edwards, Sep. 28, 1848.
  Simpson Hurst, J.P. (Sep. 28, 1848).

Pleasant H. Person and Martha Davis, Sep. 23, 1848.
John Gilbert, A.D.M. (?). (Sep. 23, 1848).
Elisha Hollan and Eliza Oliver, Sep. 26, 1848. J. S.
M. Dickinson, J.P. (Sep. 27, 1848).
Thomas Wallis and Lurinda Sanders, Oct. 6, 1848. Thos.
J. (?) Person. (Oct. 8, 1848).
Spencer King and Emaline Hamblin, Oct. 11, 1848. W.
H. Harpe, M.G. (Oct. 12, 1848).
George M. Lewis and Cyntha Fulps, Sep. 16, 1848. John
M. Burch, J.P. (Sep. 17, 1848).
Nicholas M. Roberts and Martha Thomas, Sep. 20, 1848.
J. S. M. Dickinson, J.P. (Sep. 20, 1848).
Isreal Cole and Francis Jane Louden, Oct. 17, 1848.
No return.
Abraham Carmack and Delila A. Dunn, Oct. 21, 1848.
James Chick, J.P. (Oct. 22, 1848).
Isaac Grabill and Nancy Russell, Oct. 25, 1848. J. G.
Palmer, J.P. (Oct. 26, 1848).
William Minton and Polly A. Cusley, Nov. 1, 1848. John
M. Burch, J.P.
Lenard G. Harper and Louisa Carpenter, Nov. 5, 1848.
Simpson Hurst, J.P. (Nov. 5, 1848).
J. W. Smith and Lucinda Ford, Nov. 7, 1848. James
Shoemaker, J.P. (Nov. 9, 1848).
James Brown and Elizabeht Chick, Nov. 11, 1848. No
return.
Lafayette Evans and Sarah Huff, Nov. 11, 1848. No
return.
Henry Ayers and Lack G. Marcum, Nov. 20, 1848. James
Chick, J.P. (Nov. 24, 1848).
King Eldrige and Sarah Mink, Nov. 21, 1848. No return.
James D. Hurst and Elisabeth M. Farmer, Nov. 25, 1848.
Asa Routh (?), M.G. (Nov. 26, 1848).
Binson (?) Sweet and Rebecca Prestley, Nov. 27, 1848.
No return.
James Rosan and Angelina Sanders, Dec. 4, 1848. John
Easley, J.P. (Dec. 10, 1848).
Henry Nash and Emily B. Rogers, Dec. 6, 1848. Jesse
Rogers, J.P. (Dec. 14, 1848).
Benjamin Pike and Elizabeth Wells, Dec. 15, 1848. William
Needham, J.P. (Dec. 17, 1848).
William Dotson and Mary J. Kelley, Dec. 19, 1848. James
Johnston, J.P. (Dec. 25, 1848).
Jacob Cupp and Mary A. Falkner, Dec. 22, 1848. G.
Ford, M.G. (Dec. 22, 1848).
Sterling Nunn and Angeline Vennoy, Dec. 25, 1848.
Simpson Hurst. (Jan. 4, 1849).
Pleasant M. Hodges and Orleana Cloud, Dec. 30, 1848.
No return.
Harper Rice and Eliza Hurst, Dec. 30, 1848. James
Ritter, J.P. (Dec. 31, 1848).
John Simmons and Emaly Stone, Jan. 1, 1849. Simpson
Hurst. (Jan. 22, 1849).
A. W. Harrell and Malinda I. (?) Bartlett, Jan. 1,
1849. Simpson Hurst, J.P. (Jan. 5, 1849).

John Falkner and Lucinda Hollan, Jan. 10, 1849.  Levi
  Goin, J.P.  (Jan. 14, 1849).
Peter Hollan and Emaline Helton, Jan. 14, 1849.  Elisha
  Clark, J.P.  (Jan. 18, 1849).
John Johnson and Elender Barnet, Jan. 18, 1849.
  Jeremiah Singleton.  (Jan. 19, 1849).
Lemuel Ball and Ann Eliza Powers, Jan. 18, 1849.  James
  Shoemaker, J.P.  (Jan. 18, 1849).
Isaac Guim and Louisa Marie Willis, Jan. 21, 1849.
  John Easley, J.P.  (Jan. 23, 1849).
Preston Sparks and Mary Eley, Jan. 24, 1849.  No return.
Calvin Masengale and Louisa Roark, Jan. 27, 1849.  No
  return.
James Garner and Elisabeth Lenard, Jan. 27, 1849.  J.
  Chick, J.P.  (Jan. 28, 1849).
Carey Myers and Pasefy Timey (?) Lewis, Jan. 29, 1849.
  Wm. Bullard, J.P.  (Feb. 1, 1849).
James Price and Pheby Hicks, Feb. 1, 1849.  Levi Goin,
  J.P.  (Feb. 8, 1849).
William Brown and Nancey (?) Wien (?), Feb. 2, 1849).
  No return.
Russel Breeding and Mary I. Dunsmore, Feb. 3, 1849.
  Hiram Hurst, M.G.  (Feb. 3, 1849).
William R. Hayse and Adaline Devault, Feb. 5, 1849.
  James Ritter, J.P. (Feb. 22, 1849).
Jonathan Barnard and Lemira Barnard, Feb. 12, 1849.
  Jeremiah Singleton.  (Feb. 13, 1849).
Jeremiah Burchfield and Sarah Welch, Feb. 21, 1849.
  William Bullard, J.P.
Thos. Zicks and Cacey Thacker, Feb. 24, 1849.  Simpson
  Hurst, J.P.  (Feb. 25, 1849).
Andrew Presley and Rebecca Hicks, Feb. 24, 1849.  M.
  Cunningham, J.P.  (Feb. 24, 1849).
Hesakiah Moyers and Rachal Harrison, Mar. 1, 1849.
  Levi Goin, J.P.  (Mar. 4, 1849).
Joseph Beelon (?) and Hariet Branscome, Mar. 5, 1849.
  Jesse Rogers, J.P.  (Mar. 8, 1849).
Henry Poore and Vina Calone, Mar. 10, 1849.  James
  Shoemaker, J.P.  (Mar. 11, 1849).
Asa Rosan (?) and Emaline Mallicoat, Mar. 23, 1849.
  J. G. Palmer, J.P.  (Mar. 25, 1849).
Moses Smith and Polly Kesterson, Mar. 24, 1849.  James
  Chick, J.P.  (Mar. 26, 1849).
Camadore Rogers and Mary Grimes, Mar. 25, 1849.  James
  Chick, J.P.  (Mar. 26, 1849).
John Hodges and Alley Cuningham, Mar. 26, 1849.  James
  Ritter, J.P.  (Mar. 28, 1849).
Péruda Sowder and Elisabeth Ausmus, Apr. 2, 1849.
  (Apr. 6, 1849).
John M. Sawyers and Marian J. E. Martin, Apr. 3, 1849.
  No return.
Nathaniel S. Havlaen (?) and Sarah M. Poindexter,
  Apr. 18, 1849.  E. E. Crockett, J.P.  (Apr. 18, 1849).
Joseph Carden and Adalade B. Noel, May 2, 1849.  W. G.
  E. Cuningham (?).  (May 2, 1849).

William F. Toney (?) and Orleany Johnson, May 5, 1849.
Simpson Hurst, J.P. (May 5, 1849).
William N. McWilliams and Emaley Brusten, May 11, 1849.
R. E. Crockett, J.P. (May 24, 1849).
John McMahon and Elisabeth Wilson, May 19, 1849. Isaac
Thomas, J.P. (May 19, 1849).
Richard H. Harper and Frankey Hopper, May 19, 1849.
Levi Goin, J.P. (May 24, 1849).
Benjamin L. Huddleston and Sarah Vanderpool, May 19,
1849. J. B. S. Leforee (?), J.P. (May 24, 1849).
Joseph Eastes and Priscilla Cox, May 24, 1849. Mark
Hurst, M.G. (May 24, 1849).
Josiah Wyatt and Jane Jones, May 28, 1849. Hughes
W. Taylor, M.G. (May 31, 1849).
Robert Southern and Martha Ann Henderson, May 31, 1849.
Mark Hurst, M.G. (May 31, 1849).
M. B. Nunn and Sarah Furgerson, Apr. 7, 1849. James
Chick, J.P.
Samuel Colwell and Amelia York, Apr. 19, 1849. J. S.
M. Dickinson, J.P. (Apr. 19, 1849).
Elonza D. Butcher and Martha Jane Vaughn, June 11,
1849. J. Chick, J.P. (June 12, 1849).
Isral Coles and Sarah A. Peck, June 13, 1849. James
Chick, J.P. (June 14, 1849).
Wm Upton and Polly Burns, June 13, 1849. John Brown,
J.P. (June 15, 1849).
Benjamin Dickinson and Matilda Garnett, June 21, 1849.
W. G. E. Cuningham. (June 21, 1849).
Isaac Stuart and Sarah Hurst, June 24, 1849. W. G. E.
Cunningham, M.G. (June 24, 1849).
James Walker and Mary Ann Campbell, July 20, 1849.
No return.
Zachariah Whicker (?) and Martha Hurst, July 18, 1849.
Simpson Hurst, J.P. (July 11, 1849).
William M. Rite and Mary Linch, June 5, 1849. Wm. L.
Smith, M.G. (June 6, 1849).
William Bayley and Zilpha J. Frasher, June 25, 1849.
James Chick, J.P. (June 26, 1849).
James M. Hicks and Lucy Green, July 4, 1849. Mark
Hurst, M.G. (July 10, 1849).
William Hase and Sarah A. Brooks, July 9, 1849.
Jeremiah Singleton. (July 10, 1849).
John H. Kelley and Ann Jane Sewell, July 11, 1849. W.
G. E. Cunningham, M.G. (July 11, 1849).
John Evans and Malasha Hurst, July 15, 1849. Jas.
Johnson, J.P. (July 15, 1849).
Ganeum McBee and Rebecca Fulps, July 16, 1849. No
return.
Alvis Hunnacutt and Martha Presley, July 18, 1849. Levi
Goin, J.P. (July 19, 1849).
Josiah Crawford and Sally Shofner, July 21, 1849. J. G.
Palmer, J.P. (July 22, 1849).
Samuel McBee and Alemida (?) Stubblefield, July 21,
1849. No return.

B. H. M. Cole and Mary E. Butcher, July 23, 1849. John
Easley, J.P. (July 23, 1849).
Wesley Simmons and Nancy Owens, Aug. 2, 1849. J.
Chick, J.P. (Aug. 3, 1849).
William B. Lane and Thersa Ann Willis, Aug. 4, 1849.
John Easley, J.P. (Aug. 5, 1849).
Eli Goins and Rachel Edwards, Aug. 8, 1849. Levi
Goin, J.P. (Aug. 9, 1849).
John J. F. Eastes and Rebecca Friar, Aug. 15, 1849.
James Chick, J.P. (Aug. 16, 1849).
Richard Crabtree and Betsy Ann Grimes, Aug. 16, 1849.
J. Chick, J.P. (Aug. 17, 1849).
Henry C. Hodges and Manervy Devault, Aug. 23, 1849.
Simpson Hurst, J.P. (Aug. 23, 1849).
Henry Carroll and Mary Englant, Sep. 1, 1849. James
Shoemaker, J.P. (Aug. 3 (?), 1849).
Thomas Rite and Mary Sexton, Sep. 8, 1849. Aaron
Lynch, J.P. (Sep. 15, 1849).
Thomas Marlom and Catherine Cress, Sep. 9, 1849. W.
H. Harpe, M.G. (Sep. 12, 1849).
Edwards Fields and Orlena Hix (Hicks), Sep. 11, 1849.
Mark Hurst, M.G. (Sep. 17, 1849).
William K. Sharp and Mary Lemar, Sep. 15, 1849. Wm L.
Smith, M.G. (Sep. 20, 1849).
McKindry Ellerson and Manerva Lynch, Sep. 15, 1849.
Wm. Williams. (Oct. 2, 1849).
Jackson Berry and Elizabeth Eads, Sep. 18, 1849. Levi
Goin, J.P. (Sep. 19, 1849).
Elias Presley and Jane A. Calon, Sep. 19, 1849. R. E.
Crockett, J.P. (Sep. 20, 1849).
Robert Cheek and Peggy Cox, Sep. 22, 1849. James
Chick, J.P.
John Hacker and Lety Smith, Sep. 22, 1849. Asa Routh,
M.G. (Oct. 5, 1849).
William Baker and Frankey I. (?) Mills, Sep. 26, 1849.
Wm. Bullard, J.P. (Sep. 26, 1849).
Morgan J. Woodson and Elizabeth Ramsey, Sep. 28, 1849.
Wm. Bullard, J.P. (Sep. 28, 1849).
Wm. McBee and Lilly J. Owens, Sep. 29, 1849. Isaac
Thomas, J.P. (Oct. 5, 1849).
Wilborn Pendleton and Anna Huddleston, Oct. 2, 1849.
Henry Beach, J.P. (Oct. 4, 1849).
Robert C. Woodson and Lucy Jane Fugate, Oct. 3, 1849.
John Easley, J.P. (Oct. 4, 1849).
John Carmon and Phebe Price, Oct. 3, 1849. John Easley,
J.P. (Oct. 4, 1849).
Charles Covey and Dianna Luttrell, Oct. 6, 1849. James
Long, M.G. (Oct. 7, 1849).
William H. Carroll and Nancy Bawldridge, Oct. 8, 1849.
R. E. Crockett, J.P. (Oct. 11, 1849).
James Hunter and Thirsa McVey, Oct. 10, 1849. Wm.
Williams, M.G. (Oct. 12, 1849).
James Doyle and Louisanna Green, Oct. 10, 1849. M.
Cunningham, J.P. (Oct. 10, 1849).

Spencer Ousley and Susan Skaggs, Oct. 17, 1849. J. M.
Burch, J.P. (Oct. 21, 1849).

Woobery Robinson and Nancy Evans, Oct. 18, 1849. Aaron
Lynch, J.P. (Oct. 26, 1849).

John Strevels and Mary Ann Sherac (?), Oct. 19, 1849.
James (?) Shoemaker, J.P. (Oct. 21, 1849).

David Huddleston and Telitha Vanderpool, Oct. 23, 1849.
J. B. S. Leforce, J.P. (Oct. 24, 1849).

Philip Minton and Rachel M. Hodges, Oct. 4, 1849. John
M. Burch, J.P. (Oct. 5, 1849).

James P. Cunningham and Orleana Jane Adams, Oct. 8, 1849.
J. S. M. Dickinson, J.P. (Oct. 8, 1849).

Elisha Kirby and Lucinda Rice, Nov. 2, 1849. J. S. M.
Dickinson, J.P. (Nov. 3, 1849).

Alfred Tredaway and Rebecca Gresly (?), Nov. 3, 1849.
John Easley, J.P. (Nov. 3, 1849).

William Camran and Rachel Hart, Nov. 5, 1849. R. E.
Crockett, J.P. (Nov. 10, 1849).

Samuel McBee and Nancy I. Lewis, Nov. 6, 1849. No
return.

Ezekiel Robinson and Winney Vandergriff, Nov. 15, 1849.
No return.

Cleveland McCrary and Elizabeth Lay, Nov. 17, 1849.
Isaac Thomas, J.P. (Dec. 16, 1849).

George McCrary and Elender Venable, Nov. 17, 1849.
Isaac Thomas, J.P. (Nov. 18, 1849).

Joseph Southern and Jennetter Brooks, Nov. 19, 1849.
J. Chick, J.P. (3d _____, 1849).

Abraham Balis and Elizabeth Pressley, Nov. 28, 1849.
Levi Goin, J.P. (Nov. 29, 1849).

Arthur L. Jones and Mary Dobins, Nov. 28, 1849. M.
Cunningham, J.P. (Nov. 28, 1849).

Solomon (?) Wesley and Sarah J. Richardson, Nov. 28,
1849. John Easley, J.P. (Nov. 28, 1849).

Joseph Neal and Margaret Margraves, Nov. 29, 1849. J.
M. Kelley, M.G. (Nov. 29, 1849).

Flemon Willis and Mary J. Harper, Nov. 13, 1849.
Simpson Hurst, Esq. (Nov. 13, 1849).

William L. Venoy and Lucy S. Venoy, Nov. 29, 1849. John
Easley, J.P. (Dec. 1, 1849).

Mathew Sharp and Manerva Carr, Dec. 4, 1849. Wm McBee,
J.P. (Dec. 6, 1849).

Sterling Person and Elizabeth Davis, Dec. 8, 1849.
Jeremiah Singleton, Minister. (Dec. 9, 1849).

William H. Hopper and Anna Gowin, Dec. 9, 1849. Levi
Goins, J.P. (Dec. 13, 1849).

Peter Owens and Lucinda Eastes, Dec. 10, 1849. J.
Chick, J.P. (Dec. 12, 1849).

Joseph Branscome and Rachel Dunn, Dec. 15, 1849. Jesse
Rogers, J.P. (Dec. 20, 1849).

Lewis Lucker (?) and Calvina Lee, Dec. 17, 1849. R. E.
Crockett, J.P. (Dec. 17, 1849).

Henry Sharp and Cathrine Sowder, Dec. 22, 1849. Wm
Williams. (Jan. 1, 1850).

CLAIBORNE COUNTY MARRIAGES

William McNeil and Nancy L. Carter, Dec. 22, 1849.
  Jacob J. Parks, J.P. (Dec. 27, 1849).
John Brock and Sarah Longworth, Dec. 22, 1849. John
  Brown, J.P. (Dec. 23, 1849).
Samuel Lane and Sarah Keith, Dec. 27, 1849. J. G.
  Palmer, J.P. (Dec. 27, 1849).
Tilman H. Moor and Mary A. Burket, Dec. 29, 1849. J.
  B. G. Leeforce (?). (Dec. 25, 1849).
Riley Clark and Emily Chumbly, Jan. 1, 1850. No return.
Thos. Redmon and Martha J. Carr, Jan. 4, 1850. Isaac
  Thomas, J.P. (Jan. 6, 1850).
Robert Harrell and Mahala Hurst, Jan. 5, 1850. John
  Easley, J.P. (Jan. 6, 1850).
William Hamons and Elender Hamons, Jan. 8, 1850. Wm.
  Bullard, J.P.
John Bright and Mary Hardy, Jan. 9, 1850. Wm. McBee.
  (Jan. 10, 1850).
James Dikes and Mary Holton, Jan. 14, 1850. Levi
  Goin, M.G. (Jan. 17, 1850).
William P. Dean and Rachel Salyers, Jan. 15, 1850.
  A. D. Woodson (?), J.P.
Robert C. Luster and Julia Hamelton, Jan. 18, 1850.
  A. D. Woodson, J.P.
Doctor H. Owens and Jane Chick, Jan. 22, 1850. J.
  Chick, J.P. (Jan. 23, 1850).
Enas Allin and Sarah Lay, Jan. 23, 1850. Thos. P.
  Ensor. (Jan. 24, 1850).
George W. Wilson and Cerena Hurst, Jan. 26, 1850. J.
  G. Palmer, J.P. (Jan. 27, 1850).
Joseph P. Johnson and Elender E. Goins, Jan. 29, 1850.
  A. D. Woodson, J.P. (Jan. 29, 1850).
Asa Brogan and Leta Sharp, Feb. 4, 1850. J. G. Palmer,
  J.P. (Feb. 7, 1850).
Elijah Braden and Lucinda Lynch, Feb. 5, 1850. Aaron
  Lynch, J.P. (Feb. 10, 1850).
John S. Cain and Barberry Lynch, Feb. 8, 1850. Wm.
  Williams. (Feb. 12, 1850).
Zackariah Trent and Matilda Scelf (?), Feb. 12, 1850.
  No return.
John F. Berry and Susan A. Moses, Feb. 14, 1850. J. G.
  Palmer, J.P. (Feb. 14, 1850).
William L. Munday and Margret R. Norvell, Feb. 14, 1850.
  No return.
Thomas Colson and Manervay Bales, Jan. 30, 1850. James
  Chick, J.P. (Feb. 3, 1850).
Preston Dunsmore and Beste A. Hodges, Feb. 2, 1850.
  No return.
Elbert Rice Cook and Emily L. Whitaker, Feb. 14, 1850.
  Mark Hurst, M.G. (Feb. 14, 1850).
Prior L. Vance and Catherine Felps, Feb. 19, 1850.
  John M. Burch, J.P. (Feb. 22, 1850).
Bowyer Beeler and Rebecca Lewis, Feb. 20, 1850. John
  M. Burch, J.P. (Feb. 21, 1850).
James M. Honeycutt and Nancy Woodward, Mar. 4, 1850.
  J. G. Palmer, J.P. (Mar. 4, 1850).

41

Bales Shomate and Rebecca Colson, Mar. 4, 1850. R. E. Crockett, J.P. (Mar. 7, 1850).

William F. Ball and V. A. Cottrell, Mar. 11, 1850. Thos. P. Ensor. (Mar. 19, 1850).

H. M. Sharp and Matilda E. Jones, Mar. 15, 1850. Wm. Bruce, L.E. (?). (Mar. 19, 1850).

Noah Harrel and Nancy E. Green, Mar. 14, 1850. James Johnston, J.P. (Mar. 17, 1850).

David Chadwell and Nancy Rennels, Mar. 26, 1850. James Chick, J.P. (Mar. 28, 1850).

David Cardwell and Elizabeth Cailor, Mar. 26, 1850. J. M. Kelley, M.G. (Mar. 26, 1850).

Welsey Chittam and Malinda Neil, Mar. 26, 1850. Thos. P. Ensor. (Mar. 26, 1850).

William Louis and Elizabeth Howel, Apr. 2, 1850. A. D. Woodson, J.P. (Apr. 2, 1850).

P. Dunsmore and B. A. Husyes (?), Apr. 2, 1850. H. Hurst, M.G. (Mar. 3, 1850 (?)).

Watesel Lay and Milley Chumbley, Apr. 9, 1850. A. D. Woodson.

William M. Clevelan and Eliza A. Jennings, Apr. 17, 1850. James Johnston, J.P. (Apr. 17, 1850).

McKenna Dulin and Eliza Kesterson, Apr. 17, 1850. M. Cunningham, J.P. (Apr. 17, 1850).

Daniel Spillars and Julia Qualls, Apr. 18, 1850. John Easley, J.P. (Apr. 18, 1850).

Sterling Nunn and Mariah Herrell, Apr. 19, 1850. No return.

John Cloud and Adaline Campbell, Apr. 5, 1850. James Chick, J.P. (Apr. 7, 1850).

Thomas Evans and Nancy Day, Apr. 20, 1850. Hiram Hurst, M.G. (Apr. 21, 1850).

Ephraim Dobbs and Mahala Dinkins, Apr. 20, 1850. Simpson Hurst, J.P. (Apr. 21, 1850).

Neil Breeding and Rebecca Hurst, Apr. 23, 1850. James Ritter, J.P. (Apr. 28, 1850).

John H. Carr and Mahala Seals, Apr. 24, 1850. Levi Goin, J.P. (Apr. 26, 1850)

Lewis C. Pridda and Elen Davis, Apr. 28, 1850. John M. Burch, J.P. (Apr. 28, 1850).

Ralph Burket and Orlena Lee, May 2, 1850. Aaun (?) Lynch, J.P.

Wilbourne Hooper and Nancy Rutledge, May 2, 1850. J. M. Kelley, M.G. (May 2, 1850).

Jacob Davis and Elen Pridda, May 7, 1850. No return.

B. F. Cloud and Nancy Middleton, May 10, 1850. James Chick, J.P. (May 14, 1850).

John Minton and Evaline Lynch, May 15, 1850. J. M. Burch, J.P. (May 16, 1850).

John Campbell and Mary Ann Chadwell, May 15, 1850. John Brown, J.P. (May 16, 1850).

Hiram Ausmus and Sarah Ballinger, May 15, 1850. Jesse Rogers, J.P. (May 20, 1850).

James Burket and Lidda Green Lee, May 18, 1850. Aaua Lynch, J.P.

Simpson Casey and Elizabeth Dulin, May 21, 1850.  John
    Brown, J.P.  (May 21, 1850).
Wm. P. Bales and Russilla Ann Houston, June 4, 1850.
    Robt. Glenn, M.G.  (June 4, 1850).
Isaac Gibson and Cathrine Biggs, June 17, 1850.  Simpson
    Hurst, J.P.  (June 17, 1850).
Daniel Littrell and Nancy A. Hinton, June 28, 1850.
    James Chick, J.P.  (June 28, 1850).
Thomas Hatfield and Nancy J. Upton, July 4, 1850.
    James Chick, J.P.  (July 6, 1850).
Dawson Lamb and Geminia Jackson, July 15, 1850.  Simpson
    Hurst, J.P.  (July 15, 1850).
James Harp and Nancy Tate, July 15, 1850.  Levi Goin,
    J.P.  (July 15, 1850).
Robert Beard and Martha Davis, July 20, 1850.  No return.
Garrett Southern and Elizabeth Willis, July 16, 1850.
    J. S. M. Dickinson, J.P.  (July 17, 1850).
John W. Walker and Lucretia Campbell, July 21, 1850.
    No return.
Nathaniel Brooks and Lucinda Dobkins, July 27, 1850.
    J. S. M. Dickinson, J.P.  (July 28, 1850).
William Norvell and Elizabeth Rolin, July 30, 1850.
    R. E. Crockett, J.P.  (Aug. 4, 1850).
Hamelton Sanders and Anjaline Maden, July 30, 1850.
    James Ritter, J.P.  (Aug. 1, 1850).
Edmund Murry and Polly Welch, Aug. 2, 1850.  J. G.
    Palmer, J.P.  (Aug. 1 (?), 1850).
Jonas Snavely and Lena Fletcher, Aug. 3, 1850.  James
    Chick, J.P.  (Aug. 4, 1850).
George Allen and Emaline Pitman, Aug. 3, 1850.  Simpson
    Hurst, J.P.  (Aug. 7, 1850).
David Sanders and Polly Geasley, Aug. 5, 1850.  J. G.
    Palmer, J.P.  (Aug. 7, 1850).
William Itson and Polly Sullivan, Aug. 7, 1850.
    Jeremiah Singleton, Parson.  (Aug. 8, 1850).
John Lynch and Elizabeth Kesterson, Aug. 8, 1850.  J.
    S. M. Dickinson, J.P.  (Aug. 8, 1850).
Edward Bray and Emily Campbell, Aug. 10, 1850.  Jacob
    J. Parks, J.P.  (Aug. 11, 1850).
Solomon Dobkins and Nancy Adams, Aug. 10, 1850.  Jacob
    J. Parks, J.P.  (Aug. 11, 1850).
Thos. Baldridge and Martha Wilbourne, Aug. 16, 1850.
    R. E. Crockett, J.P.  (Aug. 17, 1850).
John Wagby (?) and Eliza Vanbebber, Aug. 19, 1850.
    Isaac Thomas, J.P.  (Aug. 15 (?), 1850).
William L. Monday and Margret R. Norvell, Aug. 22,
    1850.  No return.
William Sulfridge and Martha Seabolt, Aug. 30, 1850.
    No return.
James McKenny and Elizabeth Mills, Aug. 31, 1850.
    W. G. Payne, J.P.  (Aug. 12, 1852).
Andrew Hatfield and Rachel Loson, Sep. 2, 1850.  John
    Brown, J.P.  (Sep. 5, 1850).
Joshua Moyers and Sindney Bunch, Sep. 3, 1850.  (Sep.
    4, 1850).

Wm Capps and Louisa E. Jones, Sep. 4, 1850.  J. G.
   Palmer, J.P.  (Sep. 4, 1850).
Marshal Seals and Louisa Houston, Sep. 4, 1850.  J. G.
   Palmer, J.P.  (Sep. 4, 1850).
Peter Wolfenbarger and R. Collins, Sep. 4, 1850.  Wm.
   H. Harpe, M.G.  (Sep. 9, 1850).
Samuel L. Minton and Cesear Susong, Sep. 13, 1850.
   James Chick, J.P.  (Oct. 3, 1850).
John Baker and Polly Ramsey, Sep. 15, 1850.  John
   Easley, J.P.  (Sep. 15, 1850).
Hugh G. White and Magret Powers, Sep. 17, 1850.  James
   Chick, J.P.
Robert Garrett and Nancy Spurlock, Sep. 18, 1850.  J.
   S. M. Dickinson, J.P.  (Sep. 18, 1850).
Daniel Hooper and Rachel Hunter, Sep. 25, 1850.  Wm.
   Williams, M.G.  (Sep. 26, 1850).
William W. Yoakum and Nancy Poff, Sep. 26, 1850.
   Aaun (?) Lynch, J.P.  (Dec. 30, 1850).
James Maples and Mary A. Strevels, Sep. 28, 1850.
   J. G. Palmer, J.P.  (Sep. 21 (?), 1850).
Sterling Nunn and Mariah J. Herrell, Oct. 4, 1850.
   Simpson Hurst, J.P.  (Oct. 5, 1850).
Samuel Harris and Sela George, Sep. 27, 1850.  No return.
John Massey and Cynthia M. Tucker, Oct. 10, 1850.  J.
   G. Palmer, J.P.  (Oct. 10, 1850).
G. W. Myers and Martha F. Guinn, Sep. 28, 1850.  No
   return.
W. M. W. Anderson and Elizabeth Johnson, Oct. 12, 1850.
   Jessy Singleton.  (Oct. 13, 1850).
George W. Jones and Elender Chumbley, Oct. 14, 1850.
   A. D. Woodson, J.P.  (Oct. 14, 1850).
Daniel Frior and Eliza Jane Roark, Oct. 22, 1850.
   James Chick, J.P.  (Oct. 23, 1850).
Jacob Massa and Elizabeth Brummet, Oct. 29, 1850.
   Wm. H. Harpe, M.G.  (Oct. 31, 1850).
William Spradling and Mary Carpenter, Oct. 31, 1850).
   No return.
Wm. F. Collinsworth and Louisa Roland, Nov. 2, 1850.
   No return.
Peter Marcum and Abigail Sutton, Nov. 9, 1850.  No
   return.
Martin V. Shultz and Margret V. Dunsmore, Nov. 13, 1850.
   No return.
Henry Wilborne and Margret Devault, Nov. 21, 1850.  No
   return.
Timothy Eastrage and Lucy J. Furgason, Nov. 23, 1850.
   No return.
A. Barnett and (?) Baughman, Nov. 25, 1850.  No return.
David Leach and Cathrine Proffit, Nov. 30, 1850.  No
   return.

CAMPBELL COUNTY, TENNESSEE

Marriages, 1838-1853

Richard Smith to Rachel Terry, Jan. 8, 1839 (?). R.
    Pennington, J.P. (Jan. 16, 1839 (?)).
John Elliott to Eliza Jane Bailey, Jan. 19, 1838.
    Isaac Gross, J.P. (Jan. 19, 1838).
Jesse Hix to Mary Duncan, Jan. 20, 1838. Allen McDonald,
    J.P. (Jan. 20, 1838).
Jeremiah Ridenour to Rebecca Day, Jan. 23, 1838. Isaac
    Gross, J.P. (Jan. 23, 1838).
Alfred Dossett to Ann Elliott, Jan. 23, 1838. J. C.
    Petree, J.P. (Feb. 1, 1838).
George Cooper to Emily Wilson, Jan. 23, 1838. Isaac
    Gross, J.P. (Jan. 25, 1838).
Archibald Murphy to Margaret Stephens, Jan. 26, 1838.
    P. Pennington, J.P. (Jan. 26, 1838).
David Ellington to Rebecca Martin, Feb. 27, 1838. No
    return.
Luke Adkins to Sarah Woosley, Feb. 11, 1838. Allen
    McDonald, J.P. (Feb. 11, 1838).
Manuel Phillips to Lanner Sexton, Feb. 11. 1838. Allen
    McDonald, J.P. (Feb. 11, 1838).
Daniel Richardson, Jr. to Polly Wilhite, Feb. 10,
    1838. Thos. Douglas, J.P. (Feb. 11, 1838).
Samuel Brown to Mary Graves, Mar. 1, 1838. Isaac Gross,
    J.P. (Mar. 29, 1838).
Zachariah David to Nancy McDonald, Mar. 3, 1838. Allen
    McDonald, J.P. (Mar. 3, 1838).
Shampson Wilson to Sarah Walker, Sep. 22, 1849. J. H.
    Grant, J.P. (Oct. 4, 1849).
James Parker to Elizabeth Ann Brooks, Feb. 2, 1856.
    James H. Grant, J.P. (Feb. 28, 1856).
Charlie Williamson to Sarah Greece, Nov. 11, 1850.
    J. H. Grant, J.P. (Nov. 15, 1850).
Levi Smith to Martha Reid, Dec. 28, 1850. J. H. Grant,
    J.P. (Jan. 2, 1851).
Ewen Baker to Rachel Irvin, Apr. 18, 1851. J. H. Grant,
    J.P. (Apr. 20, 1851).
Daniel Foust to Esther Strader, Feb. 21, 1840. (Mar.
    5, 1840).
C. Waters to Nelly McMinn, Mar. 16, 1840. J. H. Grant,
    J.P. (Mar. 21, 1843).
Moses Dagley to Nancy J. Curnut, Feb. 16, 1848. J. H.
    Grant, J.P. (Feb. 20, 1848).

Elias Parker to Lorancy Wilson, Dec., 1851. J. H.
Grant, J.P. (Dec. 28, 1851).
Peter Mayatt to Mary Wilson, Sep. 13, 1864. No return.
William Ridenour to Susan Cox, Feb. 20, 1860. James
H. Grant. (Feb. 20, 1860).
Lindsay Hill to Nancy Sharp, Dec. 8, 1840. J. H.
Grant, J.P. (Jan. 10, 1864).
John Flatford to Lucinda Craig, Nov. 1, 1848. J. H.
Grant, J.P. (Nov. 2, 1848).
Henderson Lay to Sarilda Heatherly, Nov. 20, 1862. No
return.
John Black to Nancy Fouse, Jan. 22, 1858. James H.
Grant, J.P. (Jan. 23, 1858).
James Morton to Mahaley Longmire, Feb. 26, 1842. No
return.
Paskel G. Briant to Margaret Adkins, Jan. 15, 1838.
Michael Broyles, M.G. (Mar. 15, 1838).
Nelson Lynch to Sarah Dossett, Mar. 17, 1838. Isaac
Gross, J.P. (Mar. 1, 1838).
William G. Henderson to Nancy Sowders, Mar. 21, 1838.
Ruconvy Pennington, J.P. (Mar. 21, 1838).
David Willis to Elizabeth Canter, Mar. 22, 1838. Elijah
Hill, J.P. (Mar. 22, 1838).
Charles G. Martin to Elizabeth Runnels, Mar. 27, 1838.
M. Broyles, M.G. (Mar. 27, 1838).
John Suttle to Cilly Ann Bratcher, Apr. 4, 1838. Wm.
Bruce. (Apr. 5, 1838).
Jesse Cox to Martha McDy, Apr. 18, 1838. Michael
Broyles, M.G. (Apr. 12, 1838).
Pharoh M. Right to Nancy Blankenship, Mar. 23, 1838.
Matthew Douglas, J.P. (Apr. 22, 1838).
John Newman to Sarah Wilhite, May 5, 1838. Isaac Gross,
J.P. (May 3, 1838).
William Oaks to Elizabeth Campbell, May 3, 1838. Matthew
Douglas, J.P. (May 3, 1838).
James Meaders to Francis Creekmore, May 13, 1838. M.
Broyles, M.G. (May 13, 1838).
Lear Wiles to Mary L. Miller, May 18, 1838. Abrm.
Hayer, J.P. (May 31, 1838).
Daniel Cox to Mary Ann Zachary, May 17, 1838. Joshua
Duncan, J.P. (May 17, 1838).
Calvin Barrons to Canny Baird, May 31, 1838. Michael
Broyles, M.G. (May 31, 1838).
S. E. Herring to Delilah Maffort, May 31, 1838. C. H.
Boatright, M.G. (June 19, 1838).
Cornelius Reynolds to Elizabeth McCarty, June 2, 1838.
John Pebley, J.P. (June, 1838).
William Bruce to Cinthy Ann Mopin, June 9, 1838.
William Bargess, M.G. (June 19, 1838).
Wm. J. Rogers to Elgina Williams, July 14, 1838. Thomas
Douglas, J.P. (July 14, 1838).
Jesse Lovett to Hester Thompson, Apr. 2, 1838. John E.
Wheeler, J.P. (Aug. 2, 1838).
Russell Williams to Mary Barnett, Aug. 3, 1838. J. C.
Petree, J.P. (Apr. 5, 1838).

Gabriel Ruth to Susey Poteet, Apr. 15, 1838. John L. Smith, J.P. (Aug. 19, 1838).

Thomas Chambers to Jane Owens, Sep. 2, 1838. R. Pennington, J.P. (Sep. 2, 1838).

Jacob Seabolt to Ann Garland, Sep. 3, 1838. John Jones, J.P. (Sep. 18, 1838).

John Goad to Lucreta Phillips, Sep. 11, 1838. Allen McDonald, J.P. (Sep. 11, 1838).

Feelden Beams to Matilda Richmond, Sep. 13, 1838. Michael Broyles, M.G. (Sep. 13, 1838).

William Beard to Nancy Barron, Sep. 19, 1838. Matthew Douglas, J.P. (Sep. 19, 1838).

Daniel Vinzant to Susan Page, Sep. 20, 1838. Thos. Hope, J.P. (Sep. 21, 1838).

William Pennington to Nancy Jones, Sep. 23, 1838. Matthew Douglas, J.P. (Sep. 23, 1838).

James Rains to Sarah Standly, Sep. 27, 1838. Michael Broyles, M.G. (Sep. 27, 1838).

A. T. Miller to Sarah Ann Wiley, Sep. 27, 1838. John Pebley, J.P. (Oct. 4, 1838).

Davis Hatfield to Elizabeth Walden, Oct. 3, 1838. Michael Broyles, M.G. (Oct. 7, 1838).

Greenberry Foley to Ann Ingle, Oct. 8, 1838. John Jones, J.P. (Oct. 8, 1838).

James Cannon to Martha Tuder, Oct. 8, 1838. John Jones, J.P. (Oct. 8, 1838).

Preston Carnutt to Elizabeth Campbell, Oct. 15, 1838. No return.

Washington Wise to Rebecca Brown, Oct. 15, 1838. No return.

George Ousley to Wilena Silver, Oct. 28, 1838. Michael Broyles, M.G. (Oct. 28, 1838).

William Watson to Lucindy Day, Oct. 31, 1838. No return.

Andrew Jackson to Katharine Lay, Nov. 4, 1838. Michael Broyles, M.G. (Nov. 4, 1838).

George Bryant to Lydia Penington, Nov. 4, 1838. Michael Broyls, M.G. (Nov. 11, 1838).

Wm. Blankenship to Mary Ann Wilson, Nov. 19, 1838. Matthew Douglas, J.P. (Nov. 19, 1838).

Jesse Hackler to Sarah Potter, Nov. 26, 1837. Matthew Douglas, J.P. (Nov. 26, 1837).

Harry None to Polley Smith, Dec. 9, 1838. No return.

Joel Parrott to Catherine Marlow, Dec. 9, 1838. No return.

Jackson Rose to Ann Crowley, Dec. 16, 1838. Matthew Douglas, J.P. (Dec. 16, 1838).

John Douglas to Lucinda Bell, Dec. 29, 1838. Matthew Douglas, J.P. (Dec. 29, 1838).

Richard Smith to Racehl Terry, Jan. 8, 1839. M. R. Pennington, J.P. (Jan. 16, 1838).

William Childers to Nancy Langherty, Jan. 9, 1839. Allen McDonald, J.P. (Jan. 9, 1839).

John Bryant to Elizabeth Loe (Lee), Jan. 11, 1839. Matthew Douglas, J.P. (Jan. 11, 1839).

John Allen to Nancy Brown, Jan. 13, 1839. Michael
Broyles, M.G. (Jan. 13, 1839).
Elias Miller to Sarah Gray, Jan. 26, 1839. Isaac
Gross, J.P. (Jan. 26, 1839).
James Adkins to Margaret Tye, Jan. 28, 1839. Matthew
Douglas, J.P. (Jan. 28, 1839).
William Conner to Elizabeth Agee, Jan. 20, 1838. C.
H. Boatright, M.G. (Jan. 28, 1838).
Thomas Angel to Nancy Elmore, Feb. 9, 1839. Joshua
Duncan, J.P. (Feb. 9, 1839).
Robert Stewart to Susan Faulkner, Feb. 10, 1839.
Matthew Douglas, J.P. (Feb. 10, 1839).
Oliver Hill to Ann Oaks, Feb. 20, 1839. A. W. Lindsay,
J.P. (Feb. 24, 1839).
Reuben Standley to Nancy Branham, Feb. 20, 1890.
(Feb. 20, 1890).
John Barbee to Nancy Jones, Feb. 24, 1839. J. C.
Petree, J.P. (Feb. 24, 1839).
John Mosier to Mary Murray, Mar. 1, 1839. Aron Hatmaker,
J.P. (Mar. 6, 1839).
Andrew Heatherly to Sarah Craig, Mar. 2, 1839. No return.
Reubin Craig to Polley Cannon, Mar. 4, 1839. John Jones,
J.P. (Mar. 4, 1839).
Jeremiah Meadors to Mary Creekmore, Mar. 10, 1839.
Matthew Douglas, J.P. (Mar. 10, 1839).
Anthony Blevins to Margaret Carson, Mar. 18, 1839.
Joshua Duncan, J.P. (Mar. 18, 1839).
Saml. Douglas to Lak Campbell, Mar. 26, 1839. Matthew
Douglas, J.P. (Mar. 26, 1839).
Solomon Standsbury to Jane Beams, Apr. 5, 1839. Michael
Broyles, M.G. (Apr. 5, 1839).
Henry Ridenour to Nancy Cox, Apr. 5, 1839. No return.
Jesse Smith to Ann Thompson, Apr. 10, 1839. P.
Pennington, J.P. (Apr. 11, 1839).
Eli Rotten to Hannah Dowel, Apr. 25, 1839. Thos. Hope,
J.P. (Apr. 25, 1839).
Daniel Bowen to Peziah Hamblin, May 2, 1839. Matthew
Douglas, J.P. (May 2, 1839).
Alais Cooper to Polley Foster, May 6, 1839. Allen
McDonald, J.P. (May 6, 1839).
James Miller to Mary Brosswhite, May 12, 1839. No
return.
Tom N. Campbell to Catherine Sharp, May 14, 1839.
Matthew Douglas, J.P. (May 14, 1839).
Jesse M. Trammell to Lavina Marcus, May 18, 1839. P.
Pennington, J.P. (May 19, 1839).
Anthony Heather to Elizabeth Keller, May 24, 1839. A.
W. Lindsay, J.P. (May 26, 1839).
John Miller to Emily Jones, May 25, 1839. No return.
Joel Stephens to Jane Thomas, May 30, 1839. William
King, J.P. (May 30, 1839).
R. Shoopman to Margaret Harness, June 13, 1839. Allen
McDonald, J.P. (June 15, 1839).
William Thornton to Sarah Ann Davis, June 16, 1839.
M. Broyles, M.G. (June 16, 1839).

George Smith Peters to Elizabeth Heatoh, June 20, 1839.
Isaac Gross, J.P. (June 21, 1839).
Andrew Miller to Sarah McCulley, July 1, 1839. Isaac
C. Petree, J.P. (July 7, 1839).
Edward Smith to Jane Smith, July 5, 1839. Isaac
Gross, J.P. (July 8, 1839).
Ephraim Cooper to Lavina J. Peterson, July 12, 1839.
Isaac Gross, J.P. (July 13, 1839).
Jackson Cannon to Angeline Tillery, July 18, 1839.
Isaac Gross, J.P. (July 21, 1839).
Phillip Meying to Lavina McCarty, July 18, 1839. Isaac
C. Petree, J.P. (July 22, 1839).
Isaac Smiddy to Elizabeth McFarland, July 24, 1839. Ch.
Lynch, M.G. (July 28, 1839).
Sampson Martin to Ann Baker, Aug. 1, 1839. John E.
Wheeler, J.P. (Aug. 4, 1839).
William Huckaby to Nancy Mullins, Aug. 4, 1839. Isaac
Gross, J.P. (Aug. 4, 1839).
William Lindsay to Huldah Cooper, Aug. 9, 1839. Isaac
Gross, J.P. (Aug. 10, 1839).
James Wilson to Martha Agee, Aug. 10, 1839. No return.
Moses Lay to Delila Adkins, Aug. 14, 1839. Jacob
Hill, J.P. (Aug. 15, 1839).
Jeremiah Boshears to Elly Ann Miller, Aug. 19, 1839.
(Aug. 20, 1839).
Carr Shomate to Sarah Maupin, Sep. 5, 1839. Wm. Bruce,
L.M. (Sep. 12, 1839).
Robert Gray to Francis Mallicoat, Sep. 6, 1839. No
return.
Allen Hubboard to Jane Chavis, Sep. 16, 1839. John
Jones, J.P. (Sep. 16, 1839).
Robert Dossett to Elizabeth Wilson, Sep. 20, 1839.
John Jones, J.P. (Sep. 22, 1839).
James Harness to Eliza Barns, Sep. 21, 1839. Thomas
Hope, J.P. (Sep. 22, 1839).
Jesse Hubbard to Sarah Chavis, Sep. 26, 1839. John
Jones, J.P. (Oct. 1, 1839).
Obediah Adkins to E. Shelton, Sep. 26, 1839. Allen
McDonald, J.P. (Sep. 26, 1839).
Liberty S. Sutton to Jane McFarland, Sep. 30, 1839.
M. Broyles, M.G. (Sep. 30, 1839).
Enos King to Nancy Angel, Aug. 22, 1839. Joshua
Dunkin, J.P. (Aug. 22, 1839).
William Ryan to Polley Trammell, Aug. 22, 1839. Joshua
Duncan, J.P. (Aug. 22, 1839).
Welcome Stephens to Morgan Williamson, Aug. 23, 1839.
'John Jones, J.P. (Sep. 3, 1839).
J. M. Tucker to Martha Gray, Oct. 9, 1839. Isaac
Gross, J.P. (Oct. 10, 1839).
Elijah Burriss to Polly Jarman, Oct. 9, 1839. Aaron
Hatmaker, J.P. (Oct. 13, 1839).
Benj. Richardson to Elizabeth L. Perkins, Oct. 27,
1839. Michael Broyles, M.G. (Oct. 27, 1839).
Henderson Murray to Rebecca Delap, Nov. 3, 1839.
Thos. Douglas, J.P. (Nov. 3, 1839).

Fielding Pennington to Elizabeth Chambers, Nov. 9, 1839. R. Pennington, J.P. (Nov. 26, 1839).
Calvin Little to Nancy J. Jackson, Nov. 10, 1839. Michael Broyles, M.G. (Nov. 10, 1839).
Sanford Higgs to Dornelia Haley, Nov. 25, 1839. Wm. Bruce, L.P. (Nov. 28, 1839).
Hardin Thomas to Melinda Bodkins, Nov. 28, 1839. Matthew Douglas, J.P. (Nov. 28, 1839).
William N. Ballard to Elizabeth Smith, Nov. 18, 1839. Thomas Douglas, J.P. (Nov. 19, 1839).
Jesse Lay to Canny Lay, Dec. 8, 1839. Joab Hill, J.P. (Dec. 8, 1839).
Joel Parrott to Catherine Marlow, Dec. 9, 1839. Matthew Douglas, J.P. (Jan. 14, 1840).
Thomas Brown to Catherine Honeycutt, Dec. 10, 1839. Joshua Duncan, J.P. (Dec. 10, 1839).
John Thomas to Barbary Grimes, Dec. 16, 1839. William Bruce, J.P. (Dec. 19, 1839).
Robert Ross to Martha Dial, Dec. 16, 1839. Isaac Gross, J.P. (Dec. 20, 1839).
David Harness to Elizabeth Arnott, Jan. 2, 1840. R. Pennington, J.P. (Jan. 2, 1840).
Andrew Chitwood to Elizabeth M. Colten, Jan. 5, 1840. R. Pennington, J.P. (Jan. 5, 1840).
Enoch Nelson to Polley Moore, Jan. 6, 1840. John Lower, J.P. (Jan. 6, 1840).
Edward Sweaton to Jane Pendleton, Jan. 15, 1840. M. A. W. Sampson, J.P.
Campbell Reid to Patsy Chitwood, Jan. 23, 1840. Allen McDonald, J.P. (Jan. 23, 1840).
Preston McClary to Eliza Brassfield, Jan. 29, 1840. No return.
Isaac W. Colten to Christian Jeffers, Feb. 8, 1840. R. Pennington, J.P. (Feb. 9, 1840).
Alfred Murray to Mary Sharp, Feb. 14, 1840. Aaron Hatmaker, J.P. (Feb. 14, 1840).
Reuben Standley to Nancy Branham, Feb. 20, 1840. Michael Broyles, M.G. (Feb. 20, 1840).
Daniel Faust to Elizabeth Strader, Feb. 29, 1840. No return.
Archibald Mobley to Vicey Young, Mar. 1, 1840. Michael Broyles, M.G. (Mar. 1, 1840).
Eliza Bowman to Nancy Douglass, Mar. 5, 1840. Matthew Douglas, J.P. (Mar. 5, 1840).
Andrew Dossett to Isa Cain, Mar. 11, 1840. Isaac C. Petree, J.P. (Mar. 15, 1840).
James Hatmaker to Delila Carver, Mar. 14, 1840. Archibald W. Lindsay, J.P. (Mar. 14, 1840).
James Carver to Alcey Jackson, Mar. 14, 1840. No return.
Henry Ridenour to Eclid Miller, Mar. 17, 1840. Isaac Gross, J.P. (Mar. 17, 1840).
Ransom Smith to Hannah Gibson, Apr. 7, 1840. Wm. Bruce, L.J. (Apr. 9, 1840).

William Daugherty to Catherine Sweet, Apr. 12, 1840.
R. Pennington, J.P. (Apr. 12, 1840).
Andrew Loyd to Mary Jeffers, Apr. 10, 1840. Allen
McDonald, J.P. (Apr. 16, 1840).
William Jackson to Mahala Cooper, Apr. 25, 1840.
Isaac Gross, J.P. (Apr. 26, 1840).
Ousley Huckaby to Mary Bullock, May 2, 1840. Aaron
Hatmaker, J.P. (May 3, 1840).
Joseph Campbell to Rena Nelson, May, 1840. No return.
William Price to Matilda Adkins, May 10, 1840. Michael
Broyles, M.G. (May 10, 1840).
Peter Dewel to Lucinda Lovett, May 13, 1840. M. A. W.
Simpson, J.P. (May 19, 1840).
Matison Glenn to Elizabeth Miller, May 17, 1840. J.
C. Petree, J.P. (May 18, 1840).
John Ellison to Julian Boyers, June 7, 1840. Michael
Broyles, M.G. (June 7, 1840).
William Kay to Sarah Douglas, June 4, 1840. Matthew
Douglas, J.P. (June 4, 1840).
Joseph Smith to Nancy Baker, June 8, 1840. Matthew
Douglas, J.P. (June 14, 1840).
O. P. Broughton to Martha Cain, June 14, 1840. Michael
Broyles, M.G. (June 14, 1840).
Samuel Douglas to Eliza Carter, June 14, 1840. Matthew
Douglas, J.P. (June 14, 1840).
James Hutson to Gabella Gray (Isabella Gray), June 17,
1840. No return.
Jesse B. Stamper to Martha Smith, June 21, 1840. C.
Fulton, E.M.E.C. (June 20, 1840).
John Harnes to Jane Smith, June 25, 1840. R. Pennington,
J.P. (June 25, 1840).
Isaac Reed to Feriby McDonald, June 26, 1840. Allen
McDonald (?), J.P. (June 28, 1840).
James Lumpkins to Susan Chavis, July 8, 1840. Jacob
Petree, J.P. (July 24, 1840).
Joseph Beard to Sally Smith, July 9, 1840. Michael
Broyles, M.G.
Bartholomew Neal to Kesiah Whitman, July 10, 1840. C.
H. Boatright, M.G. (July 12, 1840).
Robert Lindsay to M. E. Green, July 16, 1840. W. C.
Reynolds, M.G. (July 16, 1840).
Joseph Meader to Cintha Crickmore (Creekmore), July 26,
1840. Matthew Douglas, J.P.
William Bridges to Delila Nelson, Aug. 3, 1840. John
Lower, J.P. (Aug. 3, 1840).
William McClary to Nancy McGloshlier, Aug. 5, 1840.
Anderson Smith. (Sep. 8, 1840).
John Hatfield to Elizabeth Hatfield, Aug. 11, 1840.
William Bruce, L.D. (Aug. 12, 1840).
Sampson Shumtate to Doley Barber, Aug. 11, 1840.
William Bruce, L.D. (Aug. 15, 1840).
John C. Bratcher to Martha Gray, Aug. 21, 1840. J. C.
Petree, J.P. (Aug. 24, 1840).
H. L. Foreman to Mahala Brooks, Aug. 24, 1840. Thos.
Hope, J.P. (Aug. 30, 1840).

Wm. H. Williams to Dualla Newport, Aug. 26, 1840. No return.

Jeremiah Adkins to Valentine Bowl, Sep. 4, 1840. Matthew Douglas, J.P. (Sep. 4, 1840).

Cornelius Dabney to Sarah Dagley, Sep. 9, 1840. Thos. Hope, J.P. (Sep. 9, 1840).

Haywood Gilbert to Nancy Clark, Sep. 15, 1840. J. C. Petree, J.P. (Sep. 15, 1840).

Michael Lay to Lydia Beard, Sep. 20, 1840. Matthew Douglas, J.P. (Sep. 20, 1840).

Jonas Baker to Nancy Thomas, Sep. 24, 1830. No return.

Lewis Wilson to Elizabeth Henby, Sep. 24, 1840. No return.

Albert Williamson to Louisa J. Brantlett, Oct. 5, 1840. Jacob Petree, J.P. (Oct. 8, 1840).

James Campbell to Barbary Glenn, Oct. 8, 1840. J. C. Petree, J.P. (Oct. 10, 1840).

William M. Strunk to Malinda Lego (Lebo), Oct. 15, 1840. Joshua Duncan, J.P. (Oct. 15, 1840).

James Lay to Iris Grant, Oct. 17, 1840. No return.

Lyn Boulton to Ann Cox, Oct. 22, 1840. Matthew Douglas, J.P. (Oct. 22, 1840).

Hiram Boulton to Rhoda Standley, Oct. 22, 1840. Matthew Douglas, J.P. (Oct. 22, 1840).

James Ford to Ann Ford, Nov. 3, 1840. Thomas Douglas, J.P. (Nov. 8, 1840).

W. D. Durham to Mary Little, Nov. 4, 1840. Thomas Douglas, J.P. (Nov. 8, 1840).

William Wilson to Sarah Pitman, Nov. 11, 1840. James Owen, J.P. (Nov. 12, 1840).

John Smith to Nancy W. Colten, Nov. 14, 1840. R. Pennington, J.P. (Nov. 15, 1840).

Isaac Bunch to Dolley McGee, Nov. 28, 1840. Isaac Gross, J.P. (Nov. 26, 1840).

Moris Foster to Rhoda Costin, Nov. 28, 1840. Joshua Duncan, J.P. (Nov. 28, 1840).

Andrew Dibbley to Rachel Goin, Dec. 10, 1840. Michael Broyles, M.G. (Dec. 10, 1840).

Elijah Adkins to Pelina Jane McCarty, Dec. 10, 1840. Michael Broyles, M.G. (Dec. 11, 1840).

Joshua Duncan to Lucy Chambers, Dec. 13, 1840. James Cooper, J.P. (Jan. 2, 1841).

Henry Wheeler to Ann Agee, Dec. 20, 1840. No return.

Christopher Foust to Susan Nelson, Dec. 20, 1840. No return.

Henry Sharp to Catherine Cooper, Dec. 23, 1840. No return.

Richard C. Lawson to Lucinda Siler, Dec. 26, 1840. Michael Broyles, M.G. (Dec. 26, 1840).

Ephraim Langley to Mary Murray, Jan. 5, 1841. Matthew Douglas, J.P. (Jan. 4, 1841).

James Risterson to Margaret Lovedy, Jan. 13, 1841. Isaac Gross, J.P. (Jan. 14, 1841).

Samuel Harness to Mary Howett, Jan. 14, 1841. Allen McDonald, J.P. (Jan. 14, 1841).

# CAMPBELL COUNTY MARRIAGES

David Acres to Sarah Stanley, Jan. 15, 1841. Joshua
Duncan, J.P. (Jan. 15, 1841).
Benjamin Graier to Jones Wilson, Jan. 19, 1840. No
return.
Edward Wilson to Hulda Cooper, Jan. 20, 1841. No
return.
Nelson Eads to Didaman Delk, Jan. 28, 1841. James
Owens, J.P. (Jan. 28, 1841).
Joseph York to Reuben Duncain (Duncan), Feb. 5, 1840.
Michael Broyles, M.G. (Feb. 5, 1840).
Joel Champman to Margaret Woods, Feb. 8, 1841. James
Cooper, J.P. (Feb. 9, 1841).
Martin Canada to Rachel Ward, Feb. 9, 1841. W. Bruce,
L.D. (Feb. 11, 1841).
Matthew Luallen (Lewellen or Lewyellen) to Susan Lawson,
Feb. 11, 1841. Allen McDonald, J.P. (Feb. 11, 1841).
Asa Eads to Sarah Adkins, Mar. 4, 1841. James Owens,
J.P. (Mar. 12, 1841).
Dusta Goin to D. A. King, Mar. 10, 1841. No return.
James Baker to Delila Kay, Mar. 25, 1841. Matthew
Douglas, J.P. (Mar. 25, 1841).
Levi Ingram to Nancy Morgan, Mar. 28, 1841. Matthew
Douglas, J.P. (Mar. 28, 1841).
Peter Tuttle to Elizabeth Smith, Apr. 8, 1841. Jacob
Hill, J.P. (Apr. 13, 1841).
John M. Leach to Angeline Chapman, Apr. 15, 1841. James
Cooper, J.P. (Apr. 15, 1841).
David Lovett to Matilda Bird, May 26, 1841. Matthew
Douglas, J.P. (May 26, 1841).
James Paul to Malinda Boshears (Bashears or Beathshears),
May 22, 1841. No return.
Eli Stiner to Luisa Jane Heatherly, June 10, 1841.
James Cooper, J.P. (June 19, 1841).
William Nelson to Mary Ann Smith, June 12, 1841. John
Sower, J.P. (June 13, 1841).
Gowel Williams to Margaret Siler, June 13, 1841. Matthew
Douglas, J.P. (June 13, 1841).
Archibald Briton to Martha Woods, June 20, 1841.
Matthew Douglas, J.P. (June 20, 1841).
Pryor Herrin to Margaret Pouder, Aug. 28, 1841.
Jacob Petree, J.P. (Aug. 29, 1841).
James Boswell to Cintha Honeycutt, July 3, 1841. James
Owens, J.P. (July 7, 1841).
Joseph Phillips to Elizabeth Hicks, July 14, 1841.
James Owens, J.P. (July 25, 1841).
William C. Kirk to Irena Miller, July 16, 1841. Moses
A. W. Sampson, J.P. (July 16, 1841).
William Simpkins to Minerva Dossett, July 18, 1841.
No return.
Pleasant Chitwood to Polley Thompson, Aug. 6, 1841.
Joshua Duncan, J.P. (Aug. 7, 1841).
Campbell Taylor to Mary Henderson, Aug. 6, 1841. Matthew
Douglas, J.P. (Aug. 6, 1841).
William Lawson to Elizabeth Benit, Aug. 19, 1841.
Matthew Douglas, J.P. (Aug. 19, 1841).

A. Bowlinger to Dally Robinson, Aug. 30, 1841. No
return.
William Dagley to Amanda Dagley, Aug. 26, 1841. Robert
Kimbraugh, M.G. (Aug. 26, 1841).
Pryor Herrin to Margaret London, Aug. 28, 1841. Jacob
Petree, J.P. (Aug. 29, 1841).
William Dagley and Amanda Dagley, Aug. 26, 1841. Robert
G. Kimbraugh, M.G. (Aug. 26, 1841).
Pryor Herrin to Margaret London, Aug. 28, 1841. Jacob
Petree, J.P. (Aug. 29, 1841).
James Hewith to Elizabeth Anderson, Aug. 30, 1841. No
return.
John Murphy to Levina Stephens, Sep. 1, 1841. Joshua
Duncan, J.P. (Sep. 2, 1841).
William Carter to Elizabeth Adkins, Oct. 26, 1841.
Matthew Douglas, J.P. (Oct. 26, 1841).
Jas. D. Campbell to C. A. Nelson, Sep. 7, 1841. No
return.
John Duncan to Matilda Loyd, Sep. 8, 1841. James Owens,
J.P. (Sep. 12, 1841).
Benjamin Baker to Sarah Vines, Sep. 9, 1841. James
Owens, J.P. (Sep. 7, 1841).
William Sigo to Martha Trammel, Sep. 16, 1841. Matthew
Douglas, J.P. (Sep. 16, 1841).
Henry Lawson to Sarah Rose, Sep. 27, 1841. Matthew
Douglas, J.P. (Sep. 27, 1841).
Pascal Smith to Susan McClary, Oct. 14, 1841. Matthew
Douglas, J.P. (Oct. 17, 1841).
James Logan to Lucinda Woord, Oct. 17, 1841. Matthew
Douglas, J.P. (Oct. 17, 1841).
Samuel Douglas to Thursey Barton, Oct. 27, 1841. James
Cooper, J.P. (Oct. 31, 1841).
A. D. Smith to Summerfield Miller, Nov. 6, 1841.
William Bruce, L.D. (Nov. 10, 1841).
William Sanders to Clarissa Glandon, Nov. 11, 1841.
Thomas Douglas, J.P.
Edmond Gray to Dolly Wilson, Nov. 13, 1841. Isaac
Gross, J.P. (Nov. 14, 1841).
Joseph Gray to Nancy Farmer, Nov. 10, 1841. Isaac
Gross, J.P. (Nov. 14, 1841).
Alexander Loyd to Lucinda McDonald, Nov. 20, 1841.
Cutbirth Webb, M.G. (Nov. 21, 1841).
Joshua Wilson to Jane Creekmore, Dec. 12, 1841. Matthew
Douglas, J.P. (Dec. 12, 1841).
Richmond Taylor to Sarah Ryan, Dec. 17, 1841. Matthew
Douglas, J.P. (Dec. 17, 1841).
Wm. Ephrin Moore to Susan Davis, Dec. 17, 1841.
Matthew Douglas, J.P. (Dec. 17, 1841).
Ota T. Claiborn to Mary Smith, Dec. 24, 1841. Anderson
Smith, M.G. (Dec. 26, 1841).
Anthony Hutson to Elizabeth Bowling, Dec. 23, 1841. C.
H. Boatright, M.G. (Dec. 26, 1841).
Robert Hayslip to Elizabeth Lay, Dec. 25, 1841. Matthew
Douglas, J.P. (Dec. 25, 1841).

CAMPBELL COUNTY MARRIAGES

Isham Sharp to Nancy Adkins, Dec. 25, 1841. James
    Owens, J.P. (Dec. 30, 1841).
D. M. Manley to Nancy Archer, Jan. 4, 1842. No return.
John Hutson to Nancy Sweat, Jan. 6, 1842. No return.
Milton Stanfill to Rachael Beard, Jan. 15, 1842.
    Michael Broyles, M.G. (Feb. 3, 1842).
Edward Wilson to Hulda Cooper, Jan. 20, 1842. Aaron
    Hatmaker, J.P. (Jan. 20, 1842).
D. M. Sharp to Sarah Smith, Jan. 20, 1842. J. G.
    Petree, J.P. (Jan. 27, 1842).
William Hatmaker to Mary Heatherly, Jan. 22, 1842.
    Isaac Gross, J.P. (Jan. 23, 1842).
Calam Barron to Nancy Perkins, Feb. 13, 1842. Matthew
    Douglas, J.P. (Feb. 13, 1842).
Christopher Adkins to Elizabeth Martin, Feb. 1, 1842.
    Matthew Douglas, J.P. (Feb. 11, 1842).
John Wiley Hilhite to Catherine Carter, Feb. 1, 1842.
    Matthew Douglas, J.P. (Feb. 1, 1842).
David Lawson to Ann Lawson, Feb. 18, 1842. James Owens,
    J.P. (Feb. 18, 1842).
Malekeer Hatmaker to Elizabeth Murray, Feb. 24, 1842.
    Aaron Hatmaker, J.P. (Feb. 27, 1842).
James Martin to Mahala Longmire, Feb. 26, 1842. No
    return.
Thomas Pritchard to Louise Walker, Feb. 22, 1842.
    Matthew Douglas, J.P. (Feb. 27, 1842).
Thomas Miller to Margaret Loops, Mar. 1, 1842. J. C.
    Petree, J.P. (Mar. 6, 1842).
Green B. Suttle to Hannah Miller, Mar. 8, 1842. J. C.
    Petree, J.P. (Mar. 10, 1842).
Samuel Carroll to Ann Debby, Mar. 23, 1842. J. A.
    Hollingsworth, J.P. (Mar. 23, 1842).
Jackson Miller to Polly Paulson, Mar. 30, 1842. J. C.
    Petree, J.P. (Apr. 3, 1842).
Franklin Miller to Polly Paulson, Mar. 30, 1842.
    (Apr. 12, 1842).
James V. Sullivan to James M. Sheans, Apr. 3, 1842.
    Matthew Douglas, J.P. (Apr. 3, 1842).
James Strunk to Polly King, May 12, 1842. Wm. Dickson,
    J.P. (May 12, 1842).
Reubin Hampton to Cyntha Reeves, June 1, 1842. Jos. H.
    Delap, J.P. (June 2, 1842).
Cornelius Anderson to Emily Davis, June 11, 1842. Wm.
    Dickson. (June 11, 1842).
Alexander Lofty to Matilda Prock, June 23, 1842. Calvin
    Peterson, J.P. (June 23, 1842).
Hickman Carroll to Elizabeth McCulley, July 1, 1842.
    'No return.
Isaac Hutson to Polly Ford, July 4, 1842. Joseph H.
    Delap, J.P. (July 4, 1842).
William Douglas to Catherine Lay, July 10, 1842.
    Matthew Douglas, J.P. (July 10, 1842).
William Blevins to Susan Puree, Apr. 11, 1842. R. G.
    Goin, M.G. (Apr. 11, 1842).

Francis Chandoin to Elizabeth Heath, Apr. 11, 1842.
No return.
William Tankestley (Tankersley) to Ann Beams, Apr. 14,
1842. Matthew Douglas, J.P. (Apr. 14, 1842).
John Smith to Olley Jones, Apr. 17, 1842. Matthew
Douglas, J.P. (Apr. 17, 1842).
Elisha Childress to Lucy Meaders, Apr. 21, 1842. J. A.
Hollingsworth, J.P. (Apr. 25, 1842).
William Campbell to Sarah Graves, Apr. 21, 1842. J. C.
Petree, J.P. (Apr. 21, 1842).
Jackson H. King to Eliza Angel, Apr. 24, 1842. Matthew
Douglas, J.P. (Apr. 24, 1842).
Joseph Keeney to Lavina Huff, July 14, 1842. Robert G.
Kinbrough, M.G. (July 14, 1842).
Leander King to Polley Smith, July 20, 1842. J. C.
Petree, J.P. (July 21, 1842).
William Shumate to Cornelius C. Reed, July 20, 1842.
No return.
Milton Gatliff to Sarilda Cummins, July 22, 1842.
Matthew Douglas, J.P. (July 22, 1842).
Silas Williams to Catherine Smith, July 22, 1842. No
return.
Joseph M. Laws to Elizabeth Belew, July 25, 1842. No
return.
Willie Graham to Clarissa Montgomery, July 27, 1842.
Robert C. Kinbrough, M.G. (Aug. 21, 1842).
John Brock to Rebecca Langley, Sep. 6, 1842. Joseph
H. Delap, J.P. (Sep. 7, 1842).
Ivory F. Hamly to Sarah Bedkin, Sep. 11, 1842. Matthew
Douglas, J.P. (Sep. 11, 1842).
G. E. Ridenour to Sarah Brantley, Sep. 17, 1842. No
return.
Martin Terry to Nancy Thompson, Sep. 17, 1842. No
return.
Samuel Petrey to Elizabeth Bryant, Sep. 25, 1842.
Matthew Douglas, J.P. (Sep. 25, 1842).
Elijah Cosier to Eliza Steel, Aug. 29, 1842. Matthew
Douglas, J.P. (Aug. 29, 1842).
James M. Stringer to Monday McFall, Aug. 30, 1842.
Matthew Douglas, J.P. (Aug. 30, 1842).
Moses Gatliff to Elizabeth Stanfill, Oct. 4, 1842.
Matthew Douglas, J.P. (Oct. 4, 1842).
Aaron Broyles to Lavina Thomas, Oct. 5, 1842. Michael
Broyles, M.G. (Oct. 6, 1842).
James Dabney to Malinda Reeves, Oct. 19, 1842. C. H.
Boatright, J.P. (Oct. 23, 1842).
Samuel Beard to Ann Palina, Oct. 20, 1842. Matthew
Douglas, J.P. (Oct. 20, 1842).
Robert Dossett to Minerva Cain, Oct. 20, 1842. No
return.
John Rains to Lanija Nartin, Oct. 27, 1842. Matthew
Douglas, J.P. (Oct. 27, 1842).
Thomas Drain to Belinda Polly, Nov. 3, 1842. Matthew
Douglas, J.P. (Nov. 3, 1842).

Curtis Blakely to Synthia Bord, Nov. 3, 1842. Matthew
   Douglas, J.P. (Nov. 10, 1842).
William Broyles to Rhoda Douglas, Nov. 10, 1842.
   Matthew Douglas, J.P. (Nov. 10, 1842).
Thomas York to Sarah Johnson, Dec. 8, 1842. Matthew
   Douglas, J.P. (Dec. 8, 1842).
Elias Paulston to Gemima Still, Dec. 14, 1842. (Dec.
   15, 1842).
John E. Bayer to Nancy F. Stinger, Dec. 20, 1842.
   Matthew Douglas, J.P. (Dec. 20, 1842).
Amos Bratcher to Elizabeth Goin, Dec. 24, 1842. John
   Adkins, J.P. (Jan. 1, 1842).
Joseph Adkins to Eliza Smith, Dec. 25, 1842. John
   Adkins, J.P. (Dec. 25, 1842).
Joshua Moses to Sarah Creekmore, Dec. 27, 1842. Matthew
   Douglas, J.P. (Dec. 27, 1842).
Wm. Wells to Nancy Faulkner, Jan. 1, 1843. Matthew
   Douglas, J.P. (Jan. 1, 1843).
P. J. P, Follon to Lucinda Harris, Jan. 1, 1843. Wm.
   Graves, M.G. (Jan. 1, 1843).
Wm. Albright to Nancy Stout, Jan. 4, 1843. No return.
William Duke to Tansey Sharp, Jan. 4, 1842. Isaac
   Gentry, M.G. (Jan. 8, 1842).
Samuel Shelby to Sally McCulley, Jan. 4, 1843. No
   return.
Litcher Stanfield to Hannah Beard, Jan. 9, 1843. Michael
   Broyles, M.G. (Jan. 19, 1843).
Fielding Loe to Sarah Carrolle, Jan. 12, 1843. Matthew
   Douglas, J.P. (Jan. 12, 1843).
George Reeves to Sarah Shadowen, Jan. 15, 1842. Matthew
   Douglas, J.P. (Jan. 15, 1842).
Henry Burriss to Polley Gray, Jan. 17, 1843. Calvin
   Peterson, J.P. (Jan. 19, 1843).
John Hitch to Fany Sharp, Jan. 18, 1843. Isaac Wilson,
   J.P. (Jan. 22, 1843).
Starn Wilhite to Catherine Carter, Jan. 29, 1843.
   Matthew Douglas, J.P. (Jan. 29, 1843).
F. F. Hunt to Jane Adkins, Jan. 30, 1843. (Married
   by J.P.)
Jas. Johnson to Eliza Adkins, Feb. 4, 1843. Peter
   Burriss, J.P. (Feb. 5, 1843).
Tapley J. Henson to Malinda McCarty, Feb. 7, 1842.
   Alvis Kincaid, J.P. (Feb. 12, 1842).
Wm. Dossett to Eliza Hope, Feb. 9, 1843. Alivs
   Kincaid, J.P. (Feb. 16, 1843).
George Washington Rogers to Catharine Powel, Feb. 28,
   1843. Matthew Douglas, J.P. (Feb. 28, 1843).
Charles M. Johnson to Nancy Craig, Mar. 6, 1843. No
   return.
Arthur Marcum to Nancy Delk, Mar. 6, 1843. Jno. Akins,
   J.P. (Mar. 7, 1843).
Milton Wyatt to Nancy Ann Allison, Mar. 15, 1843.
   Matthew Douglas, J.P. (Mar. 15, 1843).
Champ Waters to Nelly McMann, Mar. 16, 1843. No
   return.

David Adkins to Nancy Faulkner, Mar. 16, 1843. Matthew
 Douglas, J.P. (Mar. 16, 1843).
Henderson Lay to Sally Stout, Mar. 11, 1843. No return.
Henry Wilson to Sarah Campbell, Mar. 18, 1843. Peter
 Burris, J.P. (Mar. 18, 1843).
Wm. Johnson to Desse Adkins, Mar. 25, 1843. Peter
 Burriss, J.P. (Mar. 26, 1843).
H. W. Marcum to Mary Ann Hanks, Apr. 3, 1843. John
 Adkins, J.P. (Apr. 5, 1843).
Robert Parker to Lanor Chapman, Apr. 3, 1843. Allen
 McDonald, J.P. (Apr. 10, 1843).
Benjamin H. Brown to Harriet H. Swan, Apr. 6, 1843.
 J. Backley, J.P. (Apr. 6, 1843).
Stephen Gibson to Elizabeth Smith, Apr. 9, 1843. Allen
 McDonald. (Apr. 9, 1843).
Wm. B. Davis to Olive P. Allison, Apr. 9, 1843. Matthew
 Douglas, J.P. (Apr. 9, 1843).
Joseph A. Pelkington to Susan Martin, Apr. 20, 1843.
 S. Buckley, J.P. (Apr. 20, 1843).
James Miller to Nancy McCully, Apr. 22, 1843. John
 Jones, J.P. (Apr. 23, 1843).
Balantine Lovit to Louisa Anderson, Apr. 20, 1843.
 Matthew Douglas, J.P. (Apr. 20, 1843).
Wm. Bowman to Susan McClain, May 2, 1843. No return.
John Grimes to Nancy J. Kincaid, June 4, 1843. Wm.
 Bruce, J.P. (June 4, 1843).
M. L. Phillisp to Mary C. Hickox, June 6, 1843. Robert
 G. Kimbrough, M.G. (June 7, 1843).
Jno. Cox to Elizabeth Branham, June 10, 1843. Peter
 Burriss, J.P. (June 11, 1843).
Wm. Agee to Mariah M. Maden, June 18, 1843. John
 Jones, J.P. (June 18, 1843).
Stephen Thomas to Sarah Reed, July 3, 1843. Allen
 McDonald, J.P. (July 5, 1843).
Joseph Davis to Clender McCidy, July 6, 1843. Matthew
 Douglas, J.P. (July 6, 1843).
Jos Peterson to Eliza Keeny, July 12, 1843. R. G.
 Kimbrough, J.P. (July 12, 1843).
Wm. Sweat to Frances McCarty, July 29, 1843. John
 Jones, J.P. (July 30, 1843).
Silas Adkins to Cenia Wright, Aug. 6, 1843. Matthew
 Douglas, J.P. (Aug. 6, 1843).
A. Miller to Elizabeth Graves, Aug. 10, 1843. Alvis
 Kincaid. (Aug. 13, 1843).
David F. Creekmore to Elizabeth Meadors, Aug. 13, 1843.
 Matthew Douglas, J.P. (Aug. 13, 1843).
Jno. Chapman to Orpha Kiggs, Aug. 19, 1843. James
 Cooper, J.P. (Aug. 20, 1843).
Wm. King to Martha Richardson, Aug. 21, 1843. Reuben
 Rogers, J.P. (Aug. 22, 1843).
Robt. R. Hope to Martha Ann Isley, Aug. 25, 1843.
 Reubin Rogers, J.P. (Aug. 27, 1843).
Franklin Kincaid to Ann Cain, Aug. 28, 1843. W. Bruce,
 J.P. (Aug. 28, 1843).

CAMPBELL COUNTY MARRIAGES

Jno. Hinson to Sarah Lovett, Aug. 30, 1843.  J.
  Buckley, M.G.  (Aug. 30, 1843).
Wm. Smith to Lockey Cox, Sep. 5, 1843.  Peter Burriss,
  J.P.  (Sep. 10, 1843).
James Cox to Mary Wilson, Sep. 5, 1843.  Peter Burriss,
  J.P.  (Sep. 10, 1843).
Hiram Richardson to Martha Pearce, Sep. 6, 1843.  No
  return.
Enoch Archer to Susannah Boulten, Sep. 9, 1843.  Matthew
  Douglas, J.P.  (Sep. 9, 1843).
Henry Woods to Ann Rice, Sep. 12, 1843.  Isaac Wilson,
  J.P.  (Sep. 14, 1843).
Martin Terry to Nancy Thompson, Sep. 17, 1843.  No
  return.
Wm. Woodson to Leah Ford, Oct. 4, 1843.  Joe F. Delap,
  J.P.  (Oct. 8, 1843).
Silas Ingram to Sarah Hampton, Oct. 4, 1843.  Joe.
  F. Delap, J.P.  (Oct. 5, 1843).
James Stephens to Hannah Thomas, Oct. 9, 1843.  Michael
  Broyles, M.G.  (Oct. 10, 1843).
James A. McColloch to Nancy Siler, Oct. 15, 1843.  Mat-
  thew Douglas, J.P.  (Oct. 15, 1843).
Joel Ryan to Jane Creekmore, Oct. 19, 1843.  Matthew
  Douglas, J.P.  (Oct. 19, 1843).
Willie D. Alder to Sarah Meadors, Oct. 24, 1843.  No
  return.
Jno. N. Suttle to Diecy M. Smith, Nov. 8, 1843.  No
  return.
Valentine Turner to Lucinda Malone, Nov. 20, 1843.  No
  return.
James W. Moore to Mary Hall, Nov. 23, 1843.  Matthew
  Douglas, J.P.  (Nov. 23, 1843).
Spencer Hunter to Louisa Jarmon, Nov. 24, 1843.  (Nov.
  24, 1843).
Isaac Hutten to Mary Ann Carroll, Nov. 25, 1843.  No
  return.
Jos. Cabirth to Thuray Ann McKeehan, Nov. 26, 1843.
  Matthew Douglass.  (Nov. 26, 1843).
Jno. Surritt to Mary E. Moore (Mason), Nov. 20, 1843.
  No return.
Joseph Nix to Amariah Holt, Nov. 30, 1843.  Matthew
  Douglas, J.P.  (Nov. 30, 1843).
Wyly Thomas to Cinthia Polly, Dec. 3, 1843.  Michael
  Broyles, M.G.  (Dec. 7, 1843).
J. W. Plaster to V. C. Maupin, Dec. 18, 1843.  T.
  Buckley, M.G.  (Dec. 21, 1843).
Burton Buck to Lavina Miller, Nov. 2, 1843.  No return.
Wm. Peterson to Sarah Sweat, Dec. 21, 1843.  Reuben
  Rogers, J.P.  (Dec. 24, 1843).
Joseph Culbirth to Nancy Beams, Dec. 22, 1843.  Matthew
  Douglas, J.P.  (Dec. 22, 1843).
Nathan Shelly to Nancy Faulkner, Dec. 23, 1843.  Matthew
  Douglas, J.P.  (Dec. 24, 1843).
James Riggs to Elizabeth Smith, Jan. 2, 1844.  Peter
  Burris, J.P.  (Jan. 6, 1844).

# CAMPBELL COUNTY MARRIAGES

John Willoby to Catherine Vanderpoll, Jan. 3, 1844.
J. A. Hollingsworth, J.P. (Jan. 7, 1844).
J. D. Barkley to Nancy Green, Jan. 3, 1844. R. W.
Patty, M.G. (Jan. 4, 1844).
Jacob Lawson to Vicia Luallen (Lewellen), Jan. 5, 1844.
Allen McDonald, J.P. (Jan. 5, 1844).
George Brooks to Sarah Bratcher, Jan. 6, 1844. Matthew
Douglas, J.P. (Jan. 6, 1844).
James Perkins to Sarah Richmond, Jan. 7, 1844. Matthew
Douglas, J.P. (Jan. 7, 1844).
Jackson Campbell to Elizabeth Perkins, Jan. 18, 1844.
Matthew Douglas, J.P. (Jan. 18, 1844).
Edwin Hicks to Michael Beams, Jan. 18, 1844. Matthew
Douglas, J.P. (Jan. 18, 1844).
Andrew Lawson to Elizabeth Case, Jan. 21, 1844. Matthew
Douglas, J.P. (Jan. 21, 1844).
Wm. Duff to Leah Murray, Jan. 25, 1844. Joseph F.
Delap, J.P. (Jan. 26, 1844).
Peter Cooper to Rebecca Burton, Jan. 24, 1844. Peter
Burriss, J.P. (Jan. 24, 1844).
James Ball to Elizabeth McFarland, Jan. 25, 1844.
Matthew Douglas, J.P. (Jan. 25, 1844).
Thomas Brooks to Elizabeth Lay, Jan. 31, 1844.
Matthew Douglas, J.P. (Jan. 31, 1844).
Henry C. Grimes to Polly Fleming, Feb. 19, 1844.
R. S. Kimbrough, M.G.
Reubin Smiddy to B. A. Phillips, Feb. 27, 1844. Jackson
Wilhite, J.P. (Mar. 9, 1844).
David Rogers to Lena Williams, Feb. 29, 1844. Reubin
Rogers, J.P. (Feb. 29, 1844).
Daniel Chambers to Phoebe Phillips, Mar. 5, 1840.
Matthew Douglas, J.P. (Mar. 5, 1840).
Thomas Phillips to Ester Terry, Mar. 17, 1844. Allen
McDonald, J.P. (Mar. 17, 1844).
Samuel Burge to Polly Luallen (Lewellen), Mar. 18,
1844. Allen McDonald, J.P. (Mar. 21, 1844).
Calvin Smiddy to Elizabeth Hicks, Mar. 19, 1844.
Jackson Wilhite, J.P. (Mar. 28, 1844).
L. B. Crowly to Winney Lay, Mar. 28, 1844. Matthew
Douglas, J.P. (Mar. 28, 1844).
Fleming Nickleson to Sarah Skoans, Mar. 28, 1844.
Matthew Douglas, J.P. (Mar. 28, 1844).
Wm. Adams to L. N. McCall, Mar. 30, 1844. J. H. Delph,
J.P. (Mar. 30, 1844).
Jno. Siler to Harriet Owens, Mar. 31, 1844. Matthew
Douglas, J.P. (Mar. 31, 1844).
James McDonald to Melinda Lawson, May 1, 1844. Wiley
Chambers, J.P. (May 2, 1844).
John Tanner to Mary Pearce, May 6, 1844. John Jones,
J.P. (May 19, 1844).
Nelson Phillips to Rebecca Morgan, May 26, 1844.
Matthew Douglas, J.P. (May 26, 1844).
Speed Nicholson to Malinda Faulkner, May 30, 1844.
Matthew Douglas, J.P. (May 30, 1844).

Jeremiah Boshears to Sarah Malicoat, June 3, 1844.
   Peter Burriss, J.P. (June 3, 1844).
Isaac Petree to Martha Ford, June 8, 1844. Jacob
   Petree, J.P. (June 13, 1844).
John Vanderpool to Anna Dossett, June 19, 1844. Jacob
   Petree, J.P. (June 24, 1844).
John C. Ford to Ann Petree, June 20, 1844. James
   Parker, D.D. (4th Sunday in June, 1844).
Holley D. Moses to Sarah Malissa Candler, June 27, 1844.
   Matthew Douglas, J.P. (June 27, 1844).
Ezra Davenport to Elizabeth Lego (Lebo), June 27, 1844.
   Matthew Douglas, J.P. (June 27, 1844).
Thomas Griffy to Nancy Wilson, July 18, 1844. Peter
   Burriss, J.P. (July 18, 1844).
Vinsen Riggs to Mary Ballard, July 20, 1844. James
   Cooper, J.P. (July 2, 1844).
Arch Monday to Sarah Paulson, Aug. 6, 1844. Reubin
   Rogers, J.P. (Aug. 7, 1844).
Andrew McHone to Eliza Jackson, Aug. 8, 1844. Isaac
   Wilson, J.P. (Aug. 8, 1844).
John Chavis to Nancy Tate, Aug. 20, 1844. No return.
Milton Plaster to Elizabeth Hayter, Aug. 23, 1844.
   J. C. Petree, J.P. (Aug. 25, 1844).
John Nix to Mary Rains, Aug. 25, 1844. Matthew
   Douglas, J.P. (Aug. 25, 1844).
Wm. Reeves to Nancy Longmire, Sep. 7, 1844. Joseph
   H. Delap, J.P. (Sep. 7, 1844).
Isaac Neal to Sarah Gross, Oct. 19, 1844. R. Rogers,
   J.P. (Oct. 20, 1844).
Berry Thompson to Calia Lay, Sep. 30, 1844. Jackson
   Wilhite, J.P. (Sep. 30, 1844).
Shanklin Engle to Matilda J. Elliott, Sep. 30, 1844.
   Matthew Douglas, J.P. (Sep. 30, 1844).
James Vinsant to Elizabeth Douglas, Oct. 2, 1844.
   Reubin Rogers, J.P. (Oct. 3, 1844).
Jno. Hunter to Talitha Hart, Oct. 3, 1844. Reubin
   Rogers, J.P. (Oct. 6, 1844).
James M. Marshall to Elizabeth Smith, Oct. 14, 1844.
   Jack Buckley, M.G. (Oct. 17, 1844).
James Gray to Mary Tally, Oct. 17, 1844. James
   Johnson, J.P. (Oct. 23, 1844).
Jno. H. Stout to Orlena Wilhite, Oct. 17, 1844. No
   return.
Edmund Witt to Lucinda Lay, Nov. 1, 1844. Isaac Wilson,
   J.P. (Nov. 3, 1844).
Thomas L. Blevins to Elizabeth Yancy, Nov. 21, 1844.
   No return.
James B. Tackett to Biddy Hatfield, Nov. 26, 1844.
   Michael Broyles, M.G. (Nov. 26, 1844).
Bluford Burris to Francis Tally, Dec. 7, 1844. John
   Jones, J.P. (Aug. 8, 1844).
Henry Lawson to Lucinda Bennet, Dec. 15, 1844. Matthew
   Douglas, J.P. (Dec. 15, 1844).
Sampson Hodges to Parmelia Ann Angel, Dec. 16, 1844.
   Matthew Douglas, J.P. (Dec. 16, 1844).

James Johnson to Lucinda Carnutt, Dec. 17, 1844. No
  return.
Wm. Peters to Catharine Smith, Dec. 17, 1844. J.
  Buckley, M.G. (Dec. 26, 1844).
Ben Wilhite to Elmira Edwards, Dec. 23, 1844. J. H.
  Delap, J.P. (Dec. 26, 1844).
L. D. Bridgmon to Mary A. Queener, Dec. 26, 1844.
  C. H. Boatright, M.G. (Dec. 26, 1844).
Jno. M. Carnutt to Louisa Albright, Dec. 31, 1844. No
  return.
David Beard to Martha Jane Adkins, Jan. 2, 1845.
  Matthew Douglas, J.P. (Jan. 2, 1845).
Adison Gentry to Rebecca Rice, Jan. 6, 1845. Isaac
  W. Wilson, J.P. (Jan. 12, 1845).
William Blackwell to Elizabeth Salvage, Jan. 16, 1845.
  Isaac Wilson, J.P. (Jan. 16, 1845).
James Queener to Una Jackson, Jan. 28, 1845. No return.
Ota T. Cliborne to America Monday, Feb. 4, 1845. Isaac
  Petree, J.P. (Feb. 9, 1845).
Caloway Heron to Mary Bratcher, Feb. 6, 1865. Jacob
  Petree, J.P. (Feb. 9, 1865).
Hardy Honeycutt to Nancy Smith, Feb. 10, 1865. Champ
  Duncan, J.P. (Feb. 13, 1865).
G. W. Smith to Julia Ann Smith, Feb. 10, 1846. Jackson
  Buckley, M.G. (Feb. 13, 1846).
Henry Duncain to Catherine Thompson, Feb. 14, 1845.
  (?) Champson, J.P. (Feb. 20, 1845).
Alexander Carroll to Patsey Ewing, Feb. 14, 1845. James
  Owens, J.P. (Feb. 14, 1845).
John Jones to Sarah Powers, Feb. 19, 1845. Matthew
  Douglas, J.P. (Feb. 19, 1845).
H. W. Boatright to Lavina Henry, Feb. 23, 1844.
  Matthew Douglas, J.P. (Feb. 23, 1844).
Pleasant W. Jones to Ester Nickleson, Feb. 27, 1845.
  Matthew Douglas, J.P. (Feb. 27, 1845).
Wm. Beams to Jarilda Walden, Feb. 28, 1845. Matthew
  Douglas, J.P. (Feb. 28, 1845).
Wm. Goin to Catharine Carroll, Mar. 3, 1845. No return.
James H. West to Elizabeth Campbell, Mar. 6, 1845.
  Matthew Douglas, J.P. (Mar. 6, 1865).
Wm. Boshears to Elizabeth Adkins, Mar. 13, 1845. M.
  Thompson Duncan, J.P. (Mar. 15, 1845).
William York to Martha Brock, Mar. 19, 1845. Jacob
  Petree, J.P. (Mar. 20, 1845).
Jos. P. Irvin to Nancy Kincaid, Mar. 26, 1845. M.
  Bruce, J.P. (Mar. 26, 1845).
Michael Baker to Mary Ann Thomas, Mar. 22, 1845.
  Matthew Douglas, J.P. (Mar. 23, 1845).
Rufus Grant to Lucy Parker, Mar. 6, 1845. No return.
William Wilson to Mariah Wilson, Mar. 26, 1845. No
  return.
Aaron Harmon to Rachel Mosier, Apr. 3, 1845. No return.
John Campbell to Sarah Duncan, Apr. 3, 1845. Matthew
  Douglas, J.P. (Apr. 3, 1845).

CAMPBELL COUNTY MARRIAGES

Thomas Perkins to Catharine Bird, Apr. 2, 1845. Michael
  Broyles, M.G. (Apr. 3, 1845).
William Brock to Sarah Newman, Apr. 25, 1845. Joseph
  H. Delap, J.P. (Apr. 6, 1845).
James Holt to Eady Tory, 1845. No return.
Robert Dossett to Minerva Cain, Oct. 20, 1842. No
  return.
John Rains to Lanij Martin, Oct. 29, 1842. Matthew
  Douglas, J.P. (Oct. 27, 1842).
Thomas Dram to Belinda Polly, Nov. 3, 1842. Matthew
  Douglas, J.P. (Nov. 3, 1842).
Curtis Blakely to Syntha Bord, Nov. 3, 1842. Matthew
  Douglas, J.P. (Nov. 10, 1842).
William Broyles to Rhoda Douglas, Nov. 10, 1842. Mat-
  thew Douglas, J.P. (Nov. 10, 1842).
Thomas York to Sarah Johnson, Dec. 8, 1842. Matthew
  Douglas, J.P. (Dec. 8, 1842).
Elias Paulston to Gemima Still, Dec. 14, 1842. John
  Adkins, J.P. (Dec. 15, 1842).
John E. Bayer to Nancy F. Stinger, Dec. 20, 1842.
  Matthew Douglas, J.P. (Dec. 20, 1842).
Amos Bratcher to Elizabeth Goin, Dec. 24, 1842. John
  Adkins, J.P. (Jan. 1, 1842).
Joseph Adkins to Eliza Smith, Dec. 25, 1842. John
  Adkins, J.P. (Dec. 25, 1842).
Joshua Moses to Sarah Creekmore, Dec. 27, 1842. Matthew
  Douglas, J.P. (Dec. 27, 1842).
Wm. Wells to Nancy Faulkner, Jan. 1, 1843. Matthew
  Douglas, J.P. (Jan. 1, 1843).
P. J. P. Follon to Lucinda Harris, Jan. 1, 1843. Wm.
  Graves, M.G. (Jan. 1, 1843).
Wm. Albright to Nancy Stout, Jan. 4, 1843. No return.
William Duke to Tansey Sharp, Jan. 4, 1842. Isaac
  Gentry, M.G. (Jan. 8, 1842).
Samuel Shelby to Sally McCully, Jan. 4, 1843. No
  return.
Litcher Stanfield to Hannah Beard, Jan. 9, 1843.
  Michael Broyles, M.G.
Fielding Loe (Lee) to Sarah Carrolle, Jan. 12, 1843.
  Matthew Douglas, J.P. (Jan. 12, 1843).
George Reeves to Sarah Shadowen, Jan. 15, 1842. Matthew
  Douglas, J.P. (Jan. 15, 1842).
Henry Burriss to Polly Gray, Jan. 17, 1843. Calvin
  Peterson, J.P. (Jan. 19, 1843).
John Hitch to Fany Sharp, Jan. 18, 1843. Isaac Wilson,
  J.P. (Jan. 22, 1843).
Starn Wilhite to Catherine Carter, Jan. 29, 1843.
  Matthew Douglas, J.P. (Jan. 29, 1843).
F. F. Hunt to Jane Adkins, Jan. 30, 1843. Married
  by J.P.
Jas. Johnson to Eliza Adkins, Feb. 4, 1843. Peter
  Burress, J.P. (Feb. 5, 1843).
Tapley J. Henson to Malinda McCarty, Feb. 7, 1842.
  Alvis Kincaid, J.P. (Feb. 12, 1842).

Wm. Dossett to Eliza Hope, Feb. 9, 1843. Alvis
Kincaid, J.P. (Feb. 16, 1843).
George Washington Rogers to Catharine Powel, Feb. 28,
1843. Matthew Douglas, J.P. (Feb. 28, 1843).
Charles M. Johnson to Nancey Craig, Mar. 6, 1843.
No return.
Arthur Marcum to Nancy Delk, Mar. 6, 1843. Jno.
Adkins, J.P. (Mar. 7, 1843).
Milton Wyatt to Nancy Ann Allison, Mar. 15, 1843.
Matthew Douglas, J.P. (Mar. 15, 1843).
Champ Waters to Nelly McMann, Mar. 16, 1843. No return.
David Adkins to Nancy Faulkner, Mar. 16, 1843. Matthew
Douglas, J.P. (Mar. 16, 1843).
Henderson Lay to Sally Stout, Mar. 11, 1843. No return.
Henry Wilson to Sarah Campbell, Mar. 18, 1843. Peter
Burress, J.P. (Mar. 18, 1843).
Wm. Johnson to Desse Adkins, Mar. 25, 1843. Peter
Burress, J.P. (Mar. 26, 1843).
G. W. Marcum to Mary Ann Hanks, Apr. 3, 1843. John
Adkins, J.P. (Apr. 5, 1843).
Robert Parker to Laner Chapman, Apr. 3, 1843. Allen
McDonald, J.P. (Apr. 10, 1843).
Benjamin H. Brown to Harriet H. Swan, Apr. 6, 1843.
J. Backley, J.P. (Apr. 6, 1843).
Stephen Gibson to Elizabeth Smith, Apr. 9, 1843. Allen
McDonald. (Apr. 9, 1843).
Wm. B. Davis to Olive P. Alison, Apr. 9, 1843. Matthew
Douglas, J.P. (Apr. 9, 1843).
Joseph A. Pelkington to Susan Martin, Apr. 20, 1843.
S. Buckley, J.P. (Apr. 20, 1843).
James Miller to Nancy McCully, Apr. 22, 1843. John
Jones, J.P. (Apr. 23, 1843).
Balintine Lovit to Louisa Anderson, Apr. 20, 1843.
Matthew Douglas, J.P. (Apr. 20, 1843).
Wm. Bowman to Susan McClain, May 2, 1843. No return.
John Grimes to Nancy J. Kincaid, June 4, 1843. Wm.
Bruce, J.P. (June 4, 1843).
M. L. Phillips to Mary C. Hickox, June 6, 1843. Robert
T. Kimbrough, M.G. (June 7, 1843).
Jno. Cox to Elizabeth Branham, June 10, 1843. Peter
Burriss, J.P. (June 11, 1843).
Wm. Agee to Moriah M. Maden, June 18, 1843. John
Jones, J.P. (June 18, 1843).
Stephen Thomas to Sarah Reed, July 3, 1843. Allen
McDonald, J.P. (July 5, 1843).
Joseph Davis to Clender McCidy, July 6, 1843. Matthew
Douglas, J.P. (July 6, 1843).
Silas Adkins to Cenia Wright, Aug. 6, 1843. Matthew
Douglas, J.P. (Aug. 6, 1843).
A. Miller to Elizabeth Graves, Aug. 10, 1843. Alvis
Kincaid. (Aug. 13, 1843).
David F. Creekmore to Elizabeth Meadors, Aug. 13, 1843.
Matthew Douglas, J.P. (Aug. 13, 1843).
Jno. Chapman to Orpha Kiggs, Aug. 19, 1843. James
Cooper, J.P. (Aug. 20, 1843).

CAMPBELL COUNTY MARRIAGES

Wm. King to Martha Richardson, Aug. 21, 1843. Reubin
Rogers, J.P. (Aug. 22, 1843).
Robt. R. Hope to Martha Ann Isley, Aug. 25, 1843.
Reubin Rogers, J.P. (Aug. 27, 1843).
Franklin Kincaid to Ann Cain, Aug. 28, 1843. W. Bruce,
J.P. (Aug. 28, 1843).
Jno. Hinson to Sarah Lovett, Aug. 20, 1843. J.
Buckley, M.G. (Aug. 30, 1843).
Wm. Smith to Lockey Cox, Sep. 5, 1843. Peter Burriss,
J.P. (Sep. 10, 1843).
James Cox to Mary Wilson, Sep. 5, 1843. Peter Burriss,
J.P. (Sep. 10, 1843).
Hiram Richardson to Martha Pearce, Sep. 6, 1843. No
return.
Enoch Archer to Susannah Boutten, Sep. 9, 1843.
Matthew Douglas, J.P. (Sep. 9, 1843).
Henry Woods to Ann Rice, Sep. 12, 1843. Isaac Wilson,
J.P. (Sep. 14, 1843).
Martin Terry to Nancy Thompson, Sep. 17, 1843. No
return.
Wm. Woodward to Leah Ford, Oct. 4, 1843. Joe F. Delap,
J.P. (Oct. 8, 1843).
Silas Ingram to Sarah Hampton, Oct. 4, 1843. Jas. F.
Delap, J.P. (Oct. 5, 1843).
James Stephens to Hannah Thomas, Oct. 9, 1843. Michael
Broyles, M.G. (Oct. 10, 1843).
James A. McColloch to Nancy Siler, Oct. 15, 1843.
Matthew Douglas, J.P. (Oct. 15, 1843).
Joel Ryan to Jane Creekmore, Oct. 19, 1843. Matthew
Douglas, J.P. (Oct. 19, 1843).
Willis D. Alder to Sarah Meadows, Oct. 24, 1843.
No return.
Jno. N. Sattle to Diecy M. Smith, Nov. 8, 1843. No
return.
Valentine Turner to Lucinda Malone, Nov. 20, 1843. No
return.
James W. Moore to Mary Hall, Nov. 23, 1843. Matthew
Douglas, J.P. (Nov. 23, 1843).
Spencer Hunter to Lonna Jarman, Nov. 24, 1843. (Nov.
24, 1843).
Isaac Hutton to Mary Ann Carroll, Nov. 25, 1843. No
return.
Jas. Cabirth to Thursy Ann McKeehan, Nov. 26, 1843.
Matthew Douglas. (Nov. 26, 1843).
Jas. Campbell to Mary Douglass, Nov. 26, 1843. Michael
Broyles, M.G. (Nov. 26, 1843).
Jno. Surritt to Mary E. Mason, Nov. 20, 1843. No return.
Jno. Lay to Elizabeth Murray, Nov. 30, 1843. Matthew
Douglas, J.P. (Nov. 30, 1843).
Joseph Nix to Amariah Holt, Nov. 30, 1843. Matthew
Douglas, J.P. (Nov. 30, 1843).
Wyly Thomas to Cintha Polly, Dec. 3, 1843. Michael
Broyles, M.G. (Dec. 7, 1843).
J. W. Plaster to V. C. Maupin, Dec. 18, 1843. T.
Buckley, M.G. (Dec. 21, 1843).

Burton Buck to Lavina Miller, Nov. 2, 1843. No return.

Wm. Peterson to Sarah Sweat, Dec. 21, 1843. Reuben Rogers, J.P. (Dec. 24, 1843).

Joseph Culbirth to Nancy Beams, Dec. 22, 1843. Matthew Douglas, J.P. (Dec. 22, 1843).

Nathan Shelly to Nancy Faulkner, Dec. 23, 1843. Matthew Douglas, J.P. (Dec. 24, 1843).

James Riggs to Elizabeth Smith, Jan. 2, 1844. Peter Burris, J.P. (Jan. 6, 1844).

John Willoby to Catherine Vanderpool, Jan. 3, 1844. J. A. Hollingsworth, J.P. (Jan. 7, 1844).

J. L. Barkley to Nancy Green, Jan. 3, 1844. R. W. Patty, M.G. (Jan. 4, 1844).

Jacob Lawson to Vicia Luallen, Jan. 5, 1844. Allen McDonald, J.P. (Jan. 5, 1844).

George Brooks to Sarah Bratcher, Jan. 6, 1844. Matthew Douglas, J.P. (Jan. 6, 1844).

James Perkins to Sarah Richmond, Jan. 7, 1844. (Jan. 7, 1844).

Jackson Campbell to Elizabeth Perkins, Jan. 18, 1844. Matthew Douglas, J.P. (Jan. 18, 1844).

Edwin Hicks to Michael Beams, Jan. 18, 1844. (Jan. 18, 1844).

Andrew Lawson to Elizabeth Case, Jan. 21, 1844. Matthew Douglas, J.P. (Jan. 21, 1844).

George Brooks to Sarah Bratcher, Jan. 6, 1844. Matthew Douglas, J.P. (Jan. 6, 1844).

James Perkins to Sarah Richmond, Jan. 7, 1844. Matthew Douglas, J.P. (Jan. 7, 1844).

Jackson Campbell to Elizabeth Perkins, Jan. 18, 1844. Matthew Douglas, J.P. (Jan. 18, 1844).

Edwin Hicks to Nichel Beams, Jan. 18, 1844. Matthew Douglas, J.P. (Jan. 18, 1844).

Andrew Lawson to Elizabeth Case, Jan. 21, 1844. Matthew Douglas, J.P. (Jan. 21, 1844).

Wm. Duff to Leah Murray, Jan. 25, 1844. Joseph F. Delap, J.P. (Jan. 26, 1844).

Peter Cooper to Rebecca Burton, Jan. 24, 1844. Peter Burris, J.P. (Jan. 24, 1844).

James Ball to Elizabeth McFarland, Jan. 25, 1844. Matthew Douglas, J.P. (Jan. 25, 1844).

Thomas Brooks to Elizabeth Lay, Jan. 31, 1844. Matthew Douglas, J.P. (Jan. 31, 1844).

Henry C. Grimes to Polly Fleming, Feb. 19, 1844. R. S. Kimbrough, M.G.

Reubin Smiddy to B. A. Phillips, Feb. 27, 1844. Jackson Wilhite, J.P. (Mar. 9, 1844).

David Rogers to Lena Williams, Feb. 29, 1844. Reubin Douglas, J.P. (Feb. 29, 1844).

Danl. Chambers to Phoebe Phillips, Mar. 5, 1844. Matthew Douglas, J.P. (Mar. 5, 1844).

Thomas Phillips to Ester Terry, Mar. 17, 1844. Allen McDonald, J.P. (Mar. 17, 1844).

Samuel Burge to Polly Luallen, Mar. 18, 1844. Allen McDonald, J.P. (Mar. 21, 1844).

CAMPBELL COUNTY MARRIAGES

Calvin Smiddy to Elizabeth Hicks, Mar. 19, 1844.
    Jackson Wilhite, J.P. (Mar. 28, 1844).
L. B. Crowly to Winney Lay, Mar. 28, 1844. Matthew
    Douglas, J.P. (Mar. 28, 1844).
Fleming Nickleson to Sarah Skoans, Mar. 28, 1844.
    Matthew Douglas, J.P. (Mar. 28, 1844).
Wm. Adams to L. N. McCall, Mar. 30, 1844. J. H. Delap,
    J.P. (Mar. 30, 1844).
Jno. Siler to Harriet Owens, Mar. 31, 1844. Matthew
    Douglas, J.P. (Mar. 31, 1844).
James McDonald to Melinda Lawson, May 1, 1844. Wiley
    Chambers, J.P. (May 2, 1844).
John Tanner to Mary Pearce, May 6, 1844. John Jones,
    J.P. (May 19, 1844).
Nelson Phillips to Rebecca Morgan, May 26, 1844.
    Matthew Douglas, J.P. (May 26, 1844).
Speed Nicholson to Malinda Faulkner, May 30, 1844.
    Matthew Douglas, J.P. (May 30, 1844).
Jeremiah Boshears to Sarah Malicoat, June 3, 1844.
    Peter Burriss, J.P. (June 3, 1844).
Isaac Petree to Martha Ford, June 8, 1844. Jacob
    Petree, J.P. (June 13, 1844).
John Vanderpool to Anna Dossett, June 19, 1844. Jacob
    Petree, J.P. (June 24, 1844).
John C. Ford to Ann Petree, June 20, 1844. James
    Parker, D.D. (4th Sunday in June, 1844).
Holley D. Moses to Sarah Malissa Candle, June 27, 1844.
    Matthew Douglas, J.P. (June 27, 1844).
Ezra Davenport to Elizabeth Lego (Lebo), June 27, 1844.
    Matthew Douglas, J.P. (June 27, 1844).
Thomas Griffy to Nancy Wilson, July 18, 1844. Peter
    Burriss, J.P. (July 18, 1844).
Vinsen Riggs to Mary Ballard, July 20, 1844. James
    Cooper, J.P. (July 2, 1844).
Arch Monday to Sarah Raulson, Aug. 6, 1844. Reubin
    Rogers, J.P. (Aug. 7, 1844).
Andrew McHone to Eliza Jackson, Aug. 8, 1844. Isaac
    Wilson, J.P. (Aug. 8, 1844).
John Chavis to Nancy Tate, Aug. 20, 1844. No return.
Milton Plaster to Elizabeth Hayter, Aug. 23, 1844.
    J. C. Petree, J.P. (Aug. 25, 1844).
John Nix to Mary Rains, Aug. 25, 1844. Matthew
    Douglas, J.P. (Aug. 25, 1844).
Wm. Reeves to Nancy Longmire, Sep. 7, 1844. Joseph
    H. Delap, J.P. (Sep. 7, 1844).
Berry Thompson to Celia Lay, Sep. 30, 1844. Jackson
    Wilhite. (Sep. 30, 1844).
Shanklin Engle to Matilda J. Elliott, Sep. 30, 1844.
    Matthew Douglas, J.P. (Sep. 30, 1844).
James Vinzant to Elizabeth Douglas, Oct. 2, 1844. Reubin
    Rogers, J.P. (Oct. 3, 1844).
Jno. Hunter to Talitha Hart, Oct. 3, 1844. Reubin
    Rogers, J.P. (Oct. 6, 1844).
James M. Marshall to Elizabeth Smith, Oct. 14, 1844.
    Jack Buckley, M.G. (Oct. 17, 1844).

James Gray to Mary Tolly, Oct. 17, 1844. James Johnson, J.P. (Oct. 23, 1844).

Jno. H. Stout to Orlena Wilhite, Oct. 17, 1844. No return.

Edmund Witt to Lucinda Lay, Nov. 1, 1844. Isaac Wilson, J.P. (Nov. 3, 1844).

Thomas L. Blevins to Elizabeth Yancy, Nov. 21, 1844. No return.

James B. Tacket to Biddy Hatfield, Nov. 26, 1844. Michael Broyles, M.G. (Nov. 26, 1844).

Bluford Burris to Francis Tolly, Dec. 7, 1844. John Jones, J.P. (Dec. 8, 1844).

Henry Lawson to Lucinda Bennet, Dec. 15, 1844. Matthe Douglas, J.P. (Dec. 15, 1844).

Sampson Hodges to Permelia Ann Angel, Dec. 16, 1844. Matthew Douglas, J.P. (Dec. 16, 1844).

James Johnson to Lucinda Carnutt, Dec. 17, 1844. No return.

Wm. Petree to Catharine Smith, Dec. 17, 1844. J. Buckley, M.G. (Dec. 26, 1844).

Ben Wilhite to Elmira Edwards, Dec. 23, 1844. J. H. Delap, J.P. (Dec. 26, 1844).

L. D. Bridgman to Mary H. Queener, Dec. 26, 1844. C. H. Boatright, M.G. (Dec. 26, 1844).

Jno. M. Carnutt to Louisa Albright, Dec. 31, 1844. No return.

David Beard to Martha Jane Adkins, Jan. 2, 1845. Matthew Douglas, J.P. (Jan. 21, 1845).

Adison Gentry to Rebecca Rice, Jan. 6, 1845. Isaac Wilson, J.P. (Jan. 12, 1845).

William Blackwell to Elizabeth Salvage, Jan. 16, 1865. Isaac Wilson, J.P. (Jan. 16, 1865).

James Queener to Ura Jackson, Jan. 28, 1845. No return.

Ota T. Cliborne to America Monday, Feb. 4, 1845. Isaac Petree, J.P. (Feb. 9, 1845).

Caloway Heron to Mary Bratcher, Feb. 6, 1865. Jacob Petree, J.P. (Feb. 9, 1865).

Hardy Honeycutt to Nancy Smith, Feb. 10, 1865. Champ Duncain, J.P. (Feb. 13, 1865).

G. W. Smith to Julia Ann Smith, Feb. 10, 1845. Jackson Buckley, M.G. (Feb. 13, 1845).

Henry Duncain to Catherine Thompson, Feb. 14, 1845. (?) Champson, J.P. (Feb. 20, 1845).

Alexander Carroll to Patsey Ewing, Feb. 14, 1845. James Owens, J.P. (Feb. 14, 1845).

John Jones to Sarah Powers, Feb. 19, 1845. Matthew Douglas, J.P. (Feb. 19, 1845).

H. W. Boatright to Lavina Henry, Feb. 22, 1845. No return.

Robert Bird to Nancy Blakely, Feb. 23, 1844. Matthew Douglas, J.P. (Feb. 23, 1844).

Pleasant W. Jones to Ester Nickleson, Feb. 27, 1845. Matthew Douglas, J.P. (Feb. 27, 1845).

Wm. Beams to Jarilda Walden, Feb. 28, 1845. Matthew Douglas, J.P. (Feb. 28, 1845).

CAMPBELL COUNTY MARRIAGES

Wm. Goin to Catharine Carroll, Mar. 3, 1845. No return.
James H. West to Elizabeth Campbell, Mar. 6, 1845.
Matthew Douglas, J.P. (Mar. 6, 1865).
Wm. Boshears to Elizabeth Adkins, Mar. 13, 1845. M.
Champson Duncan, J.P. (Mar. 15, 1845).
William York to Martha Brock, Mar. 18, 1845. Jacob
Petree, J.P. (Mar. 20, 1845).
Jos. P. Irvin to Nancy Kincaid, Mar. 26, 1845. M.
Bruce, J.P. (Mar. 26, 1845).
Michael Baker to Mary Ann Thomas, Mar. 22, 1845. Matthew
Douglas, J.P. (Mar. 23, 1845).
Rufus Grant to Lucy Parker, Mar. 26, 1845. No return.
William Wilson to Mariah Wilson, Mar. 26, 1845. No
return.
Aaron Harmon to Rachel Mosier, Apr. 3, 1845. No return.
John Campbell to Sarah Duncan, Apr. 3, 1845. Matthew
Douglas, J.P. (Apr. 3, 1845).
Thomas Perkins to Catharine Bird, Apr. 2, 1845. Michael
Broyles, M.G. (Apr. 3, 1845).
William Brock to Sarah Newman, Apr. 25, 1845. Joseph
H. Delap, J.P. (Apr. 6, 1845).
James C. Holt to Eady Tory, Apr. 7, 1845. Mattbew
Douglas, J.P. (Apr. 13, 1845).
Jno. C. Chesterson (Kesterson) to Martha Wilhite, Apr.
11, 1845. Rube Rogers, J.P. (Apr. 10, 1845).
Robt. Bird to Rachel Douglass, Apr. 13, 1845. Matthew
Douglas, J.P. (Apr. 13, 1845).
Bushood Withers to Elizabeth Bratcher, Apr. 16, 1845.
F. H. Bratcher, J.P. (Apr. 17, 1845).
James Powel to Martha Jones, Apr. 25, 1845. Jacob
Petree, J.P.
Joel Rector to Polly Dial, Apr. 26, 1845. Jos Owens,
J.P. (May 31, 1845).
Calvin Hatfield to Candia Bryant, Apr. 29, 1845.
Michael Broyles, M.G. (Apr. 29, 1845).
J. H. Kilsoe to Sarah Jones, May 6, 1845. William
Bruce, J.P. (May 27, 1845).
Daniel Richardson to Jane Young, May 10, 1845. Peter
Burriss, J.P. (May 11, 1845).
Wm. D. Sharp to Julia Miller, May 21, 1848. Wm.
Bruce, L.E. (May 27, 1848).
Richard Green to Mary Jane Hutson, July 16, 1845. No
return.
E. Smith to Polly Chapman, Aug. 8, 1845. Jos. Delap,
J.P. (Sep. 11, 1845).
Jno. Cross to Lucinda Acres, Aug. 12, 1845. J. C.
Petree, J.P. (Aug. 17, 1845).
Patrick H. Rogers to Elizabeth Dossett, Aug. 14, 1845.
J. C. Petree, J.P. (Aug. 27, 1845).
James Williams to Charlotte Barbee, Aug. 22, 1845. J.
C. Petree, J.P. (Aug. 27, 1845).
L. D. Low to F. Bailey, Aug. 23, 1845. No return.
Westley Higgs to Polly Huley, Aug. 30, 1845. Jos. F.
Delap, J.P. (Aug. 30, 1845).

Wm. Bailey to Nancy Chambers, Aug. 30, 1845. No return.

David Smith to Catharine St. John, Aug. 30, 1845. No return.

Jno. Carroll to Nancy Patison, Sep. 1, 1845. No return.

Henry Richardson to Pamelia Hickey, Sep. 1, 1845. No return.

Thomas Dean to Martha Evans, Sep. 6, 1845. No return.

Joel Gossadge to Mahala Plastin, Sep. 9, 1845. J. C. Petree, J.P. (Sep. 13, 1845).

John Cole to Cornelia Shumake, Sep. 12, 1845. No return.

Thomas Dunkin to Bethina Lumpkin, Sep. 26, 1845. No return.

Calvin Sweat to Melvina Todd, Oct. 10, 1845. No return.

Absolom Crabtree to Jane Cooper, Nov. 1, 1845. Jas. A. Delap. (Nov. 1, 1845).

Jno. Q. A. Sweat to Mary McCarty, Nov. 7, 1845. No return.

William Cadell to Louisa Moses, Jan. 1, 1846. Michael Broyles, M.G. (Jan. 1, 1846).

William Carver to Nancy Hatmaker, Jan. 3, 1846. Isaac Gross, J.P. (Jan. 4, 1846).

James Sharp to Polly Smith, Jan. 8, 1846. Allen McDonald, J.P. (Jan. 11, 1846).

Samuel Baker to Margaret Hatfield, Jan. 15, 1846. William L. Lay, J.P. (Jan. 19, 1846).

Colson Sharp to Anna Snodderly, Jan. 16, 1846. John Lohn Lowes, J.P. (Jan. 18, 1846).

Joseph Fox to Hannah Beams, Jan. 22, 1846. Michael Broyles, M.G. (Feb. 22, 1846).

James Thompson to Kesiah Potter, Jan. 22, 1846. Cutbeth Webb, M.G. (Feb. 22, 1846).

James R. Standfill to Seproney Adkins, Jan. 22, 1846. Michael Broyles, M.G. (Jan. 22, 1846).

Josiah Boulton to Elizabeth Standfill, Jan. 22, 1846. Michael Broyles, M.G. (Jan. 22, 1846).

Samuel Sumner to Christiana Brown, Jan. 24, 1846. Michael Broyles, M.G. (Jan. 29, 1846).

James Stanfill to Lucinda Broyles, Jan. 29, 1846. Michael Broyles, M.G. (Jan. 29, 1846).

William Perkins to Elizabeth Lay, Feb. 4, 1846. Jos. H. Delap, J.P. (Feb. 8, 1846).

Joseph Campbell to Eliza Perkins, Feb. 12, 1846. Michael Broyles, M.G. (Feb. 12, 1846).

Armstead Herrin to Susan Lukes, Feb. 13, 1846. John Lowes, J.P. (Feb. 15, 1846).

John Snodderly to Eliza Sharp, Feb. 14, 1846. Isaac Gentry, M.G. (Feb. 8, 1846).

Frederick Smith to Precilla Hutson, Feb. 19, 1846. Jas. H. Delap, J.P. (Feb. 19, 1846).

Peter Cooper to Manda Wilson, Feb. 20, 1845. Jos. H. Delap, J.P. (Feb. 20, 1846).

James Chapman to Eliza Hale, Mar. 6, 1846. F. H. Bratcher, J.P. (Mar. 8, 1846).

Mynatt McElkins to Marcum Murray, Mar. 9, 1846. Joseph
H. Delap, J.P. (Mar. 9, 1846).

Hiram Prewit to Chany M. Kidy, Mar. 12, 1846. Michael
Broyles, M.G. (Mar. 12, 1846).

James M. Pitman to Polly Gloscake, Mar. 12, 1846. L.
Lay, J.P. (Mar. 12, 1846).

James Hatmaker to Sophia Cooper, Mar. 14, 1846. John
Murray, J.P. (Mar. 14, 1846).

Josiah Crouch to Luiza Branam, Mar. 17, 1846. (Mar.
17, 1846).

Thomas Childress to Mariah Martin, Mar. 19, 1846.
Champion Duncan, J.P. (Mar. 19, 1846).

William Murray to Sally Hatmaker, Mar. 20, 1846.
(Mar. 21, 1846).

Thomas Petry to Nancy Young, Mar. 22, 1846. Michael
Broyles, M.G. (Mar. 22, 1846).

Larkin W. Cross to Henrietta Duncan, Mar. 22, 1846.
Champion Duncan, J.P. (Apr. 2, 1846).

William Douglas to Elizabeth Broyles, Mar. 26, 1846.
James Archer, J.P. (Mar. 23, 1846).

Joseph Bird to Tilitha Cook, Mar. 27, 1843. Chapman
Duncan, J.P. (Apr. 2, 1846).

Peter Perkins to Rebecca Wier, Apr. 2, 1846. Michael
Broyles, M.G. (Apr. 2, 1846).

Joseph N. Cooper to Mary Ann Hutson, Apr. 8, 1846.
C. H. Boatright, M.G. (Apr. 9, 1846).

Wm. C. Marcum to Cynthia Gentry, May 4, 1846. Chapman
Duncan, J.P. (Jan. 26, 1848).

Isaac Miller to Nancy Soaps, May 7, 1846. J. C.
Petree, J.P. (May 2, 1847).

Wm. Morgan to Susannah King, May 15, 1846. Jos. H.
Delap, J.P. (May 17, 1846).

James Smith to Nancy Pebley, June 7, 1846. No return.

James Trammel to Rebecca Hamby, June 10, 1846. No
return.

Isaac White to Lanima Sweaton, June 20, 1846. C. H.
Boatright, M.G. (July 2, 1846).

King D. Anderson to Susannah Lamore, July 4, 1846. No
return.

Irvin Deas to Lydia Meaders, July 6, 1846. W. D.
Alder, J.P. (July 7, 1846).

Eli Cooper to Polly Gross, July 11, 1846. Isaac
Gross, J.P. (July 2, 1846).

Tilman P. A. Drake to Nancy Roe, July 27, 1846. Michael
Broyles, M.G. (July 27, 1846).

Robert Stookesberry to Jane Sharp, July 27, 1846. P.
M. Rogers. (Aug. 5, 1846).

George Tudor to Sarah Blevins, Aug. 1, 1846. No return.

Andrew Shadonias (Chadoins) to Sarah Norris, Aug. 6,
1846. Michael Broyles, M.G. (Aug. 6, 1846).

David Penberton to Elizabeth Martin, Aug. 6, 1846.
James Johnson, J.P. (Aug. 9, 1846).

Joseph Allen to Martha Sharp, Aug. 14, 1846. Michael
Broyles, M.G. (Aug. 14, 1846).

Levy Brown to Elivina Douglass, Aug. 22, 1846. J. C.
  Petree, J.P. (Aug. 23, 1846).
Hamilton Brown to Sally Phillips, Aug. 23, 1846. Allen
  McDonald, J.P. (Aug. 23, 1846).
Wm. Campbell to Catharine Queener, Aug. 26, 1846. C.
  H. Boatright, M.G. (Aug. 26, 1846).
John Wilson to Francis B. Jackson, Aug. 31, 1846.
  James Johnson, J.P. (Sep. 10, 1846).
Joseph B. Bird to Alley Dabny, Aug. 31, 1846. John
  L. Fowler, M.G. (Sep. 8, 1846).
James Turner to Sally Williamson, Sep. 7, 1846. T. W.
  Page, J.P. (Oct. 4, 1846).
R. S. Standly to Rosey Hix, Aug. 3, 1846. Isaac W.
  Smith. (Aug. 3, 1846).
George Davis to Martha Ross, Sep. 7, 1846. James
  Johnson, J.P. (Sep. 7, 1846).
George Master to Mary J. Hampton, Sep. 8, 1846. Michael
  Broyles, M.D. (Sep. 8, 1846).
William Cook to Isbald Beard, Sep. 11, 1846. Champion
  Duncan, J.P. (Sep. 17, 1846).
John M. Siler to Polly Ann Stanfill, Sep. 29, 1846.
  Michael Broyles, M.G. (Sep. 29, 1846).
David Hayslip to Rachel Beams, Oct. 15, 1846. Michael
  Broyles, M.G. (Oct. 15, 1846).
William Pierce to Catharine Richardson, Oct. 15, 1846.
  T. W. Page, J.P. (Oct. 25, 1846).
Henry L. Vinzant to Malvina Pouder, Oct. 15, 1846.
  Reubin Rogers, J.P. (Oct. 25, 1846).
Absolum Lumpkins to Mary Goin, Oct. 15, 1846. Willis
  D. Alder, J.P. (Oct. 18, 1846).
Asa M. Elison to Timanda J. Vannoy, Oct. 19, 1846.
  Michael Broyles, M.G. (Oct. 19, 1846).
Wm. Brown to Nancy Carroll, Oct. 21, 1846. John
  Murray, J.P. (Oct. 13, 1846).
A. Heatherly to Sarah Ford, Oct. 25, 1846. No return.
William Williams to Martha Sharp, Nov. 11, 1846.
  James Archer, J.P. (Nov. 12, 1846).
Jesse Wilhite to Elizabeth Fox, Nov. 22, 1846. Wm. L.
  Lay, J.P. (Nov. 22, 1846).
Samuel Stooksberry to Sally Sharp, Dec. 12, 1846. John
  Murray, J.P. (Dec. 15, 1846).
A. C. Alder to Lucinda Low, Dec. 12, 1846. No return.
Henry Warfield to Merica Terril, Dec. 13, 1846. (Dec.
  13, 1846).
Daniel Hart to Nancy Bruce, Dec. 19, 1846. Reubin
  Rogers, J.P. (Dec. 19, 1846).
Thomas Harness to Elizabeth Robins, Dec. 21, 1846.
  Wm. L. Lay, J.P. (Dec. 27, 1846).
Tilmond Sharp to Cerena Adkins, Dec. 26, 1846. Wm. L.
  Lay, J.P. (Dec. 27, 1846).
Samuel McDonald to Rebecca Reid, Dec. 28, 1846. John
  Lewallen, J.P. (Jan. 14, 1849).
Abel Bryant to Eliza Duncan, Dec. 29, 1846. Joseph
  Vanpell. (Dec. 29, 1846).

CAMPBELL COUNTY MARRIAGES

Robert Irvin to Sarah Smith, Dec. 28, 1846. Wm.
  Bruce, L.E. (Dec. 29, 1846).
Sidney Lynch to Aoral Sequin, Jan. 7, 1847. Michale
  Broyles, M.G. (Jan. 7, 1847).
Henry Valentine to Francis Lovett, Jan. 7, 1847.
  Michael Broyles, M.G. (Jan. 7, 1847).
Elijah Adkins to Catherine Adkins, Jan. 10, 1847.
  Isaac Gross, J.P. (Jan. 17, 1847).
John Witt to Polly Snodderly, Jan. 14, 1847. No return.
John Vanderpool to Polly Bailey, Jan. 15, 1847. T.
  W. Page, J.P.
Squire Hunter to Francis Dabay, Jan. 27, 1847. R.
  Rogers, J.P. (Feb. 27, 1847).
Jesse Adkins to Martha Bird, Jan. 27, 1847. Champion
  Duncan, J.P. (Feb. 28, 1847).
John Roach to Margaret Anderson, Jan. 26, 1847. Isaac
  W. Smith, J.P. (Jan. 26, 1847).
Preston Burge to Clara Hewith, Feb. 2, 1847. John
  Lewallen, J.P. (Feb. 9, 1847).
Elisha Adkins to Hannah Bullock, Feb. 3, 1847. John
  Murray, J.P. (Feb. 3, 1847).
Wm. S. Ayers to S. C. Marrs, Feb. 6, 1847. Allen
  McDonald, J.P. (Feb. 14, 1847).
Alfred Lanton to Sally Thomas, Feb. 14, 1847. Allen
  McDonald, J.P. (Feb. 14, 1847).
Zebadee Baird to Mary Rose, Feb. 16, 1847. Wm. Lay,
  J.P. (Feb. 18, 1847).
Wesley Butram to Polly Canon, Feb. 21, 1847. Isaac
  W. Smith, J.P. (Feb. 21, 1847).
Thomas Sharp to Margaret Karr, Feb. 22, 1847. Michael
  Broyles, M.G. (Feb. 22, 1847).
Finly Marlow to Nancy Sharp, Feb. 27, 1847. Wm.
  Dickson, J.P. (Feb. 27, 1847).
Elitra Seaver to Polly Sweet, Mar. 8, 1847. Isaac
  W. Smith, J.P. (Mar. 8, 1847).
Jonothan Phillips to Alcey Terril, Mar. 10, 1847.
  Isaac W. Smith, J.P. (Mar. 20, 1847).
Jesse Wilson to Peggy McAnn, Mar. 11, 1847. J. L.
  Smith, J.P. (Mar. 14, 1847).
Joel A. Hampton to Nancy Benit, Mar. 21, 1847. Wm.
  Bruce, L.E. (Apr. 1, 1847).
Harvey C. Kincaid to Mary J. Ward, Mar. 22, 1847. Wm.
  Bruce, L.E. (Apr. 1, 1847).
Isaac Thomas to Winney West, Mar. 28, 1847. Isaac W.
  Smith, J.P.
Caswell Queener to Eveline Walker, Mar. 27, 1847.
  Jas. Johnson, J.P.
Wm. Bowling to Polly Curnutt, Apr. 4, 1847. No return.
John Orick to Martha Burchill, May 10, 1847. T. W.
  Page, J.P. (May 11, 1847).
Michael Cook to Tabitha Galeher, May 13, 1847. Michael
  Broyles, M.G. (May 13, 1847).
Ralph Mays to Susan Mays, June 15, 1847. Michael
  Broyles, M.G. (June 15, 1847).

James Cooper to Ada Burton, June 19, 1847. John
　　Murray, J.P. (June 19, 1847).
Pleasant W. Woods to Susan Karr, July 1, 1847. Michael
　　Broyles, M.G. (July 1, 1847).
LaFayette Muzinger to Margaret Hill, July 3, 1847. F.
　　H. Bratcher, J.P. (July 4, 1847).
A. B. Lindsay to Martha Lindsay, July 9, 1847. Jas.
　　Johnson, J.P.
John Jarman to Eleaner Brown. July 24, 1847. John
　　Murray.
Isaac Ford to Harriet Griffin, Aug. 3, 1847. John
　　Murray. (Aug. 3, 1847).
Adonijah Thomas to Mary Ann Lovely, Aug. 5, 1847.
　　Reuben Rogers, J.P. (Aug. 8, 1847).
John Peterson to Ann Ryan, Aug. 5, 1847. Joseph Vanfelt,
　　D.D. (Aug. 5, 1847).
Jourdon Owens to Hannah Fox, Aug. 18, 1847. Champion
　　Duncan, J.P. (Aug. 19, 1847).
Henry Maupin to Hester Ann Cain, Aug. 20, 1847. James
　　R. Haggard, M.G. (Aug. 26, 1847).
Edward Riggs to Jane Greer, Sep. 4, 1847. J. C. Petree,
　　J.P. (Sep. 5, 1847).
G. W. Brown to America Alder, Sep. 6, 1847. James
　　Parker, D.D. (Sep. 12, 1847).
H. G. Miller to Mary Bridges, Sep. 8, 1847. James
　　Parker, D.D. (Sep. 16, 1847).
David Lay to Lyrena Flatford, Sep. 9, 1847. No return.
Thomas Y. Douglas to Rachel Powley, Sep. 9, 1847.
　　Michael Broyles, M.G. (Sep. 9, 1847).
John Clark to Nancy Riggs, Aug. 25, 1847. Michael
　　Broyles, M.G. (Aug. 25, 1847).
Daniel McCarty to Sarah Sweat, Oct. 16, 1847. (Oct.
　　17, 1847).
Wyatt Stokes to Nancy Jane Harmon, Oct. 20, 1847.
　　John Murray.
Berry Bowlin to Vestia Brown, Oct. 25, 1847. Champion
　　Duncan, J.P. (Oct. 28, 1847).
John N. Jackson to Susan A. Elkins, Oct. 28, 1847.
　　Michael Broyles, M.G. (Oct. 28, 1847).
Levan Flatford to Elizabeth Lay, Nov. 11, 1847. No
　　return.
Rich. Bennett to Flora Wilson, Nov. 11, 1847. No
　　return.
Elisha Huckaby to Salitha Adkins, Nov. 17, 1847.
　　Champion Duncan, J.P. (Nov. 21, 1847).
John Heirs to Elizabeth Snotherly, Nov. 18, 1847.
　　Michael Broyles, M.G. (Nov. 18, 1847).
Joseph Willoughby to Rhoda Heatherly, Nov. 20, 1847.
　　T. W. Page, J.P. (Nov. 21, 1847).
James Carson to F. E. Smith, Dec. 6, 1847. No return.
Andrew Stewart to Nancy Archer, Dec. 6, 1847. Jas.
　　Johnson, J.P.
John Bailey to Polly Sharp, Dec. 7, 1847. No return.
Commodore Huckaby to Seripta S. Adkins, Dec. 22, 1847.
　　Champion Duncan, J.P. (Dec. 22, 1847).

CAMPBELL COUNTY MARRIAGES

Absolum Walker to Susan D. Haggare, Dec. 25, 1847.  No
  return.
S. D. Queener to Olive Bruce, Dec. 30, 1847.  Reubin
  Rogers, J.P.  (Dec. 31, 1847).
Jacob Queener to Sarah Ann Hope, Dec. 30, 1847. Reuben
  Rogers, J.P.  (Dec. 30, 1847).
Henry Hill Jr. to Sarah Herrin, Jan. 3, 1848.  No return.
James McGee to Polly Patterson, Jan. 8, 1848.  Champion
  Duncan, J.P.  (Jan. 10, 1848).
Jacob Siler to Margaret Petree, Jan. 3, 1848.  Calvin
  R. Barion, J.P.  (Jan. 3, 1848).
Manuel Roach to Eliza Thomspon, Jan. 5, 1848.  Champion
  Duncan, J.P.  (Jan. 5, 1848).
James H. Boatright to Susan Jones, Feb. 3, 1848.  Jas.
  Johnson, J.P.
John L. Heeny (Keeny) to Minerva J. Walker, Feb. 6,
  1848.  Jas. Johnson, J.P.
Isaac Crabtree to Sally Crabtree, Feb. 12, 1848.
  Champion Duncan, J.P.  (Feb. 12, 1848).
George Anderson to Roma Tacket, Mar. 29, 1848.  Champion
  Duncan, J.P.  (Mar. 30, 1848).
William Rose to Catherine Jackson, Apr. 14, 1848.  Michael
  Broyles, M.G.  (Apr. 14, 1848).
Nicholson Patterson to Martha Cross, Apr. 15, 1848.
  Champion Duncan, J.P.  (Apr. 18, 1848).
Samuel Sevier to Permelia Hibbard, Apr. 24, 1848.
  Michael Broyles, M.G.  (Apr. 24, 1848).
David Rider to Emily Robinson, May 24, 1848.  Thomas
  Douglas, J.P.  (May 24, 1848).
William Cain to Nancy Smith, May 29, 1848.  W. Bruce,
  L.E.  (May 30, 1848).
Gilbert Delk to Prudy Fox, July 5, 1848.  Champion
  Duncan, J.P.  (July 5, 1848).
Jesse Jones to Delany Harp, July 5, 1848.  No return.
William Walker to Anna Hampton, July 19, 1848.  J. J.
  Marrs, J.P.  (Apr. 20, 1848).
Cyrenus Bane to Julyantha Cox.  No return.
Ewel Smith to Julyan Owens, Aug. 10, 1848.  No return.
Rider Smith to Milly Ann McCoy, Aug. 15, 1848.  (Aug.
  20, 1848).
Pressly Jones to Zephy Rose, Aug. 17, 1848.  Calvin
  C. Barron, J.P.  (Aug. 17, 1848).
John Smith to Ann Skiliner, Aug. 17, 1848.  J. J.
  Marrs, J.P.  (Aug. 17, 1848).
James Stapleton to Jane Parton, Sep. 1, 1848.  Calvin
  R. Barron, J.P.  (Sep. 1, 1848).
John Lovitt to Delana Harmon, Sep. 4, 1848.  William
  Hancock, J.P.  (Sep. 5, 1848).
Richard Cox to Catharine Bane, Sep. 5, 1848.  A. R.
  Barron, J.P.  (Sep. 5, 1848).
Benjamin Siler to Martha Holt, Sep. 7, 1848.  No return.
Joseph D. Nicks to Emily Shepherd, Sep. 9, 1848.  Jas.
  Johnson, J.P.
John Sweatt to Jane Abbitt, Sep. 10, 1848.  James
  Litton, J.P.  (Sep. 10, 1848).

William P. Cloud to Martha Heatherly, Sep. 22, 1848.
No return.
Pulasky Hall to Cynthia E. Ridemour, Sep. 22, 1848.
No return.
William Williams to Phebe Herron, Sep. 24, 1848. C. R.
Barron, J.P. (Sep. 24, 1848).
George B. Meadors to Lucinda Moore, Oct. 3, 1848. Dennis
Trammell, J.P. (Oct. 3, 1848).
Jackson Keeny to Cynthia A. Huff, Oct. 12, 1848.
Isaac Gross, J.P. (Oct. 14, 1848).
John Smith to Martha St. John, Oct. 14, 1848. Jas.
Johnson, J.P.
Daniel Miller to Diana Brown, Oct. 15, 1848. Jas.
Johnson, J.P.
Henderson Sweat to Rebecca Slaven, Oct. 15, 1848. James
Litton, J.P. (Oct. 15, 1848).
Shadrack Sutton to Polly Henderson, Oct. 19, 1848.
Wm. L. Lay, J.P. (Oct. 20, 1848).
John Hutson to Reubama Johnson, Oct. 21, 1848. Thomas
Douglass, J.P. (Oct. 25, 1848).
George Lawson to Susannah Adkins, Oct. 22, 1848. C. R.
Barron, J.P. (Oct. 22, 1848).
Jas. O. Bowman to Euminta J. Hilton, Oct. 31, 1848.
Dennis Trammel, J.P. (Oct. 31, 1848).
John Flatford to Lucinda Craig, Nov. 1, 1848. No return.
William Walden to Elizabeth Guffe, Nov. 3, 1848. C. R.
Barron, J.P. (Nov. 3, 1848).
Samuel B. Turpin to Manda Gooden, Nov. 4, 1848. Dennis
Trammell, J.P. (Nov. 4, 1848).
James H. Agee to Mary Comer, Nov. 15, 1848. Isaac
Gross, J.P. (Nov. 26, 1848).
Wm. H. Ridenour to Jane Croley, Nov. 19, 1848. Calvin
R. Barron, J.P. (Nov. 19, 1848).
Andree Rector to Francis Rector, Nov. 25, 1848. Rily
Chambers, J.P. (Nov. 26, 1848).
Francis M. Sumter to Rebecca Sarton, Nov. 27, 1848.
James Litton, J.P. (Nov. 27, 1848).
John Romine to Alcy Hunter, Nov. 28, 1848. Calvin
R. Barron, J.P. (Dec. 28, 1848).
Dannis Angel to Elizabeth King, Nov. 30, 1848. Dennis
Trammell, J.P. (Nov. 30, 1848).
Benjamin Siler to Martha Holt, Dec. 7, 1848. C. R.
Barron, J.P. (Dec. 7, 1848).
Samuel Vanderpool to Nancy Brown, Dec. 7, 1848. M.
McGraw, J.P. (Dec. 8, 1848).
Henry S. Wilson to Elizabeth Housley, Dec. 9, 1848.
George W. Baker, J.P. (Dec. 15, 1848).
Ralph Izard Hope to Lucinda J. Johnston, Dec. 13,
1848. C. H. Boatright, J.P.
Pleasant Housley to Mary Dagley, Dec. 16, 1848. No
return.
James Hancock to Sarah Stout, Dec. 16, 1848. No return.
Caswell Cross to Kesiah Baker, Dec. 16, 1848. Champion
Duncan, J.P. (Dec. 21, 1848).

William Lay to Nancy Croley, Dec. 23, 1848. Calvin
  R. Barron, J.P. (Dec. 23, 1848).
Martin Griffy to Elizabeth Richardson, Dec. 23, 1848.
  William Hancock, J.P. (Dec. 24, 1848).
Elihu Turner to Dicy Richardson, Mar. 8, 1848. F. P.
  McNew, J.P. (Mar. 10, 1848).
William Malaby to Nancy Sanders, Jan. 2, 1849. John
  Lewer, J.P. (Jan. 3, 1849).
Thomas M. Douglas to Nancy Archer, Jan. 4, 1849. Calvin
  R. Barron, J.P. (Jan. 4, 1849).
George W. Johnson to Sarah J. Madden, Jan. 4, 1849. No
  return.
Jesse Swain to Polly Ball, Jan. 9, 1849. Dennis Trammell,
  J.P. (Jan. 11, 1849).
Oliver Litton to Nelly Brown, Jan. 10, 1849. James
  Litton, J.P. (Jan. 10, 1849).
William Ingram to Elizabeth Burriss, Jan. 15, 1849. S.
  D. Queener, J.P. (Jan. 18, 1849).
Joseph D. Brown to Jane Keeny, Jan. 15, 1849. James
  Parker, D.D. (Jan. 28, 1849).
James Jackson to Mahaly Wilson, Jan. 14, 1849. No
  return.
Solomon Perkins to Anna B. Crickmore (Creekmore), Jan.
  20, 1849. D. Trammell, J.P. (Jan. 23, 1849).
Hudson Bennet to Elizabeth Milton, Jan. 28, 1849.
  Calvin R. Barron, J.P. (Jan. 28, 1849).
Fountain Cooper to Leah Harris, Jan. 28, 1850. (1850).
Cornelius Litton to Eliza Chitwood, Feb. 30, 1849. Wm.
  Chitwood, J.P. (Jan. 30, 1849).
O. H. Perry to Susannah Shelton, Feb. 14, 1849. Michael
  McGraw, J.P. (Feb. 20, 1849).
Hiram Lay to Conny Lay, Feb. 15, 1849. Sampson Stanfill,
  J.P. (Feb. 18, 1849).
Martin B. Ryan to Amelia A. Hatfield, Feb. 22, 1849.
  Dennis Trammell, J.P. (Feb. 22, 1849).
Aaron Bullock to Nancy Mozier, Mar. 1, 1849. No return.
Mitchel Alexander to Sarah E. Petree, Mar. 3, 1849.
  Wm. Bruce, L.E. (Mar., 1849).
John Robbins to Nancy Harmon, Mar. 3, 1849. Isaac
  Gross, J.P. (Mar. 4, 1849).
James Acres to Emily Cross, Mar. 4, 1849. David
  Stevens, J.P. (Mar. 4, 1849).
Wymer Croley to Rebecca Pebley, Mar. 8, 1849. Calvin
  R. Barron, J.P. (Mar. 8, 1849).
Robt. H. Smith to Martha J. Chapman, Mar. 13, 1849. G.
  W. Baker, J.P. (Mar. 14, 1849).
Matison Stout to Orpha Allbright, Mar. 15, 1849.
  William Hancock, J.P. (Mar. 15, 1849).
Isaac C. Dyer to Louisa Sharp, Mar. 24, 1849. No
  return.
Daniel Strunk to Melinda Ryan, Mar. 24, 1849. Dennis
  Trammell, J.P. (Mar., 1849).
Abram E. Hamby to Elizabeth Chitwood, Mar. 24, 1849.
  Dennis Trammell, J.P. (Mar. 31, 1849).

CAMPBELL COUNTY MARRIAGES

Joseph Siler to Christian Adkins, Mar. 31, 1849.  Calvin
R. Barron, J.P.  (Apr. 1, 1849).
Lindsay Jackson to Anna Hatfield, Apr. 2, 1849.  Thomas
Douglas, J.P.  (Apr. 4, 1849).
Isham Kamar to Rebecca McFarland, Apr. 3, 1849.  Michael
McGraw, J.P.  (Apr. 4, 1849).
John Heatherly to Lucinda Cloud, Apr. 4, 1849.  No return.
Bennett Powers to Eliza S. Chandoin, Apr. 8, 1849.
Calvin R. Barron, J.P.  (Apr. 8, 1849).
Andrew Wilson to Sephrona Chitwood, Apr. 21, 1849.
Dennis Trammell, J.P.  (Apr. 21, 1849).
John E. Willson to Hannah Smith, Apr. 23, 1849.  G. W.
Baker, J.P.  (Apr. 25, 1849).
John Dagley to Cynthia Grant, Apr. 24, 1849.  No return.
David Faris to Sarah Matthews, May 19, 1849.  Calvin
R. Barron, J.P.  (May 19, 1849).
Henderson Hatmaker to Louisa Jarman, June 2, 1849.
William Hancock, J.P.  (June 2, 1849).
Hiram Perkins to Melissa Wilson, June 10, 1849.  Calvin
R. Barron.  (June 10, 1849).
Hiram R. Dickson to Nancy Ann Smith, June 10, 1849.
Dennis Trammel, J.P.  (June 10, 1849).
James Dagly to Jane Acres, June 20, 1849.  James
Litton, J.P.  (June 20, 1849).
Edmund A. Gross to Angeletta Dabney, July 9, 1849.
Isaac Gross, J.P.  (Aug. 4, 1849).
Jesse Powers to Susannah Patsy, July 21, 1849.  Calvin
R. Barron, J.P.  (July 21, 1849).
Daniel Alford to Nancy J. Lea, July 21, 1849.  Calvin
R. Barron, J.P.  (July 21, 1849).
D. F. Leach to Frances Nicholson, July 26, 1849.  Calvin
R. Barron, J.P.  (July 26, 1849).
Henry C. Tiller to Emily Hutson, July 31, 1849.  Thos.
Douglas, J.P.  (Aug. 14, 1849).
George Smith to Kisiah Neal, Aug. 4, 1849.  Isaac
Gross, J.P.  (Aug. 5, 1849).
Joseph Brantly to Timmy Hill, Aug. 10, 1849.  Wm. L.
Smith, M.G.  (Aug. 16, 1849).
Robert W. Jourdon to Louisa Virginia Nance, Aug. 14,
1849.  No return.
Thomas Gailer to Susannah Harmon, Aug. 30, 1849.  Isaac
Gross, J.P.  (Aug. 30, 1849).
Hugh Davis to Dorcas Trammell. Sep. 2, 1849.  Dennis
Trammell, J.P.  (Sep. 2, 1849).
Riley Nicholson to Emily Sceans, Sep. 9, 1849.  Calvin
R. Barron, J.P.  (Sep. 9, 1849).
George Reed to Esther Parker, Sep. 11, 1849.  No return.
William Longmire to Rebecca Graves, Sep. 11, 1849.  John
Lower, J.P.  (Sep. 13, 1849).
James M. Keehan to Obedian Richardson, Sep. 14, 1849.
Thos. Douglas, J.P.  (Sep. 14, 1849).
Thompson Wilson to Sarah Walker, Sep. 22, 1849.  No
return.
Isaac Hutson to Vica Jackson, Oct. 2, 1849.  Thos.
Douglas, J.P.  (Oct. 2, 1849).

Louis J. Johnson to Caroline Housley, Oct. 11, 1849.
  Calvin R. Barron, J.P. (Oct. 18, 1849).
Shelton Parton to Sally Fraser, Oct. 20, 1849. James
  Archer, J.P. (Oct. 29, 1849).
William H. Smith to E. S. Kincaid, Oct. 24, 1849.
  Wm. Bruce, J.P. (Oct., 1849).
Abram Strunk to Melinda Waters, Oct. 31, 1849. Dennis
  Trammell, J.P. (Oct. 31, 1849).
Allen Rowmines to Mary Moore, Nov. 2, 1849. J. W.
  Huffaker, J.P. (Nov. 13, 1849).
Jacob Hatmaker to Polly Hatmaker, Nov. 8, 1849. Isaac
  Gross, J.P. (Nov. 9, 1849).
William Burrass to Sarah K. Fleming, Nov. 10, 1849.
  Isaac Gross, J.P. (Nov. 18, 1849).
Wm. C. Shown to Mahulda Lindsy, Nov. 16, 1849. Thos.
  Douglas, J.P. (Nov. 18, 1849).
John Ayers to Martha Dagly, Nov. 18, 1849. No return.
Jesse Laxton to Jane Thompson, Nov. 20, 1849. No
  return.
Alvis Adkins to Mary Bryant, Nov. 22, 1849. Thomas
  Douglas, J.P. (Nov. 25, 1849).
Frederick Kesterson to Anna Lovely, Nov. 28, 1849.
  No return.
P. B. Turner to Mary Sweat, Dec. 7, 1849. G. W.
  Baker, J.P. (Dec. 9, 1849).
Franklin Miller to Barbary Longmire, Dec. 18, 1849.
  G. W. Baker, J.P. (Dec. 23, 1849).
Pleasant Graves to Sally Hously, Dec. 22, 1849. W. D.
  Sharp, J.P. (Dec. 23, 1849).
John Bird to Nancy Miller, Dec. 25, 1849. Jas.
  Johnson, J.P.
Allen McDonald to Christena Lawson, Dec. 25, 1849.
  Sampson Stanfil, J.P. (Dec. 25, 1849).
John Candell to Emily J. Atkins, Dec. 27, 1849. Dennis
  Trammell, J.P. (Dec. 27, 1849).
John Campbell to Fanny Rookard, Dec. 27, 1849. Calvin
  R. Barron, J.P. (Dec. 27, 1849).
Joseph Beard to Delila Walden, Nov. 28, 1849. Wm.
  L. Lay, J.P. (Dec. 29, 1849).
Jesse Lovett to Nancy Dowell, Dec. 29, 1849. Jas.
  Johnson, J.P.
John F. Murray to Marilda Siler, Jan. 3, 1850. Calvin
  R. Barron, J.P. (Jan. 3, 1850).
John Petree to Catharine Petree, Nov. 16, 1850. James
  Parker, D.D. (Nov. 21, 1850).
Phillip Anderson to Nancy Tasket, Jan. 17, 1850. No
  return.
Timothy Anderson to Jane Roach, Jan. 17, 1849. No
  return.
James Trail to Susan Frock, Jan. 18, 1850. Jas.
  Johnson, J.P.
M. C. Robertson to Ann Eliza Wheeler, Jan. 22, 1850.
  David Fleming, M.G. (Jan. 27, 1850).
James Hatmaker to Sarah Murray, Jan. 26, 1850. William
  Hancock, J.P. (Jan. 27, 1850).

Fountain Cooper to Leah Harris, Jan. 28, 1850. Thos.
  Douglas, J.P. (Feb. 3, 1850).
Josiah Smith to Elizabeth Nettles, Feb. 25, 1850.
  Wm. Chitwood, Esq. (Feb. 28, 1850).
Jonothan C. Chitwood to Sephrony Ross, Feb. 9, 1850.
  Dennis Trammel, J.P. (Feb. 10, 1850).
Wm. C. Hart to Martha J. Houskins, Feb. 8, 1850.
  Calvin R. Barron, J.P. (Feb. 8, 1850).
George M. Douglas to Nancy Lay, Feb. 7, 1850. Calvin
  R. Barron, J.P. (Feb. 7, 1850).
Daniel E. Wilson to Eliza Cox, Feb. 6, 1850. No return.
Simeon Mallicoat to Sarah Reed, Feb. 5, 1850. S. D.
  Queener, J.P. (Apr. 1, 1850).
Elihu Turner to Dicy Richardson, Mar. 4, 1850. C. R.
  Barron, J.P. (Apr. 7, 1850).
Henry Hayslip to Martha Boulton, Apr. 7, 1850. C.
  R. Barron, J.P. (Apr. 7, 1850).
Samuel Waters to Lydia Roberts, Mar. 8, 1850. Dennis
  Trammel, J.P. (Mar. 8, 1850).
Thomas B. Crickmore (Creekmore) to Mary Trammell,
  Mar. 10, 1850. C. R. Barron, J.P. (Mar. 10, 1850).
Francis F. Bryant to Malinda Skinner, Mar. 10, 1850.
  Calvin R. Barron, J.P. (Mar. 10, 1850).
Robert Chapman to Polly Mallicoat, Apr. 11, 1850.
  No return.
Josiah Leach to Lucy J. Brass, Mar. 14, 1850. C. R.
  Barron, J.P. (Apr. 15, 1850).
Thomas Gailer to Nancy Gibson, Mar. 16, 1850. Thomas
  Douglas, J.P. (Mar. 17, 1850).
Michael Mackin to Susan Collins, May 18, 1850. John
  Lower, J.P. (May 21, 1850).
Aaron Broyles to Mary Faulkner, Mar. 21, 1850. Calvin
  R. Barron, J.P. (Mar. 21, 1850).
Isaac Bryant to Elizabeth Hatfield, Mar. 21, 1850.
  Calvin R. Barron, J.P. (Mar. 21, 1850).
McGoin to Eola Kirk, Mar. 22, 1850. Michael McGraw,
  J.P. (Mar. 24, 1850).
David Brown to Sarah Phillips, Apr. 4, 1850. Jas.
  Johnson, J.P.
Harrison Head to Ibba Solomon, Apr. 6, 1850. Calvin
  R. Barron, J.P. (Apr. 6, 1850).
William Boruff to Caroline Curnutt, Apr. 10, 1850. John
  Lower, J.P. (Apr. 11, 1850).
Wm. Griffiers to Malitha Miller, Apr. 22, 1850. No
  return.
James Crabtree to Elizabeth Smith, Apr. 25, 1850.
  Sampson Stanfill, J.P. (Apr. 26, 1850).
John Bryant to Parley Hill, Apr. 27, 1850. Wm. L.
  Smith, M.G. (May 2, 1850).
Wm. Brummett to Sarah Standler, May 5, 1850. Calvin
  R. Barron, J.P.
Wm. Solomon to Mary Angones, May 6, 1850. Calvin R.
  Barron, J.P. (May 6, 1850).
S. D. Wilhite to E. S. Elkins, June 5, 1850. Thos.
  Douglas, J.P. (June 5, 1850).

Thomas Dula to Elizabeth Brooks, June 13, 1850.
Calvin R. Barron, J.P. (June 13, 1850).
James Dunkin to Matilda Row, June 23, 1850. Calvin
R. Barron, J.P. (June 23, 1850).
Sterlin Smith to Polly McNeely, July 19, 1850. Michael
McGraw, J.P. (July 20, 1850).
Enoch Bird to Ruth Faulkner, July 21, 1850. Calvin
R. Barron, J.P. (July 21, 1850).
Caswell Smith to Sarah Ann Reid, July 27, 1850. No
return.
Leonard Casey to Tiladay Tory, July 29, 1850. James
Archer, J.P. (July 29, 1850).
Davis Arvin to Francis E. Cain, Aug. 7, 1850. Calvin
R. Barron, J.P. (Aug. 7, 1850).
Elisha Siler to Elizabeth Faulkner, Aug. 8, 1850.
Calvin R. Barron, J.P. (Aug. 8, 1850).
James McCully to Eliza Right, Aug. 18, 1850. No return.
Harvey Grant to Helen Lay, Aug. 23, 1850. Jackson
Wilhite, J.P. (Aug. 29, 1850).
John Rollins to A. E. Walker, Aug. 27, 1850. J. J.
Marrs, J.P. (Aug. 27, 1850).
Isaac Oaks to Meriah Butlar, Aug. 29, 1850. No return.
Isaac Lay to Martha Dial, Aug. 31, 1850. Sampson
Stanfill, J.P. (Oct. 12, 1850).
C. S. Lindsay to Vally Bowling, Sep. 16, 1850. Squire
Hunter, J.P. (Sep. 17, 1850).
Hamilton Wilson to Matilda Siler, Sep. 2, 1850. No
return.
O. R. Kirkpatrick to H. Talley, Sep. 18, 1850. S. D.
Queener, J.P. (Sep. 18, 1850).
Joel Bryant to Nancy Siler, Sep. 24, 1850. Calvin
R. Barron, J.P. (Sep. 21, 1850).
Reuben Marlow to Anna Ervin, Sep. 26, 1850. Calvin R.
Barron, J.P. (Sep. 26, 1850).
Isaac W. Sullivan to Susan Macmand, Sep. 29, 1850. Jas.
Archer. (Sep. 29, 1850).
James Wilson to Mary Hambin, Oct. 4, 1850. Jas. Archer.
(Oct. 4, 1850).
Robert Dossitt to Mary Smith, Oct. 1, 1850. Wm. Bruce,
L.E. (Oct. 6, 1850).
Pleasant Polly to Mary Lawson, Oct. 10, 1850. Calvin
R. Barron, J.P. (Oct. 10, 1850).
Henry Boruff to Martha Jackson, Oct. 10, 1850. Calvin
R. Barron, J.P. (Oct. 10, 1850).
George W. Sharp to Louisa J. Longmire, Oct. 23, 1850.
John Lower, J.P. (Oct. 24, 1850).
Jesse Agee to Elizabeth Maddin, Nov. 8, 1850.
William Linos. (Nov. 21, 1850).
Kemuel Hill to Manda Glander, Nov. 9, 1850. John
Lower, J.P. (Nov. 10, 1850).
Charles Williamson to Sarah Green, Nov. 11, 1850.
No return.
John Petree to Catharline Ford, Nov. 16, 1850. Jas.
Parker, D.D. (Nov. 20, 1850).

James Miller to Ann Sharp, Nov. 18, 1850. Wm. Bruce, L.E. (Nov. 25, 1855).

Wm. Wright to Sarah Chapman, Dec. 5, 1850. John Hously, J.P. (Dec. 8, 1850).

Thomas W. Gray to Hannah H. Gross, Dec. 7, 1850. J. H. Grant, J.P. (Dec. 15, 1850).

John Stanfill to Lucy Vatch, Dec. 7, 1850. James Archer. (Dec. 7, 1850).

Willis Bruce to Nancy Britgerman, Dec. 12, 1850. S. D. Queener, J.P.

James Smiddy to Elizabeth Cooper, Dec. 25, 1850. S. D. Queener, J.P.

Love Smith to Martha Reid, Dec. 28, 1850. No return.

Henry L. Jackson to Mary B. Thompson, Jan. 10, 1850. Calvin R. Barron, J.P. (Jan. 10, 1850).

George McCall to Elizabeth Gatlin, Jan. 12, 1850. Calvin R. Barron. (Jan. 12, 1850).

Wm. Bride to Lockey Hill, Jan. 16, 1850. No return.

John Luits to Hester Ann Lay, Jan. 16, 1851. No return.

Thomas Brantly to Margaret Stephens, Jan. 24, 1850. James Parker, D.D. (Jan. 30, 1850).

Isaac J. Thomas to Jane Dossett, Feb. 1, 1851. No return.

John S. Gad to Mary Abner, Feb. 5, 1850. Calvin R. Barron, J.P. (Feb. 6, 1850).

Wilson Murray to Nancy C. Rollings, Feb. 6, 1851. E. E. Gillenwaters, M.G. (Feb. 6, 1851).

Mellvill Walden to Dilly Rose, Feb. 6, 1850. Calvin R. Barron, J.P. (Feb. 6, 1851).

Christopher Gaylor to Martha Walden, Feb. 9, 1851. Calvin R. Barron, J.P. (Feb. 9, 1851).

Elkanah Ayers to Lucinda Campbell, Feb. 9, 1851. Calvin R. Barron, J.P. (Feb. 9, 1851).

Green C. Hunter to Eliza Douglas, Feb. 12, 1851. S. D. Queener, J.P. (Apr. 7, 1851).

G. W. Witt to Mary Jane Smith, Feb. 17, 1851. No return.

John Langley to Elizabeth Smiddy, Feb. 17, 1851. C. R. Barron, J.P. (Feb. 19, 1851).

Wm. Chapman to Catherine Muzingo, Feb. 21, 1851. C. R. Barron, J.P. (Feb. 19, 1851).

John M. Dyer to Polly Sharp, Feb. 26, 1851. No return.

Lemuel P. Vinzant to Mary Walker. Mar. 5, 1851. E. E. Gillinwaters, M.G. (Mar. 6, 1851).

Matthew Douglas to Hannah Baird, Mar. 6, 1851. Calvin R. Barron, J.P. (Mar. 6, 1851.).

Riley Queener to Mary Hope, Mar. 13, 1851. Isaac Gross, J.P. (Mar. 13, 1851).

Alvis Siler to Rachel Campbell, Mar. 16, 1851. C. R. Barron, J.P. (Mar. 16, 1851).

A. J. Peterson to Emily M. Hollingsworth, Apr. 5, 1851. Squire Hunter, J.P. (Apr. 5, 1851).

Amos Richardson to Matilda Wilson, Apr. 3, 1851. Isaac Gross, J.P. (Apr. 3, 1851).

William Allen to Phebe Bavion, Apr. 6, 1851. Calvin R. Barron, J.P. (Apr. 6, 1851).

John Woods to Mary Martin, Apr. 15, 1851. Calvin R. Barron, J.P. (Apr. 15, 1851).

James H. Davis to Cynthia Stanfill, Apr. 17, 1851.
  Calvin R. Barron, J.P. (Apr. 17, 1851).
James Faulkner to Martha Fox, Apr. 17, 1851. C. R.
  Barron, J.P. (Apr. 17, 1851).
Ewins Baker to Rachael Irvin, Apr. 18, 1851. No return.
James Hatfield to Nancy Broyles, May 1, 1851. C. R.
  Barron, J.P. (May 1, 1851).
G. W. Baker to Jane Irvin, May 2, 1851. No return.
J. A. Patton to Elizabeth J. Smith, May 28, 1851. James
  Atkins, M.G. (May 29, 1851).
Thomas McCarter to M. J. Fullington, June 2, 1851. Wm.
  L. Smith, Minister. (June 3, 1851).
J. A. Waisman to E. Hollingsworth, June 10, 1851. S.
  D. Queener, J.P. (May 10, 1851).
Wm. P. Cooper to Sally Hutson, June 12, 1851. Wm.
  Lindsay, Preacher of the Gospel. (June 19, 1851).
Jacob Harmon to Susan Miller, July 12, 1851. John
  Murray, J.P. (July 15, 1851).
Kellis J. Hale to Patsy Harris, July 16, 1851. W. D.
  Sharp, J.P. (July 17, 1851).
Melkijah V. Nash to Matilda Sharp, July 17, 1851. No
  return.
William Smith to Elizabeth Cliborn, July 24, 1851. Wm.
  Bruce, L.E. (July 28, 1851).
Thomas Smith to Martha N. Cooper, July 24, 1851. Wm.
  Bruce, L.E. (July 31, 1851).
John C. Adams to Nancy Maze, July 25, 1851. C. R.
  Barron, J.P. (July 25, 1851).
Isham Goin to Minerva Anne Soaps, Aug. 1, 1851. Michael
  McGraw, J.P. (Aug. 10, 1851).
William Cox to Hannah Gray, Aug. 3, 1851. John
  Murray, J.P. (Aug. 4, 1851).
Russell Leach to Anna Scritchfield, Aug. 5, 1851. F.
  P. McNew, J.P. (Aug. 10, 1851).
James Gray to Elizabeth Lay, Aug. 8, 1851. No return.
Samuel Broyles to Eliza Thomas, Aug. 14, 1851. Calvin
  R. Barron, J.P. (Aug. 14, 1851).
Payton Miller to Nancy Chapman, Aug. 16, 1851. John
  Hously, J.P. (Aug. 17, 1851).
James Rutherford to Catharine Rollings, Aug. 20, 1851.
  H. C. Grimes, J.P. (Aug. 20, 1851).
Joseph Faulkner to Kisiah Powers, Aug. 21, 1851. Calvin
  R. Barron, J.P. (Aug. 21, 1851).
E. C. Kilbourne to Elizabeth Miller, Aug. 24, 1851. Wm.
  Bruce, L.E. (Aug. 28, 1851).
Robinson Leach to Fruly Adkins, Aug. 26, 1851. L.
  Rich, M.G. (Aug. 28, 1851).
John Abner to Mary Jane Clark, Aug. 31, 1851. Calvin
  R. Barron, J.P. (Aug. 31, 1851).
Samuel O. Ayers to Lucinda H. Marrs, Sep. 13, 1851.
  James M. Marshall, M.G. (Sep. 17, 1851).
Daniel Bolton to Elizabeth Higs, Sep. 14, 1851. Calvin
  R. Barron, J.P. (Sep. 14, 1851).
William H. Sharp to Sarah J. Kincaid, Sep. 22, 1851.
  James M. Marshall, M.G. (Sep. 25, 1851).

Daniel Morgan to Malinda Whitaker, Sep. 28, 1851. Calvin
R. Barron, J.P. (Sep. 28, 1851).
Wm. A. Champion to Charity H. Hogan, Sep. 30, 1851.
Calvin R. Barron, J.P. (Sep. 30, 1851).
Thomas Chapman to Milly Ann Smith, Oct. 1, 1851. Jas.
Parker, D.D. (Oct. 2, 1851).
James Carter to Kisiah Reynolds, Oct. 2, 1851. Calvin
R. Barron, J.P. (Oct. 2, 1851).
James A. Rice to Marica E. Sexton, Oct. 3, 1851. Calvin
R. Barron, J.P. (Oct. 3, 1851).
Robt. Cook to Matilda Holy, Oct. 6, 1851. R. A. McClain,
M.G. (Oct. 6, 1851).
Wm. D. Maze to Sarah Reagan, Oct. 8, 1851. Calvin R.
Barron, J.P. (Oct. 8, 1851).
Alexander Rutherford to Minerva Jane Todd, Oct. 14,
1851. No return.
Sterling Smith to Margaret Queener, Oct. 24, 1851. A.
F. Shannon, M.G. (Oct. 25, 1851).
A. J. Bryant to Susanah Lovate, Nov. 2, 1851. Calvin
R. Barron, J.P. (Nov. 2, 1851).
A. J. Savage to Sarah Loy, Nov. 3, 1851. M. Monroe,
Minister. (Nov. 6, 1851).
Wm. Dyke to Judy Ann Smith, Nov. 9, 1851. F. P. McNew,
J.P. (Nov. 11, 1851).
Calvin Row to Martha Faulkner, Nov. 9, 1851. Calvin
R. Barron, J.P. (Nov. 9, 1851).
Henry Sharp to Sarah Kincaid, Nov. 19, 1851. James M.
Marshall, M.G. (Nov. 25, 1851).
Sanford Hill to R. E. Davis, Nov. 21, 1851. Wm. L.
Smith, M.G. (Nov. 27, 1851).
Mathias Raly to Polly Robinson, Nov. 28, 1851. M.
McGraw, J.P. (Nov. 30, 1851).
Green Foly to Rachel Jones, Dec. 4, 1851. Calvin R.
Barron, J.P. (Nov. 4, 1851).
Sterling Chavis to M. Lumpkins, Dec. 5, 1851. M. McGraw,
J.P. (Dec. 7, 1851).
Cornelius Braden to Nancy Smith, Dec. 9, 1851. Wm.
Bruce, L.E. (Dec. 30, 1851).
John Wild to Elizabeth Hinson, Dec. 22, 1851. Calvin
R. Barron, J.P. (Jan. 22, 1851).
Elias Parker to Lorany Wilson, Dec. 22, 1851. No return.
Marcellus Longmire to Leah Huff, Dec. 25, 1851. J. M.
Marshall, M.G. (Dec. 25, 1851).
Danl. Thomas to Nancy Broyles, Jan. 2, 1852. Calvin R.
Barron, J.P. (Jan. 22, 1852).
George Hart to Nancy J. McKinn, Jan. 2, 1852. Calvin
R. Barron, J.P. (Jan. 2, 1852).
Joseph Elkins to Polly Hart, Jan. 5, 1852. S. D.
Queener, J.P. (Dec. 15, 1852).
John Dossett to Elizabeth McNew, Jan. 6, 1852. James
M. Marshall, M.G. (Jan. 11, 1852).
Nathaniel Woods to P. Elkins, Jan. 21, 1852. James
M. Marshall, M.G. (Jan. 21, 1852).
Rufus K. Smith to Maria Maupin, Feb. 1, 1852. James
M. Marshall, M.G. (Feb. 10, 1852).

Benj. F. Bratcher to Nancy Y. Cain, Feb. 4, 1852.
    James M. Marshall, M.G. (Feb. 12, 1852).
James A. Rogers to Mary E. Cain, Feb. 9, 1852. Wm.
    Bruce, J.P. (Feb. 12, 1852).
Forest Powel to Rebecca Teaster, Feb. 21, 1852. S. D.
    Queener, J.P. (Feb. 21, 1852).
Alfred Mahon to Sarah Siler, Mar. 4, 1852. Calvin R.
    Barron, J.P. (Mar. 4, 1852).
Alfred Williams to Matilda Hutson, Mar. 7, 1852.
    Thomas Douglas, J.P. (Mar. 11, 1852).
Isaac Lay to Rachael Rogers, Mar. 7, 1852. S. D.
    Queener, J.P. (Mar. 7, 1852).
George Morgan to Louisa Hoper, Mar. 9, 1852. John
    Lower, J.P. (Mar. 11, 1852).
Rich J. Carr to Nancy Ann Marshall, Mar. 16, 1852.
    A. F. Shannon, M.G. (Mar. 18, 1852).
David Flatford to Martha Henderson, Mar. 27, 1852.
    John Lower, J.P. (Mar. 28, 1852).
Thomas Phillips to Elizabeth Marlow, Mar. 28, 1852.
    S. D. Queener, J.P. (Mar. 28, 1852).
G. W. Walton to Catharine Smith, Apr. 4, 1852. Wm.
    Bruce, L.E. (Apr. 5, 1852).
Andrew Smith to Sarah Meadors, Apr. 5, 1852. Wm.
    Bruce, L.E. (Apr. 8, 1852).
John McNew to Elizabeth McGlathlin, Apr. 7, 1852.
    F. P. McNew, J.P. (Apr. 7, 1852).
Sampson Croley to Sabry Standle, Apr. 13, 1852. Calvin
    R. Barron, J.P. (Apr. 13, 1852).
John S. Ross to Penelope Ann Wheeler, Apr. 17, 1852.
    A. F. Cox, M.G. (Apr. 20, 1852).
Andrew J. Burk to Ann J. Longmire, Apr. 19, 1852.
    Calvin R. Barron, J.P. (Apr. 19, 1852).
Allen Biggs to Ruth Miller, May 15, 1852. A. F.
    Shannon, M.G.
Saml. Brown to Celia Walker, May 16, 1852. A. F.
    Shannon, M.G. (June 3, 1852).
E. H. Reed to Mary Smith, May 18, 1852. No return.
Lewis Baird to Mary Lay, June 10, 1852. Calvin R.
    Barron, J.P. (June 10, 1852).
Wadrick H. Vania to Martha J. Cears, June 11, 1852.
    Calvin R. Barron, J.P. (June 10, 1852).
James D. Campbell to Catharine Petree, June 16, 1852.
    Wm. Bruce, L.E. (June 17, 1852).
John Hill to Minerva J. Norton, June 25, 1852. F. P.
    McNew, J.P. (June 25, 1852).
Brackler Hackler to Mary Ann Booth, July 1, 1852.
    Calvin R. Barron, J.P. (July 1, 1852).
W. W. Lynch to Mary J. Pebly, July 9, 1852. Michael
    McGraw, J.P. (July 18, 1852).
Samuel Smith to Susan J. Campbell, July 18, 1852. Calvin
    R. Barron, J.P. (July 18, 1852).
Charles M. Powers to Nancy Faulkner, July 22, 1852.
    John Hously, J.P. (July 22, 1852).
William Riggs to Caroline Taylor, Aug. 1, 1852.
    John Hously, J.P. (Aug. 3, 1852).

CAMPBELL COUNTY MARRIAGES

Wm. Carroll to Catharine York, Aug. 6, 1852. James
S. Murray, J.P. (Aug. 8, 1852. J
James Ruckers to Elizabeth Boulton, Aug. 9; 1852.
Calvin R. Barron, J.P. (Aug. 19, 1852).
Ezekiel Willhite to Rebecca Grant, Aug. 12, 1852.
Jackson Wilhite, J.P. (Aug. 17, 1852).
James Walden to Jane Rose, Sep. 2, 1852. Calvin
Barron, J.P. (Sep. 2, 1852).
Jacob W. Gross to Jane Thomas, Sep. 4, 1852. Isaac
Gross, J.P. (Sep. 5, 1852).
Clarwell Hill to S. A. H. Walker, Sep. 5, 1852. A. F.
Shannon, M.G. (Sep. 16, 1852).
Henry Hunter to Susan Goin, Sep. 7, 1852. Joseph
Marshall, J.P. (Sep. 9, 1852).
G. W. Thomas to Arlina Flatford, Sep. 7, 1852. No
return.
Joseph M. Smith to Sarah Peterson, Sep. 8, 1852. M. M.
Graw, J.P. (Sep. 11, 1852).
Wm. Robbins to Sarah Craig, Nov. 4, 1852. No return.
Lewis Faulkner to Silattia Siler, Nov. 11, 1852.
Calvin R. Barron, J.P. (Nov. 11, 1852).
Amos Bennett to Nancy Perkins, Nov. 11, 1852. Calvin
R. Barron, J.P. (Nov. 11, 1852).
John Drum to Catharine Beadon, Nov. 22, 1852. Wm.
Bruce, L.E. (Nov. 25, 1852).
John McNeely to Martha Goin, Nov. 24, 1852. M. McGraw,
J.P. (Nov. 25, 1852).
John G. Hall to Margaret Smith, Nov. 27, 1852. A. F.
Shannon, M.G. (Dec. 2, 1852).
Thomas Hart to Martha Carey, Oct. 2, 1852. A. F.
Shannon, M.G. (Oct. 4, 1852).
John Witt to Martha C. Sharp, Oct. 4, 1852. J. M.
Keely, M.G. (Oct. 7, 1852).
Calvin Sexton to Nancy Hilton, Oct. 11, 1852. Calvin
R. Barron, J.P. (Oct. 11, 1852).
Livel Hill to Alecy Forester, Oct. 14, 1852. W. D.
Sharp, J.P. (Oct. 18, 1852).
Berry Shaufer to Sarah Shelby, Oct. 16, 1852. John
Lower, J.P. (Oct. 17, 1852).
Album Beech to Emerose Keeny, Oct. 23, 1852. William
Lindsay, M.G. (Oct. 24, 1852).
John Kincaid to Judia Ward, Oct. 25, 1852. James M.
Marshall. (Nov. 2, 1852).
George Hamblin to Rebecca Smith, Dec. 2, 1852. Calvin
R. Barron, J.P. (Dec. 2, 1852).
Hardin P. Blakely to Elizabeth Perkins, Dec. 6, 1852.
Calvin R. Barron, J.P. (Dec. 5, 1852).
H. Humphreys to Malinda Weaver, Dec. 11, 1852. John
Lower, J.P. (Dec. 12, 1852).
Thomas Thompson to Polly Lay, Dec. 9, 1852. No return.
Jacob Mozier to Eliza Hatmaker, Dec. 23, 1852. James
Hutson, Ordained Minister. (Dec. 23, 1852).
William Fox to Milly Slatton, Dec. 30, 1852. Calvin
R. Barron, J.P. (Dec. 30, 1852).

# CAMPBELL COUNTY MARRIAGES

George Hamblin to Rebecca Smith, Dec. 2, 1852. Calvin
R. Barron, J.P. (Dec. 2, 1852).
Hardin P. Blakely to Elizabeth Perkins, Dec. 5, 1852.
Calvin R. Barron, J.P. (Dec. 5, 1852).
Abraham Nelson to Louisa Stout, Feb. 5, 1853. Jas. H.
Grant, J.P. (Jan., 1853).
Franklin Richardson to Mary Peterson, Jan. 12, 1853.
A. F. Shannon, M.G. (Jan. 13, 1853).
A. P. Weaver to Eliza A. Reeves, July 14, 1853. James
M. Marshall, M.G. (Jan. 15, 1853).
Aaron Lawson to Tabitha Wilhite, Jan. 20, 1853. No
return.
Eli Brown to Kitty Gross, Jan. 27, 1853. John Murray,
J.P. (Jan. 27, 1853).
J. W. Gatliff to E. D. Goodin, Jan. 27, 1853. Calvin
R. Barron, J.P. (Jan. 27, 1853).
Esau Miller to Sarah Woods, Jan. 29, 1853. Isaac
Gross, J.P. (Jan. 30, 1853).
John Davis to Francis Hatfield, Jan. 29, 1853. Calvin
R. Barron, J.P. (Jan. 29, 1853).
William Kirk to Eliza Fullington, Feb. 3, 1853. M.
McGraw, J.P. (Feb. 4, 1853).
Willey Tiller to Lucinda Harrison, Feb. 5, 1853. James
Hutson, Ordained Minister. (Feb. 6, 1853).
William Hutson to Tempy Pebly, Feb. 7, 1853. M. McGraw,
J.P. (Feb. 5, 1853).
Samuel Sawyers to Louisa Woodard, Feb. 13, 1853. Calvin
R. Barron, J.P. (Feb. 15, 1853).
John Pinkerton to Elizabeth Jones, Feb. 13, 1853.
Jas. Williams, J.P. (Feb. 13, 1853).
John Prewit to Sarah Ann Nix, Feb. 20, 1853. Calvin R.
Barron, J.P. (Feb. 20, 1853).
David Wright to Nancy Comer, Feb. 26, 1853. No return.
Jesse C. Douglass to Susan Sawyers, Mar. 13, 1853.
Calvin R. Barron, J.P. (Mar. 13, 1853).
James Right to C. Wilson, Mar. 17, 1853. No return.
Benjamin Shepherd to Nancy Milton, Mar. 19, 1853.
Calvin R. Barron, J.P. (Mar. 19, 1853).
Joseph Lumpkins to Phebe McCarty, Mar. 20, 1853. M.
McGraw, J.P. (Mar. 20, 1853).
Arch. Smith to Mary M. Maupin, Mar. 21, 1853. James
M. Marshall. (Mar. 22, 1853).
George P. Douglas to Lucretia Wilhite, Mar. 24, 1853.
Calvin R. Barron, J.P. (Mar. 24, 1853).
George Hale to Aleey Weaver, Mar. 29, 1853. John
Hously, J.P. (Mar. 31, 1853).
'Squire Perkins to Margaret Douglas, Apr. 3, 1853.
Calvin R. Barron, J.P. (Apr. 3, 1853).
John Q. A. Early to Elizabeth Jones, Apr. 4, 1853.
Calvin R. Barron, J.P. (Apr. 7, 1853).
John Lay to Cynthia Stanfill, Apr. 7, 1853. Calvin
R. Barron, J.P. (Apr. 7, 1853).
Aaron Sharp to Nancy Walden, Apr. 7, 1853. Calvin R.
Barron, J.P. (Apr. 7, 1853).

89

Elkana Mullis to Nancy Tye, Apr. 8, 1853. Calvin R.
Barron, J.P. (Apr. 8, 1853).

Jas. C. Faulkner to Melinda Brim, Apr. 14, 1853.
Calvin R. Barron, J.P. (Apr. 14, 1853).

Hiram Cox to C. C. Wilson, Apr. 17, 1853. No return.

Manuel Marlo to Martha Stowers, Apr. 24, 1853. Calvin
R. Barron, J.P. (Apr. 24, 1853).

Evin Walden to Nancy Sharp, Apr. 28, 1853. Calvin R.
Barron, J.P. (Apr. 28, 1853).

O. P. Bridgeman to S. J. Queener, May 15, 1853. Calvin
R. Barron, J.P. (May 15, 1853).

Casely Dunkin to Martha J. Faulkner, May 19, 1853.
Calvin R. Barron, J.P. (May 19, 1853).

H. Thompson to Polly Hatfield, May 19, 1853. Larkin
W. Cross, J.P. (July 11, 1853).

Joshua Harp to Amelia More, May 21, 1853. Calvin R.
Barron, J.P. (May 21, 1853).

Thomas Jones to Nancy Sweat, May 23, 1853. James
Parker, D.D. (May 25, 1853).

Joseph Faulkner to Lucinda Tye, June 2, 1853. Calvin
R. Barron, J.P. (June 2, 1853).

Thomas Young to Artela Fox, June 25, 1853. Calvin R.
Barron, J.P. (July 25, 1853).

Joseph Holloway to Mary Hilton, July 14, 1853. John
Murray, J.P. (July 17, 1853).

Henry Cooper to Louisa Fouster, July 14, 1853. John
Murray, J.P. (July 14, 1853).

John Henly to Martha Gross, July 21, 1853. Isaac
Gross, J.P. (July 23, 1853).

James McCarroll to Nancy York, July 24, 1853. Calvin
R. Barron, J.P. (July 24, 1853).

Jourdon Huff to Patsey McKee, July 27, 1853. William
Lindsay, M.G. (July 27, 1853).

Sampson Wilson to Elizabeth Parker, July 27, 1853.
William Lindsay, M.G. (July 27, 1853).

William Milton to E. I. Ridenour, July 30, 1853. No
return.

Elias Reynolds to Torey Lay, July 31, 1853. Calvin R.
Barron, J.P. (July 31, 1853).

Leander P. Bird to Cynthia Perkins, Aug. 11, 1853.
Calvin R. Barron, J.P. (Aug. 11, 1853).

Sterlin C. Douglas to Minerva S. Snyder, Aug. 11, 1853.
Calvin R. Barron, J.P. (Aug. 11, 1853).

Silas Rutherford to Mary Stanly, Aug. 11, 1853. Calvin
R. Barron, J.P. (Aug. 11, 1853).

James Miller to Nancy Davis, Aug. 15, 1853. W. D.
Sharp, J.P. (Aug. 15, 1853).

John M. Butter to Sarah Braden, Aug. 17, 1853. Wm.
Bruce, L.E. (Aug. 18, 1853).

Danl. Hatmaker to Martha J. Harmon, Aug. 18, 1853.
James Hutson, M.G. (Aug. 18, 1853).

Job McCully to Patsy Ivy, Aug. 19, 1853. M. McGraw,
J.P. (Aug. 21, 1853).

John Wilson to Elizabeth Walker, Aug. 20, 1853. No
return.

Willy Jones to Delila Jones, Aug. 25, 1853. Calvin
R. Barron, J.P. (Aug. 25, 1853).
J. C. Winton to Louisa Richardson, Aug. 25, 1853. A.
F. Shannon, M.G. (Aug. 26, 1853).
S. C. Fleming to M. A. Stokes, Aug. 27, 1853. Isaac
Gross, J.P. (Aug. 28, 1853).
William Harrell to Susan Bullock, Aug. 28, 1853. John
Murray, J.P. (Aug. 28, 1853).
John McKeehan to Mary Sutherland, Aug. 30, 1853. J.
H. Grant, J.P. (Sep. 1, 1853).
Alford McKee to Mary Hill, Aug. 31, 1853. No return.
Amos Ivy to Eliza Ivy, Sep. 1, 1853. M. McGraw, J.P.
(Sep. 3, 1853).
John E. Smith to Elrina Butler, Sep. 1, 1853. M.
McGraw, J.P. (Sep. 4, 1853).
Pleasant Johnson to Caly Kirk, Sep. 3, 1853. M. McGraw,
J.P. (Sep. 4, 1853).
Wm. Hatmaker to Susan Murry, Sep. 15, 1853. No return.
John Meyers to Martha Miller, Sep. 24, 1853. Wm.
Bruce, L.E. (Sep., 1853).
Wm. Huddleston to Hannah Gaylor, Sep. 25, 1853. Calvin
R. Barron, J.P. (Sep. 25, 1853).
Matthew Massingale to Margaret Miller, Oct. 6, 1853.
Jas. Williams, J.P. (Oct. 6, 1853).
George Holt to Elizabeth Fox, Oct. 6, 1853. J. C.
Barron, J.P. (Oct. 6, 1853).
Thomas Reeves to Ceny Wilson, Oct. 13, 1853. John
Housley, J.P. (Nov. 1, 1853).
John Gross to Sarah Maddin, Oct. 14, 1853. James
Hutson, Ordained Minister. (Nov. 15, 1853).
LaFayette Inzly to Martha T. Hope, Oct. 19, 1853.
S. D. Queener, J.P. (Aug. 8, 1853).
John T. Greer to E. J. Brown, Oct. 22, 1853. No return.
Wesly Leach to Mahaly Smith, Oct. 29, 1853. F. P.
McNew, J.P. (Jan. 22, 1853).
B. W. S. Alexander to Love Maupin, Oct. 31, 1853.
Wm. Bruce, L.E. (Oct., 1853).
Amos Maupin to H. Hollingsworth, Nov. 1, 1853. Wm.
Bruce, L.E. (Oct., 1853).
Robert Dessett to Sarah Ann Walker, Nov. 2, 1853. S.
D. Queener, J.P. (Aug. 9, 1853).
George Webb to Lydia Griffey, Nov. 15, 1853. Isaac
Gross, J.P. (Nov. 20, 1853).
William Evans to Francis Davis, Nov. 19, 1853. Joseph
Marshall, J.P. (Nov. 20, 1853).
Arthur McFarland to Winy Geesly, Nov. 25, 1853. John
, Lower, J.P. (Nov. 27, 1853).
William Evans to Francis Davis, Nov. 19, 1853. Joseph
Marshall, J.P. (Nov. 20, 1853).
Hiram Harmon to Rebecca Roach, Dec. 2, 1853. John
Murray. (Dec. 4, 1853).
A. C. Copeland to Mary A. Stokes, Dec. 6, 1853. Isaac
Gross, J.P. (Dec. 7, 1853).
Thomas B. Davis to Rosannah Hackler, Dec. 8, 1853.
Calvin R. Barron, J.P. (Dec. 8, 1853).

Silvester Cooper to Harriet M. Kirkpatrick. No return.
C. L. Crosswhite to Elizabeth Dabny, Dec. 19, 1853.
Wm. Lindsay, M.G. (Dec. 22, 1853).
Jacob Mozier to Eliza Hatmaker, Dec. 23, 1853. No
return.
John Bolin to Catharine Cook, Dec. 29, 1853. Calvin
R. Barron, J.P. (Dec. 29, 1853).
Isaac Sanders to Lucinda Geaslow, Jan. 5, 1854. No
return.
J. J. Sergeant to N. W. Jones, Jan. 5, 1854. No return.
Isaac N. Ford to M. T. Hampton, Jan. 7, 1854. No return.
Aaron Gailor to Delila Baird, Jan. 12, 1854. Calvin
R. Barron, J.P. (Jan. 12, 1854).
J. L. Jones to Sarah Williams, Jan. 14, 1853. F. P.
McNew, J.P. (Jan. 15, 1854).
Noah Holt to Milly Lawson, Jan. 23, 1854. Calvin R.
Barron, J.P. (Jan. 24, 1854).
James R. Skeen to Armelda Owens, Jan. 29, 1854. Calvin
R. Barron, J.P. (Jan. 29, 1854).
Eli Shelton to J. E. Smith, Feb. 3, 1854. No return.
Andrew C. Baird to Martha J. Gibson, Feb. 9, 1854.
Calvin R. Barron, J.P. (Feb. 9, 1854).
Isaac Sanders to Lucinda Geaslow, Jan. 5, 1854. No
return.

Brock (cont.)
  Martha 64, 71
  Sarah 12
  William 65, 71
Brogain, Louisa 13
Brogan, Alvis 32
  Asa 41
Brooks, Andrew 35
  B. 6
  Calvin 17
  Catharine 31
  Elizabeth 16, 34, 83
  Elizabeth Ann 47
  Geo. W. 34
  George 62, 68
  Gideon 9
  Jennetter 40
  John H. 33
  Levi 35
  Mahala 53
  Mary J. 35
  Nancy 2, 9
  Nathaniel 43
  Pertilly 29
  Preston 31
  Sarah A. 38
  Susanah 7
  Thomas 62, 68
  Thos. 31
  Traves (?) 14
  Vina 35
Brosswhite, Mary 50
Broughton, O. P. 53
Brown, Benjamin H. 60, 66
  Christiana 72
  David 82
  Diana 78
  E. J.
  Eleanor 76
  Eli 89
  G. W. 76
  Hamilton 74
  Henry A. 8
  James 36
  Joseph D. 79
  Julia A. 20
  Levy 74
  Nancy 50, 78
  Nelly 79
  Rebecca 49
  Saml. 87
  Samuel 47
  Thomas 52
  Vestia 76
  William 37
  Wm. 74
Brownlow, Franky 6
Broyles, Aaron 58, 82
  Elizabeth 73
  Lucinda 72
  Nancy 85, 86
  Samuel 85
  William 59, 65
Bruce, Nancy 74
  Olive 77
  Trifany (?) 13
  William 48
  Willis 84
Bruden (?), Tennessee 5
Bruer (?), Silvey 33
Bruice (?), Jesse 11
Brummet, Elizabeth 44
Brummett, Wm. 82
Brummit, Campbell 31
  Sarah 26
Brusten, Emaley 38
Bruster, 1
Bryant, A. J. 86

Bryant (cont.)
  Abel 74
  Candia 71
  Elizabeth 58
  Francis F. 82
  George 49
  Isaac 82
  Joel 83
  John 49, 82
  Mary 81
Buchanan, John A. 13
Buck, Burton 61, 68
  William 22
  Wm. 22
Buckhanan, Sarah 15
Buice (?), E. 25
Bullard, Boyer 33
  C. B. 3
  Joseph H. 35
  Nancy 30
  Polly Ann 25
  Susan 11
Bullock, Aaron 79
  Hannah 75
  Mary 53
  Susan 91
Bully, Philip M. 21
Bunch, Elizabeth 16
  Isaac 54
  Joseph 12
  Sindney 43
  Tabitha 35
Bundran (see also Herrall),
  Rachel 14
Bundren, Arrena (?) 3
  Elizabeth 18
  Patsy 33
Burch, Bezeet (?) 12
  Elizabeth J. (?) 17
  John 10
  Mary 31
  Reuben 22
Burchett, Benjamin 24
  James D. 23
  Sarah 24
Burchfield, H. 27
  Henry A. 15
  Jeremiah 37
  Martain 11
Burchill, Martha 75
Burchitt, Ekils (?) 25
Burge, Preston 75
  Samuel 62, 68
Burgen, Belenda 13
Burk, Andrew J. 87
  James 13
  Mary A. 33
Burket, James 42
  Mary A. 41
  Ralph 42
  William 30
Burnet, Allen 8
Burns, Nancy Jane 31
  Polly 38
  Sarah 19
Burrass, William 81
Burris, Bluford 63, 70
Burriss, Elijah 51
  Elizabeth 79
  Henry 59, 65
Burton, Ada 76
  Polla 19
  Rebecca 62, 68
  William 20
Bush, Enoch 3
Bussel, Matthew 1
Bussell, Charles 3
Bussle (?), Bird 12

Bussle (cont.)
  Charles 17
Butcher, Elisha 17
  Elonza D. 38
  Jas. 2
  Joseph 1
  Mary E. 39
Butlar, Meriah 83
Butler, Elrina 91
Butter, John M. 90
Butram, Wesley 75
Cabirth, Jas. 67
  Jos. 61
Cade, Sinclar 8
Cadel, Mariah 20
Cadell, William 72
Cadle, Drueiller (?) 21
  Green B. 34
  Julia Ann 35
  Mark 2
  Martin 1
  Mary Ann 8
Cailor, Elizabeth 42
Cain, Ann 60, 67
  Francis E. 83
  Hester Ann 76
  Isa 52
  John S. 41
  Martha 53
  Mary E. 87
  Minerva 58, 65
  Nancy Y. 87
  Nathaniel D. 14
  Perlina (?) 18
  Tempy (?) A. 13
  William 77
Calar (?), Sarah 13
Calestane (?), Jane 17
Callaham (?), L. 26
Calline, Salla 19
Calon, Jane A. 39
Calone, Vina 37
Camier (?), Eliza 14
Camin (?), E. J. 25
Campbell, A. 20
  Adeline 42
  Barnet (?) 8
  Benjamin 13
  Darkey 16
  E. 22
  Eldridge 12
  Elizabeth 48, 49, 64,
    71
  Emily 43
  Emily A. 35
  George 10
  Jackson 62, 68
  James 15, 54
  James D. 87
  Jas. 67
  Jas. D. 56
  John 42, 64, 71, 81
  Joseph 53, 72
  Lak 50
  Levisa 20
  Louisa 8
  Lucinda 84
  Lucretia 43
  Lucy Ann 31
  Mary Ann 38
  Rachel 84
  Sarah 60, 66
  Susan J. 87
  Tom N. 50
  William 58
  Wm. 74
Camran, William 40
Canada, Martin 55

95

Candell, John 81
Candler, Sarah Malissa 63,
  69
Candy, Wm. H. 3
Cane, Eli D. 27
  Hugh 7
  Mary 19
Cannon, Jackson 51
  James 49
  Polley 50
  William 35
Canon, Polly 75
Canter, Elizabeth 48
  William J. 11
Cape (see also Cope), David
  27
Capps, David B. 11
  Leor (?) 30
  Wm. 44
Carden, Joseph 37
Carder, Richard 9
Cardwell, David 42
  Nancy 21
  Obediah 11
  Reuben 20
Carell, Jas. 24
Carey, Martha 88
Carmac, Isaac 1
Carmack, Abraham 36
  Isaac 1
  Levi 32
  Mary Ann 9
  William 32
Carmon, John 39
Carnard (?), Elisabeth (?)
  27
Carnutt, Jno. M. 70
  Lucinda 64, 70
  Preston 49
Carpenter, Anderson 15
  Jane 5
  Lotty 3
  Malisa 20
  Mary 44
  Nancy O. (?) 34
  Susanah 20
Carpentr (?), Anderson 19
  Elizabeth H. 21
Carpentur (?), Arminda 16
Carr, James 35
  James M. 18
  John H. 19, 42
  Manerva 40
  Martha J. 41
  Rhoda 10
  Rich J. 87
Carrol, John J. 35
Carroll, Alexander 64, 70
  Catharine 64, 71
  Henry 39
  Hickman 57
  Jno. 72
  Mary Ann 61, 67
  Nancy 74
  Samuel 57
  Sarah 1, 18
  William 4, 6
  William H. 39
  Wm. 88
Carrolle, Sarah 59, 65
Carson, James 76
  Margaret 50
Cartar, Georg (?) 21
Carter, Alexander 9
  Benjamin S. (?) 16
  Catharine 57, 59, 65
  Eliza 53
  Eliza Jane 21

Carter (cont.)
  James 86
  Joseph 33
  Lavina 18
  Nancy 16
  Nancy L. 41
  (?), Sarah 24
  Sterling B. 29
  William 56
Carver, Delila 52
  James 52
  William 72
Case, Elizabeth 62, 68
Casey, Leonard 83
  Simpson 43
Cassel (?), J. S. 23
Cassle, John R. 7
Catterel (?), Mary 14
Cauk (?), Margret 23
Cawood, John 15
Caynard, James 29
Caywood, Anna 35
  Barbara 16
Cazort, Wiley 34
Cears, Martha J. 87
Cemore, Sarah 10
Chaden (?), Spencer 13
Chadoins (see also
  Shadonias),Andrew
  73
Chadwell, David 42
  Mary Ann 42
  Pleasant 1
  Sarah 16
  Susan 3
  Susanah 22
Chadwich (?), Charaty (?)
  28
  John Y. 31
Chadwick, Josiah 29
Chambers, Daniel 62
  Danl. 68
  Elizabeth 52
  Lucy 54
  Nancy 72
  Thomas 49
Champion, Wm. A. 86
Champman, Joel 55
Chandoin, Eliza S. 80
  Francis 58
Chany (?), John 23
Chapman, Angeline 55
  James 72
  Jno. 60, 66
  John 22
  Joshua H. 18
  Laner 66
  Lanor 60
  Martha J. 79
  Nancy 85
  Polly 71
  Robert 82
  Sarah 84
  Thomas 86
  Wm. 84
Chavis, Jane 51
  John 63, 69
  Sarah 51
  Sterling 86
  Susan 53
Cheek, Catharin 8
  Granville (?) A. 6
  Nelson 33
  Robert 39
Chesnut, Franklin 35
Chesterson (see also
  Kesterson),
  Jno. C. 71

Chick, Elizabeth 36
  Jane 41
  Jefferson 15
  William 21
Childers, William 49
Childress, Elisha 58
  Thomas 73
Chittam, Welsey 42
Chittan, James 35
Chittum, William 35
Chitwood, Andrew 52
  Eliza 79
  Elizabeth 79
  Jonothan C. 82
  Patsy 52
  Pleasant 55
  Sephrona 80
Chumbley, Elender 44
  Milley 42
Chumbly, Emily 41
  Malinda 23
  Sarah 2
Chumley, Eliza 14
  William 28
Claiborn, Ota T. 56
Clapp, Elisabeth 35
Clark, Elisha 28
  John 76
  Leftrage 18
  Mary Jane 85
  Nancy 54
  Riley 41
Clarkson, Martha 15
  William 15
Clarrick (?), Thomas 13
Clause, Nancy 3
Claxton, Henry 14
Clevelan, William M. 42
Cliborn, Elizabeth 85
Cliborne, Ota T. 64, 70
Cloud, B. F. 25, 42
  Benjamin 12
  Charlota J. 35
  Elnathon 30
  John 42
  Louisa 22
  Lucinda 80
  Mariah 20
  Nancy 3
  Orleana 36
  (?), Polley 20
  William P. 78
Clouse, Adam 8
  John 7
  William 22
Cocks, Nancy 32
Code, Samuel D. 10
  Sarah 10
Cole, B. H. M. 39
  George 10
  Isreal 36
  John 72
  Margret 29
Coleman, Sterling G. 23
Coles, Isral 38
Collensworth, Coventan 3
  Elzera 2
Collins, Abadiah 7
  Alexr. 8
  Anderson 9
  Arthur 33
  Brison 14
  Catharine 21
  Crispin 14
  Jesse 2
  Margaret 8
  Mary Ann 18

Collins (cont.)
    Nathan 14
    Prudy (?) 14
    R. 44
    Stewart 21
    Susan 82
    Thos. 30
Collinsworth, Wm. F. 44
Colson, John C. 17
    Rebecca 42
    Sarah 14
    Thomas 41
Colten, Elizabeth M. 52
    Isaac W. 52
    Nancy W. 54
Colwell, Samuel 38
Comer, Mary 78
    Nancy 89
Conner, Jno. 3
    William 50
Cook, Ann Jane 31
    Catharine 92
    Elbert Rice 41
    M. A. 28
    Michael 75
    Reuben M. 33
    Robt. 86
    Tilitha 73
    William 74
Cookard (?), Polly 12
Cooper, Alias 50
    Catharine 54
    Eli 73
    Elizabeth 84
    Ephraim 51
    Fountain 79, 82
    George 47
    Henry 90
    Hulda 55, 57
    Huldah 51
    James 76
    Jane 72
    Joseph N. 73
    Mahala 53
    Martha N. 85
    Peter 62, 68, 72
    Silvester 92
    Sophia 73
    Wm. 85
Cope (see also Cape),
    David 27
Copeland, A. C. 91
Cosier, Elijah 58
Costin, Rhoda 54
Cottral, Prsley 19
Cottrell, V. A. 42
Covey, Charles 39
Covy, Mary 2
Cox, Ann 54
    Daniel 48
    Eliza 82
    Hiram 90
    James 61, 67
    Jesse 48
    Jno. 60, 66
    John 29
    Julyantha 77
    Lockey 61, 67
    Mary 21
    Nancy 50
    Peggy 39
    Priscilla 38
    Richard 77
    Susan 48
    Thomas 7
    William 6, 7, 25
Crabtree, Absolom 72
    Elizabeth 7

Crabtree (cont.)
    Fereby 10
    Isaac 77
    James 82
    Richard 27, 39
    Sally 77
Crafford, Thos. 29
Crage, Sarah 27
Craig, Lucinda 48, 78
    Nancey 66
    Nancy 59
    Reubin 50
    Sarah 50, 88
Crank, Deborah 11
Crawford, Josiah 38
Creekmore (see also
    Crickmore),
    Anna B. 79
    Cintha 53
    David F. 60, 66
    Francis 48
    Jane 56, 61, 67
    Mary 50
    Sarah 59, 65
    Thomas B. 82
Cress, Catherine 39
Crickmore (see also
    Creekmore),
    Anna B. 79
    Cintha 53
    Thomas B. 82
Crisp, John W. 22
Crockett, Elizabeth J. 34
Croley, Jane 78
    Nancy 79
    Sampson 87
    Wymer 79
Cromwell (?), A. F. 20
Cross, Caswell 78
    Emily 79
    Jno. 71
    Larkin W. 73
    Martha 77
Crosswhite, C. L. 92
Crouch, Josiah 73
Crowley, Ann 49
Crowly, L. B. 62, 69
Croxdale (?), Nancy 26
Crumbley, F. 21
    Polley 28
Crumbly, Belenda 2
Crutchfield, Susan 2
Culbirth, Joseph 61, 68
Cumber (?), Rachael 7
Cummins, Sarilda 58
Ciningham, Alley 37
    Prior 19
Cunningham, J. 21
    James P. 40
    William 17
Cup, George W. 9
Cupp, Daniel 24
    Jacob 36
    Polly 11
    Ransam 5
Curnut, Nancy J. 47
Curnutt, Caroline 82
    Polly 75
Cusley, Polly A. 36
Cyraus, Frances 12
Dabay, Francis 75
Dabney, Angeletta 80
    Cornelius 54
    James 58
Dabny, Alley 74
    Elizabeth 92
Daey (?), Ollely (?) 33
Dagley, Amanda 56

Dagley (cont.)
    John 80
    Mary 78
    Moses 47
    Sarah 54
    William 56
Dagly, James 80
    Martha 81
Daiel, Henry 26
Danahoo, Mary Ann 14
Daniel, William 29
Daugherty, William 53
Davenport, Ezra 63, 69
David, Zachariah 47
Davis, Edmon 22
    Elen 42
    (?), Elizabeth 18, 40
    Emily 9, 18, 57
    Francis 91
    George 74
    Heston 24
    Hugh 80
    Jacob 42
    James H. 2, 85
    John 89,
    John A. 15
    Johnson 30
    Joseph 60, 66
    Louisa 28
    Lucindy 13
    (?), M. 24, 28
    Martha 29, 36, 43
    Mary 6
    Nancy 90
    Patey 32
    R. E. 86
    Sarah Ann 50
    Susan 56
    Susannah 10
    Tempy (?) 19
    Thomas B. 91
    Walter 13
    Wm. B. 60, 66
Day, Charley M. 17
    Eliza 18
    Elizabeth 5
    Enas 11, 21
    Lewis 10
    Louisa 29
    Lucindy 49
    Nancy 42
    Ransam (?) 17
    Rebecca 47
    Sarah 9, 30
Dean, Thomas 72
    William E. 14
    William P. 41
Deans, Christopher 31
    William 33
Dearnal, Wm. 2
Deas, Irvin 73
Debby, Ann 57
Dees, Rhoda 18
Delap, Rebecca 51
Delk, Didaman 55
    Gilbert 77
    Nancy 59, 66
Denny, John 30
Dessett, Robert 91
Devault, Adaline 37
    George 32
    Manervy 39
    Margret 44
Dewel, Peter 53
Dial, Martha 52, 83
    Polly 71
Dibbley, Andrew 54
Dickinson, Benjamin 38

Faulkner (cont.)
Nancy 59, 60, 61, 65,
66, 68, 87
Ruth 83
Susan 50
Faust, Daniel 52
Felps, Catherine 41
Fernay (?), James F. 18
Fernell, Eliza 34
Ferrel, Catharin 12
Ferrell, Amanda 34
Ferrile, Emily 8
Field (?), Effy 4
Fields, Abner 25
Edwards 39
Elender 19
George 28
Fips, Peter 22
Flatford, Arlina 88
David 87
John 48, 78
Levan 76
Lyrena 76
Fleming, Polly 62, 68
S. C. 91
Sarah K. 81
Flemming (?), Marcus 16
Fletcher (?), John 29
Lena 43
Mary Ann 17
Sally 7
Foley, Greenberry 49
Follon, P. J. P. 59, 65
Foly, Green 86
Forber, George 7
Ford, Ann 54
Catharline 83
Green B. W. 5
Greenberry 2
Isaac 76
Isaac N. 92
James 54
James T. 33
John C. 83, 89
Lavina 5
Leah 81, 87
Lucinda 36
Martha 63, 69
Polly 57
Sarah 74
William B. 33
Fordy (?), James 19
Foreman, H. L. 53
Forester, Alecy 88
Forgerson, Elisabeth (?)
24
John 6
Fortiner, Sarah 12
Fortner, Jesse 3
Sarah 11
Foster, Moris 54
Fostnez, Preston 8
Fouse, Nancy 48
Foust, Christopher 54
Daniel 47
Fouster, Louisa 90
Fox, Artela 90
Elizabeth 74, 91
Hannah 76
Joseph 72
Martha 85
Prudy 77
William 88
Fraser, Sally 81
Frasher, Zilpha J. 38
Freeman, Jane 24
Rebecca 5
Freemon, Celia 2

Friar, Rebecca 39
Thos. 33
Timothy 15
Frier, Abigal 33
Frior, Daniel 44
Fritts, Henry 24
Frock, Susan 81
Frost, William S. 28
Fugate, Eli 10
Hendly 15
Lucy Jane 39
Rachel 8
Fulks, David 16
Fullington, Eliza 89
M. J. 85
Fulp, Jane 11
Fulps, Abigail (?) 5
Cyntha 36
Rebecca 38
Fults, Frederick 27
Orlena J. 29
Furgason, Lucy J. 44
Furgerson, Sarah 38
Furry, Hiram 12
Margaret 7, 8
Mary 4
Randolph 2
Sarah 2
Fusian, Elizabeth 4
Gad, John S. 84
Gailer, Thomas 80, 82
Gailor, Aaron 92
Gains, William 16
Galeher, Tabitha 75
Garland, Ann 49
(?), Lewis 19
Garner, James 37
Garnett, Matilda 38
Garrett, Robert 44
Gatliff, J. W. 89
Milton 58
Moses 58
Gatlin, Elizabeth 54
Gaylor, Christopher 84
Ezanas 91
Geacolf (?), Jesse J. 5
Geasley, Polly 43
Geaslow, Lucinda 92
Geesly, Windy 91
Gentry, Adison 70
Cynthia 73
Elizabeth 5
George, Ellis 33
Sela 44
Gibbs, Carroll 24
Wm. 19
Gibert, Polly 6
(?), Susannah 11
Gibson, Drury D. 30
Hannah 52
Isaac 43
Isom 17
James 32
Martha J. 4, 92
Nancy 82
(?), Saviour (?) 13
Stephen 60, 66
William F. 18
William R. 14
Gideans, Martha 1
Gilbert, Abejah 4
D. I. 21
Haywood 54
Nancy 6, 21
Thos. 32
(?), William 11
Gipson, Mastin 29
Givin, George 4

Glanden, Silas 6
Glander, Manda 83
Glandon, Clarissa 56
Glenn, Barbary 54
Mary A. 34
Matison 53
Robert 16
Gloscake, Plooy 73
Goad, John 49
Goforth, James 13
Preston C. 13, 23
Sarah Matilda 11
Goin, Dusta 55
E. 25
Elizabeth 59, 65
Isham 85
Martha 88
Mary 74
Rachel 54
Susan 88
Wm. 64, 71
Goinbral, Drueiller 20.
Going, Cass (?) Ann 15
Jno. L. 15
Goins, Elender E. 41
Eli 39
Jane 32
Mohaby (?) 22
Gooden, Ezekiel 13
Manda 34
Goodin, E. D. 89
Ezekiel 34
Gossadge, Joel 72
Gowin, Ama 32
Anna 40
Isaac 7
Martha J. 2
Nelson 6
Sturling 6
Gowins, Nancy 28
Uriah 28
Grabill, Isaac 36
Grace, R. 28
Rosamial (?) 10
Seperia (?) 15
William 21
Gracelclose, Catharin 13
Graham, Eliza J. 4
Hugh 32
Jane 27, 29
M. A. 27
Margaret E. 7
William 32
Willie 58
Graier, Benjamin 55
Grammer, John W. 31
Grant, Harvey 83
Iris 54
Rebecca 88
Rufus 64, 71
Graves, Elizabeth 7, 60,
66
John 8, 20
Mary 47
Pleasant 81
Rebecca 80
Sally 8
Sarah 8, 58
Gray, Edmond 56
Gabella 53
Hannah 85
Isabella 53
James 63, 70, 85
John E. R. 3
Joseph 56
Martha 51, 53
Polley 59
Polly 30, 65

Gray (cont.)
　Robert 51
　Sarah 50
　Thomas W. 84
Greece, Sarah 47
Green, Eliza 1
　James D. 17
　John 17, 22
　Louisanna 39
　Lucy 38
　M. E. 53
　Nancy 62, 68
　Nancy E. 42
　Richard 71
　Sarah 83
　T. 35
　William 2
Greer, Jane 76
　John T. 91
　Manervy 14
　Permelia 6
　Robert 23
Gresly (?), Rebecca 40
Griffey, Lydia 91
Griffiers, Wm. 82
Griffin, Harriet 76
Griffy, Martin 79
　Thomas 63, 69
Grigery, Susan 28
Grimes, Barbary 52
　Betsy Ann 39
　Henry C. 62, 68
　Isaac A. 2
　James 9, 20
　John 22, 60, 66
　John M. 32
　Mary 37
　(?), Polly 9
　Sarah 31
Grocecloce. Anny 18
Groseclose (?), Adam 8
Gross, Edmund A. 80
　Hannah H. 84
　Jacob W. 88
　John 91
　Kitty 89
　Martha 90
　Polly 73
　Sarah 63
Grubb, Jno. 22
Guffe, Elizabeth 78
Guim, Isaac 37
Guinn, Martha F. 44
Guthery, Hannah 17
Guthry, William 5
Hacker, John 39
Hackler, Brackler 87
　Jesse 49
　Rosannah 91
Haggare, Susan D. 77
Hail, Camfret 1
　Susan 2
Hale, Eliza 72
　George 89
　Kellis J. 85
Haley, Dornelia 52
Hall, Elisha 32
　John G. 88
　John W. 32
　Mary 61, 67
　Nancy 7
　Pulasky 78
　S. 24
Hambin, Mary 83
Hamblin, Emaline 36
　George 88, 89
　Juda 26
　Leroy 26

Hamblin (cont.)
　Peziah 50
Hamby, Abram E. 79
　Rebecca 73
Hamelton, G. W. 24
　George 35
　Joshua 2
　Julia 41
　Martha 11
　Nancy 4
　Polly 6
　Sarah 5
　Wm. 4
Hammack, Becky 27
Hammock, Betsy 9
　Sterling 16
Hammons, Moab (?) 11
Hamons, Elender 41
　Sally 27
　William 41
Hampton, Anna 77
　Joel A. 75
　M. T. 92
　Mary J. 74
　Reubin 57
　Sarah 61, 67
Hamly, Ivory F. 58
Hancock, James 78
Hanks, Mary Ann 60, 66
Hansard, Abner C. 13
Hardy, Mary 42
　Susan M. 32
Harlis, James 31
Harmon, Aaron 64, 71
　Andrew J. 17
　Delana 77
　Hiram 91
　Jacob 85
　Martha J. 90
　Nancy 79
　Nancy Jane 76
　Susannah 80
Harnes, John 53
Harness, David 52
　James 51
　Margaret 50
　Samuel 54
　Thomas 74
Harp, Delany 77
　James 43
　Joshua 90
Harpe, Benager 34
　Leonard G. 36
　Mary J. 40
　Richard 34
　Richard H. 38
Harral, Wilmirth 12
Harrel, Noah 42
Harrell, A. W. 36
　Alexander 26
　Margaret 3
　Phoeby 22
　Robert 41
　Sylvester 35
　William 91
Harris (?), Anny 12
　E. J. 21
　Leah 79, 82
　Lucinda 59, 65
　Martin 6
　Meeley (?) 13
　Patsy 85
　Samuel 44
　Wm. P. 25
Harrison, Lucinda 89
　Rachal 37
Harry, Henry F. 14
Hart, Daniel 74

Hart (cont.)
　George 86
　Polly 86
　Rachel 4
　Talitha 63, 69
　Thomas 88
　Wm. C. 82
Hase, William 38
Hatfield, Adam 6
　Amelia A. 79
　Andrew 43
　Anna 80
　Biddy 63, 70
　Calvin 71
　Davis 49
　E. 22
　Elizabeth 53, 82
　Francis 89
　Henry 9
　James 85
　Jeminia 15
　John 53
　Lynch 7
　Manervy 15
　Margaret 72
　Mary 26
　Moses 31
　Polly 81, 90
　Ralph 14
　Thomas 43
　(?), Walter (?) 22
Hatmaker, Danl. 90
　Eliza 88, 92
　Henderson 80
　Jacob 81
　James 52, 73, 81
　Malekeer 57
　Nancy 72
　Sally 73
　William 57
　Wm. 91
Havely (?), Charles H. 27
　(?), Mary (?) 22
Havlaen (?), Nathaniel S.
　　37
Hawkins, Eli 19
Hawley (?), M. B. 24
Hays (?), Elizabeth 16
Hayslip, David 74
　Henry 82
　Robert 56
Hayse, William R. 37
Hayter, Elizabeth 63, 69
Hazelwood (?), Emaley 22
Hazs, Jos. 22
Head, Harrison 82
Heath, Elizabeth 58
Heather, Anthony 50
Heatherly, A. 74
　Andrew 50
　John 80
　Luisa Jane 55
　Martha 78
　Mary 57
　Rhoda 76
　Sarilda 48
Heatoh, Elizabeth 51
Heeny (see also Keeny),
　　John L. 77
Heirs, John 76
Hellon (?), Arnold (?) 19
Helton, Caroline 14
　Emaline 37
Henby, Elizabeth 54
Henderson, Adaline 23
　Carolein 11
　Christian 3
　Clementina N. 35

Henderson (cont.)
Martha 87
Martha Ann 38
Mary 55
Perlina 23
Polly 19, 78
William G. 48
Hendrix, Molinda 9
Henly, John 90
Henry, Lavina 64, 70
Henson, Tapley J. 59, 65
Herell (?), M. E. 22
Herllon, Mathew A. 29
Hermen, James 30
Hernen (?), Baley 29
Heron, Caloway 64, 70
Herral, Elizabeth 15
Herrall (see also Bundran)
James C. 14
Rachel 14
Herrel, Matilda (?) 21
Herrell, Elender 32
Elvira (?) M. 24
Levica 24
Levisa 24
Mariah 42
Mariah J. 44
Montgomery 29
Herrin, Armstead 72
Pryor 55, 56
Sarah 77
Herring, S. E. 48
Herron, Phebe 78
Hetton, Alson (?) 14
Hewith, Clara 75
James 56
Hibbard, Permelia 77
Hickey, Pamelia 72
Hickox, Mary C. 60, 66
Hicks (see also Hix)
Edwin 62, 68
Elizabeth 55, 62, 69
James M. 38
Jane 20
John 19, 27
Martha 17
Orlena 39
Pheby 37
Rebecca 37
Higgs, Sanford 52
Westley 71
Higs, Elizabeth 85
Hilhite, John Wiley 57
Hill, Alexander 34
Barthena 7
Clarwell 88
Clary 26
Edward N. 20
Elvis 32
Haisel (?) 31
Henry (Jr.) 77
John 87
Kemuel 83
Lindsay 48
Livel 88
Lockey 84
Mahaley 30
Margaret 76
Mariel 29
Mary 91
Oliver 50
Parley 82
S. 22
Sanford 86
Timmy 80
Hilton, Euminta J. 78
Mary 90
Nancy 88

Hinshilder (?), Matthias
(?) 17
Hinson, Elizabeth 86
Jno. 61, 67
Hinton, Nancy A. 43
Hitch, John 59, 65
Hix (see also Hicks)
Jesse 47
Orlena 39
Rebeckey 25
Rosey 74
Hobbs, Ann 31
Elisabeth Jane 23
R. 33
Hodge, Jane 18
Rebecca 3
Wm. 20
Hodges, Beste A. 41
Elijah 33
Elisabeth 33
Fielding 33
Henry C. 39
John 37
Louisa 26, 32
Mary 14
Pleasant M. 36
Rachel M. 40
Sampson 63, 70
Hogan, Charity H. 86
Holden, W. 34
Washington 33
Hollan, Elisha 36
Lucinda 37
Peter 37
Hollensworth, Madison 2
Hollin, Barbra 28
Hollingsworth, E. 85
Emily M. 84
H. 91
Hollon, Nancy 34
Holloway, Joseph 90
Holt, Amariah 61, 67
George 91
James 65
James C. 71
Kindruk (?) 21
Lavesa 15
Martha 77, 78
Noah 92
Holton (?), Lewrittey (?)
21
Mary 41
Holy, Matilda 86
Honeycut, Austin 4
Honeycutt, Catherine 52
Cintha 55
Elizabeth 5, 9
Hardy 64, 70
James M. 41
Hooper, Daniel 44
Jessee 1
Malinda 17
Wilbourne 42
Hope, Eliza 59, 66
Mary 84
Martha T. 91
Ralph Izard 78
Robt. R. 60, 67
Sarah Ann 77
Hoper, Louisa 87
Hopkins, Arthor (?) 18
Bilenda (?) 17
Catharin J. 11
Elisa (?) 23
Elizabeth 27
Isaac 15
J. R. 23
James M. 17

Hopkins (cont.)
Jobies (?) 27
Mary Ann 15
N. 28
Noah 27
Polly 27
Stephen 7
Stuphin (?) 15
Hopper, Ann 32
Frankey 38
Jeremiah 5
(?), Jesse 23
Loucinda 6
Nancy 23
Rachel 32
Sarah (?) Jane 9
Susannah 32
William H. 40
Hopson, Harid (?) 30
Harrod 33
James 20
Richard 22
Syntha A. 15
William 15, 33
Hornis (?), William 19
Hose, Ransam (?) 24
Hoskins, E. 25
Elisabeth 25
Elizabeth 18
Esther (?) 8
Heram 1
Hiram 19
Hoult, Lucy 3
Householder, Mary 17
Housholder, A. J. 20
Houskins, Martha J. 82
Housley, Caroline 81
Elizabeth 78
Pleasant 78
Hously, Sally 81
Houston, John 29
Louisa 44
Russilla Ann 43
(?), Wm. 9
Howel, Elizabeth 42
(?), Neoma 27
Howerton, Catharine 16
Howett, Mary 54
Hubbard, Andrew 15
Jesse 51
Hubbert, Samuel 21
Hubboard, Allen 51
Huckaby, (Com.) 76
Elisha 76
Ousley 53
William 51
Huddleston, Anna 39
Benjamin L. 38
David 6, 40
Effy 7
Flemman (?) 16
Wm. 91
Hudson, Elijah 17
Huff, Cynthia A. 78
Jourdon 90
Lavina 58
Leah 86
Sarah 36
Huffaker, Sally 4
Huley, Polly 71
Humphreys, H. 88
Huneycutt, Moses 10
Hunnacutt, Alvis 38
Hunnicutt, Malinda 23
Hunt, F. F. 59, 65
Hunter, (Squire)
Alcy 76
Eve 14

Longmire (cont.)
Louisa J. 83
Mahala 57
Mahaley 48
Marcellus 86
Nancy 63, 69
William 80
Longworth, George 30
Matilda 33
Sarah 41
Loops, Margaret 57
Lorton (?), John 16
Loson, Rachel 43
Louden, Francis Jane 36
Louis, William 42
Louthr (?), Jas. 26
Lovate, Susanah 86
Lovedy, Margaret 54
Lovely, Anna 81
Mary Ann 76
Loves (?), Esom 18
Lovett, David 55
Francis 75
Jesse 48, 81
Lucinda 53
Sarah 61, 67
Lovit, Balantine 60, 66
Lovitt, John 77
Low, L. D. 71
Lucinda 74
Lowe, J. M. 19
Loy, Sarah 86
Loyd, Alexander 56
Andrew 53
Matilda 56
Luallen (see also Lewellen
& Lewyellen)
Matthew 55
Polly 62, 68
Vicia 62, 68
Lucker (?), Lewis 40
Luits, John 84
Lukes, Susan 72
Lumpkin, Bethina 72
Lumpkins, Absolum 74
James 53
Joseph 89
M. 86
Lunday, John 17
Lussey, Rachael 9
Luster (?), Henry P. 8
Robert C. 41
Luttrell, Dianna 39
Lynch, Barberry 41
David 17
Evaline 42
Jeptha 28
Jesse 5
John 27, 43
Lucinda 41
Manerva 39
Margret Elviny (?) 25
Nancy 5, 17
Nelson 48
Phebe 7
Respy 3
Sarah 5
Sidney 75
V. W. 87
William W. 31
Lyngar, James H. 14
Mabane, Susan 31
Mackin, Michael 82
Macmand, Susan 83
Madden, Sarah J. 79
Maddin, Elizabeth 83
Sarah 91
Maddy, Mahala 2

Maddy (cont.)
Sarah 1
Maden, Anjaline 43
Mariah M. 60
Moriah M. 66
Nancy 29
Maffort, Delilah 48
Mahon, Alfred 87
Malaby, William 79
Malicoat (?), Anderson 18
Sarah 63, 69
Mallicoat, Emaline 37
Francis 51
Polly 82
Simeon 82
Malone, John 18
Lucinda 61, 67
Manley, D. M. 57
Mannon, Mark 30
(?), Nancy 14
Maples, Betsy 4
James 44
Wm. 9
Marcum (?), Alford 24
Arthur 59, 66
(?), Elizabeth Jane 21
G. W. 66
George 25
H. W. 60
Lack G. 36
M. C. 20
Mary A. H. 13
Nancy 17
Peter 44
Roday (?) H. 23
Wm. C. 73
Marcus, Lavina 50
Margraves, Margaret 40
Mary 11
Marian (?), Elijah 21
Marion (?), A. 24
Marler (?), Mary 21
Marlo, Mauel 90
Marlom, Thomas 39
Marlow, Catherine 49, 52
Elizabeth 87
Finly 75
John 11
Reubin 83
Marrs, Lucinda H. 85
S. C. 75
Marshall, James M. 63, 69
Nancy Ann 87
Martain, James M. 11
Viney 8
Marteal, William 17
Martin, Charles G. 48
Elizabeth 57, 73
James 57
Lanij 65
Mariah 73
Marian J. E. 37
Martha Ann 25
Mary 84
Rebecca 47
Sampson 51
Susan 60, 66
Masan, Delpha 27
Sarah 10
Masengale, Calvin 37
Maser, Michael 8
Masingil, K. 26
Mason, Caroline 30
Elvisy (?) 19
Mary Ann 4
Mary E. (see also
Moore, Mary E.) 61,
67

Mason (cont.)
Nancy 21
Massa, Jacob 44
Massengale, K. 26
Massey, John 44
Massingale, Matthew 91
Master, George 74
Mathes, Jno. D. 4
Thomas 10
Matthews, Sarah 80
Mattox, Nancy 9
Maupin, Amos 91
Henry 76
Love 91
Maria 86
Mary M. 89
Sarah 51
V. C. 61, 67
Maurae, Levisa (?) 12
Mayatt, Peter 48
Mayers, Abraham 32
Mayes, Ann 35
Mays (?), Jemina 14
Jerrice (?) D. 10
John 16
Martha Jane 12
(?), Nancy 13
Ralph 75
Susan 75
Susanah 30
Thos. 25
Maze, Nancy 85
Wm. D. 86
Mcafee, Moses 20
McAffee (?), James 23
McAmis, A. A. 7
McAnalla, Manila 31
Mcanally (?). S. 22
McAnelly, Hamelton 10
James 10
Mcanlush (?), William A.
A. (?) 28
McAnn Peggy 75
McBee, Burton 33
Calvin 28
Claiborne 7
Emeline 28
Ganeum 38
Granville 32
Houston 34
Sally 1
Samuel 38, 40
William C. 6
Wm. 39
McCall, George 84
L. N. 62, 69
McCankey (?), S. 24
McCard (?), Janes T. (?)
18
McCarroll, James 90
McCarter, Thomas 85
McCarty, Daniel 76
Elizabeth 48
Frances 60
James 10
Lavina 51
Malinda 59, 65
Mary 72
Pelina Jane 54
Phebe 89
McCidy, Clender 60, 66
McClain, Susan 60, 66
McClane, Thomas 2
McClary, Preston 52
Susan 56
William 53
McColloch, James A. 61,
67

McConkuy (?), Mary 19
McConnel, A. 8
McCoy, Milly Ann 77
McCrary, Cleveland 40
  George 40
  Jane 15
  Louisa 27
  N. 18
McCulley, Elizabeth 57
  Sally 59
  Sarah 51
McCully, James 83
  Job 90
  Nancy 60, 66
  Sally 65
McCullough, Samuel 14
McCullum, James 30
McDonald, Allen 81
  Feriby 53
  James 62, 69
  Lucinda 56
  Nancy 47
  Samuel 74
McDonel, Mathew C. 29
McDy, Martha 48
McElkins, Mynatt 73
McFall, Monday 58
McFarland, Arthur 91
  Elizabeth 51, 62, 68
  Jane 51
  Rebecca 80
  William 32
Mcfarlin, Margaret 10
McGee, Dolley 54
  James 77
  Luckrisha (?) 24
McGlathlin, Elizabeth 87
McGloshlier, Nancy 53
McGoin 82
McGoingal, Henry 15
McHenry, Francis J. 6
  Wm. 4
McHone, Andrew 63, 69
Mckchan, Nancy (?) 3
McKee, Alford 91
  Patsey 90
McKeehan, John 91
  Thuray Ann 61
  Thursy Ann 67
Mckehan, Nancy 4
McKenny, James 43
McKinn, Nancy J. 86
McMahan, Permealy (?) 27
McMahon, John 38
Mcmakan, John 3
McMann, Nelly 59, 66
McMillion, Lidia 30
McMinn, Nelly 47
McNeal, William 6
McNeelence, Fanny 35
McNeely, John 88
  Polly 83
McNeil, Ann 13
  Jane 25
  Malenda 10
  William 41
McNew, Elizabeth 86
  Isaac 21
  Jno. 8
  John 87
  Martha Jane 7
  Sarah 31
  Wm. J. 22
McNielin (?), Margaret 12
McVay, Milley 34
McVey, Thirsa 39
McWilliams, Joseph 19
  William N. 38

Meader, Joseph 53
Meaders, James 48
  Lucy 58
  Lydia 73
Meadors, Elizabeth 60, 66
  George B. 78
  Jeremiah 50
  Sarah 61, 87
Meadows, Sarah 67
Mebane, Susan
Meeler, Surrena 3
Meelor, John 34
Meotor (?), William 12
Messer, Hiram 34, 35
Meyers, John 91
Meying, Phillip 51
Middleton, Nancy 42
Miles, Benjamin D. 9
Miller, A. 60, 66
  A. T. 49
  Andrew 51
  Daniel 78
  (?), David 9
  Eclid 52
  Elias 50
  Elizabeth 53, 85
  Elly Ann 51
  Emaley 30
  Esau 89
  Franklin 57, 81
  George W. 8
  H. G. 76
  Hannah 57
  Irena 55
  Isaac 22, 73
  Jackson 57
  James 50, 60, 66, 84
    90
  James Laugh 33
  John 50
  Julia 71
  Lavina 61, 68
  Malitha 82
  Margaret 91
  Martha 91
  Mary L. 48
  Nancy 81
  Payton 85
  Pleasant 7
  Polly 5
  (?), Russell 8
  Ruth 87
  S. 26
  Summerfield 56
  Susan 85
  Thomas 57
Millis, J. B. 21
Mills, Elizabeth 43
  Frankey I. (?) 39
  Henry 30
  James 7
  Reubin 22
  William 7
Milton, Elizabeth 79
  Nancy 89
  William 90
Mink, Sarah 36
Minks, Phelin 17
Minter (?), Landax (?) C.
  11
Minton (?), Catharine 13
  Elizabeth 23
  James 32
  John 15, 42
  Philip 40
  Samuel L. 44
  Vardamon 2
  William 36

Mitchel, Mary Ann 19
Mitchell, Manila 10
Mobley, Archibald 52
Molana (?), John 17
Moncy (?), John J. 31
Monday, America 64, 70
  Arch 63, 69
  William L. 43
Moner, Nicalis (?) 30
Monk, James M. 11
Montgomery, Clarissa 58
  Mary 11
  Rebecco 12
Moody, Margret K. 33
Moor, Eliza Jane 27
  Betty 23
  John 27
  Lucy 3, 4
  Mary 30
  Nancy A. 23
  Samuel 5
  Shadrick 22
  Tilman H. 41
Moore, Caroline 32
  Chastin (?) S. 9
  Elisabeth J. 34
  James W. 61, 67
  Joseph 14
  Lucinda 78
  Mary 2, 81
  Mary E. (see also Mason,
    Mary E.) 61
  Nathan H. 19
  Polley 52
  Wm. Ephrin 56
Mopin, Cinthy Ann 48
More, Arnelia 90
Morgan, Daniel 86
  George 87
  Nancy 55
  Preston 4
  Rebecca 62, 69
  Wm. 73
Morris, Delila 19
  Julia 25
Morton, James 48
Mosby, Sarah 26
Moser, Mahaley 30
Moses, Holley D. 63, 69
  Joshua 59, 65
  Louisa 72
  Susan A. 41
Mosier, John 50
  Rachel 64, 71
Moyer, Vincent 11
Moyers, Cany (?) 27
  H. (?) 8
  Hesakiah 37
  Joseph B. 13
  Joshua 43
  William 20
  Wm. N. 8
Mozier, Jacob 88, 92
  Nancy 79
Mulhos, A. I. 19
Mullens, Eldrege 34
Mullins, Nancy 51
Mullis, Elkana 90
Muncy, Lucy 2
Munday, Malissa 35
  William L. 41
Mundy, Pleasant C. 9
Murphy, Archibald 47
  John 56
  Leeby (?) Ann (?) 25
Murray, Alfred 52
  Elizabeth 57, 67
  Henderson 51

Murray (cont.)
John F. 81
Leah 62, 68
Marcum 73
Mary 50, 54
Sarah 81
William 73
Wilson 84
Murry, Anna 25
Edmund 43
Susan 91
Muzinger, LaFayette 76
Muzingo, Catherine 84
Myers, Carey 37
G. W. 44
John 16
Mynett, Andrew 2
Myres, Isham 26
Nance, Louisa Virginia 80
Polly 34
Napeer (see also Napier)
Edmand 16
Napier (see also Napeer)
Edmand 16
Nartin, Lanija 58
Nash, Amanda 28
Elizabeth 8, 12
Henry 36
Manda 26
Melkijah V. 85
Wm. 26
Neal, Bartholomew 53
Isaac 63
Joseph 40
Kisiah 80
Needham, George B. 12
Neil, Edney I. 21
Ellerlley (?) 30
Malinda 42
Mary Ann 4
Royal 14
Sarah 13
William 7
Nelson, Abraham 89
C. A. 56
Delila 53
Enoch 52
John 26
Rena 53
Susan 54
William 55
Nettles, Elizabeth 82
Newman, John 48
Sarah 65, 71
Newport, Dualla 54
Nicely, David 34
Melvina 5
Nicholson, Frances 80
Riley 80
Speed 62, 69
Nickleson, Ester 64, 70
Fleming 62, 69
Nicks, Joseph D. 77
Nighbert, Hugh 3
Nix, John 63, 69
Joseph 61, 67
Sarah Ann 89
No (?), Susan 21
Noel, Adalade B. 37
None, Harry 49
Norris, Agness 15
Obadiah 5
Reubin 23
Sarah 73
Norton, James W. 35
Minerva J. 87
William H. 34
Norvell, Margret R. 41, 43

Norvell (cont.)
Rebecco J. 17
William 43
Nove (?), L. T. 23
Nuckels, John 13
Num (?), Silvester (?) 24
Nunn, Abner 3
Bartheny 12
Delpha 27
Elisha 2
(?), Emaley 27
Nunn, Flurrender 9
Fruatan 34
Harry 35
Louisa 2
Lugana 35
M. B. 24, 38
Russell 9
Silvester 24
Sterling 36, 42, 44
Vineny 12
William 27
Oaks, Ann 50
Elender (?) 22
Isaac 83
Mary 25
William 48
Odell, E. J. 33
Oliver, Eliza 36
Oneil, Polley Ann 22
Orick, John 75
Osborn (?), James H. 21
Ousley, George 49
Spencer 40
Overton, M. 25
Matilda 32
Milbern 28
Wm. L. 8
Owens, Archable 19
Armelda 92
Elisabeth (?) 19
H. (Dr.) 41
Harriet 62, 69
Jane 49
John 29, 32
Jourdon 76
Julyan 77
Lilly J. 39
Louisa 31
Lucinda 34
Martha 24
Mary 16
Nancy 39
Peter 40
Rodden F. 34
Roman 33
William 19
Wm. 16
Owin, Ruthy 18
Owsley, Charity 2
John 19
Mary 16
Wm. 21
Page, Susan 49
Pain, Joannes (?) 15
Palina, Ann 58
Pall, Jane 1
Palmer, Jesse Green 14
Parker, A. I. (?) W. 28
Elias 48, 86
Elisabeth 90
Esther 80
James 47
John B. 24
(?), Louisa 27
Lucy 64, 71
Mary 11
Nancy 24

Parker (cont.)
Robert 60, 66
William 34
Parkey, Barbary 8
Elisabeth S. 28
Rebecco 15
Thos. 34
William 25
Parks, Louisa 34
Simpson 25
Parrat (?), Wm. 20
Parratt, Judy (?) 25
Parrot, Joel 52
Parrott, Joel 49
Mourning 28
Wesley 19
Partan, Calvin 11
Parten, James 18
Parton, Emelia 3
Jane 77
Mary 21
Shelton 81
Patison, Nancy 72
Patsy, Susannah 80
Patterson, Nicholson 77
Polly 77
Patton, J. A. 85
Paul, James 55
(?), Susan 8
Paulson, Polly 57
Sarah 63
Paulston, Elias 59, 65
Payne, Wm. G. 23
Peace (?), Banajah 4
(?), Simon (?) 4
Pearce, Martha 61, 67
Pearce, Mary 62, 69
Pearson, Catharin 13
Pebley, Nancy 73
Rebecca 79
Pebly, Mary J. 87
Tempy 89
Peck, Nancy 35
Sarah A. 38
Pelkington, Joseph A. 60,
66
Penberton, David 73
Pendleton, Jane 52
Wilborn 39
Penington, Lydia 49
Pennington, Fielding 52
William 49
Perkey, James 23
Perkins, (Squire) 89
Cynthia 90
Eliza 72
Elizabeth 62, 68, 88,
89
Elizabeth L. 51
F. 4
Hiram 80
James 62, 68
Nancy 57, 88
Peter 73
Solomon 79
Thomas 65, 71
William 72
Perry, O. H. 79
Person, Emaley 29
Pleasant H. 36
Sterling 40
Peters, George Smith 51
Wm. 64
Peterson, A. J. 84
John 76
Jos. 60
Lavina J. 51
Mary 89

Riggs (cont.)
  James 61, 68, 89
  Nancy 76
  Vinsen 63, 69
  William 87
Right, Eliza 83
  Elisabeth 10
  Greenberry 9
  Pharoh M. 48
Riley, C. 25
Risterson, James 54
Ritchie, James 8
Rite, Thomas 39
  William M. 38
Ritter, Catharine 27
  Charlotta 26
  Elisabeth M. 33
  Elmira 7
  Hanner 22
  John 5
  (?), Orlina (?) 7
  Polly 30
  Sary Ann 29
  William 28
Roach, Jane 81
  John 75
  Manuel 77
  Rebecca 91
Roark, Eliza Jane 44
  Elizabeth 2
  Louisa 37
Roarks, John 26
  (?), Sintha 23
  Timothy 8
Robbins, John 79
  Wm. 88
Roberson, Daniel 16
Roberts, Lydia 82
  Martha 32
  Nicholas M. 36
Robertson, Allen 11
  M. C. 81
Robins, Elisabeth 74
Robinson, Dally 56
  Eliza 11
  Emily 77
  Ezekiel 40
  James 5
  John 6, 33
  Labitha 1
  Polly 86
  Rebecca 4
  Thomas 10
  Viatt J. 6
  Wm. 6
  Woobery 40
Roe, Nancy 73
Rogers, Camadore 37
  Canada 28
  Caroline M. 22
  Cornelius 22
  David 62, 68
  Dicey M. 30
  (?), E. 23
  Emily B. 36
  F. H. 24
  George Washington 59, 66
  Henderson 35
  Hugh L. W. 16
  James A. 87
  James K. 12
  M. M. 28
  Martha L. 33
  Patrick H. 71
  Rachael 87
  (?), Rebecca 6
  William 3
  Wm. 4

Rogers (cont.)
  Wm. J. 48
  Wm. M. 8
Roland, Louisa 44
Roley, Vincen 19
Rolin, Elizabeth 43
  Rachal 28
Rollings, Catharine 85
  Nancy C. 84
Rollins, John 83
  Mary 32
Romine, John 78
Romines, William 6
Rookard, Fanny 81
Root, Olive 11
Rosan (?), Asa 37
  James 36
Rossan (?), Joshua 17
  (?), Mary 12
Rose, Dilly 84
  Emily 32
  Jackson 49
  Jane 88
  Jefferson 12
  Mary 75
  Sarah 56
  William 77
  Zephy 77
Ross, John S. 87
  Martha 74
  Robert 52
  Sephrony 82
Rotton, Eli 50
Row, Calvin 86
  Matilda 83
Rowark, Polly Ann 16
Rowatt (?), Morris P. (?)
  16
Rowe, Elizabeth 7
  Washington 7
  Wiley 29
Rowland, Creed 13
  Ruthy S. 18
Rowlett, M. S. E. 6
  Macknep 2
Rownines, Allen 81
Ruckers, James 88
Ruha (?), Robert 26
Runnalds, Winney 7
Runnels, Elizabeth 48
Runnions, Martha J. 33
Runnyans, Charles W. 5
Runolds (?), Ann 9
Russel, A. S. 21
Russell, Elizabeth 6
  James L. 24
  Josiah 5
  Nancy 36
  Serena 25
Ruth, Gabriel 49
Rutherford, Alexander 86
  James 85
  Silas 90
  Wm. 9
Rutledge, Caleb W. 16
  Nancy 42
  William 6
Ryan, Ann 76
  Joel 61, 67
  Martin B. 79
  Melinda 79
  Sarah 56
  William 51
Salvage, Elizabeth 70
Salyers, Rachel 41
Sanders, Angelina 36
  David 43
  Hamelton 43

Sanders (cont.)
  Isaac 92
  Jno. 3
  Lavina 6
  Lurinda 36
  Luritta 20
  Nancy 79
  Rawsy (?) 6
  Robert 18
  William 56
Sarton, Rebecca 78
Sattle, Jno. N. 67
Savage, A. J. 86
Sawyers, Ambrose 35
  John M. 37
  Mary J. 35
  Samuel 89
  Susan 89
  Thos. L. 5
Sceans, Emily 80
Scelf (?), Matilda 41
Scivofield (?), Clarkis
  14
Scofield (?), M. A. 20
Scott, Dosha 29
  John 35
  Nathaniel M. 24
Scritchfield, Anna 85
Seabolt, Jacob 49
  Martha 43
Seafield (?), Jesse 26
Seal, Elizabeth 11
Seals, Annice 32
  Mahala 42
  Manervy 14
  Marshal 44
  Patsy 25
  Peggy 6
Seaver, Elitra 75
Sebolt, Alby (?) 30
Semmonds, Lavina 6
Sensabagh, John L. 31
Sequin, Aoral 75
Sergeant, J. J. 92
Sevier, Samuel 77
Sewell, Ann Jane 38
Sexton, Calvin 88
  Lanner 47
  Marica 86
  Mary 39
  William 4
Shadonias (see also
  Chadoins)
  Andrew 73
Shadowenm Sarah 59, 65
Shanon (?), Wm. 20
Sharp, Aaron 89
  Ambros 33
  Ann 84
  Catharin L. 24
  Catherine 50
  Colson 72
  D. M. 57
  Eliza 72
  Esaw 11
  Fany 59, 65
  George W. 83
  H. M. 42
  Henry 2, 40, 54, 86
  Isham 57
  Jacob 8
  James 72
  Jane 73
  Jonathan 25
  Larkin D. 31
  Leta 41
  Levi 7
  Louisa 6, 79

Sharp (cont.)
   Martha 73, 74
   Martha C. 88
   Mary 14, 24, 52
   Mathew 40
   Matilda 85
   Nancy 20, 48, 75, 90
   Neely 8, 29
   Permelia 31
   Polly 76, 84
   Polly Ann 29
   Sally 74
   Sarah 14, 18
   Tansey 59, 65
   Thomas 75
   Tilmond 74
   William H. 85
   William K. 39
   Wm. D. 71
   Wm. H. 22
Shaufer, Berry 88
Sheans, James M. 57
Sheckels (?), Nancy 20
Shelby, John 20
   Samuel 59, 65
   Sarah 23, 88
   Susannah 17
Shelly, James 32
   Nathan 61, 68
Shelton, E. 51
   Eli 30, 92
   Susannah 79
   Teney 33
Shelvy (?), Isaac 30
Shepherd, Benjamin 89
   Emily 77
Sherac (?), Mary Ann 40
Sherman, Thompson 17
Shields, James T. 34
Shishen, John M. T. 35
Shoemaker, Mary 18
Shofner, Elizabeth 33
   Sally 38
Shofny, Margret 26
Shomate, Bales 42
   Carr 51
   John W. 26
   (?), L. B. 26
   Menervy J. 29
   (?), Nancy L. 23
Shoopman, R. 50
Short, Greenberry 12
Shown, Wm. C. 81
Shultz, Elisabeth M. 25
   Martin V. 44
Shumake, Cornelia 72
Shumate, Ann 1
   Eliza 12
   William 58
Shumtate, Sampson 53
Sigo, William 56
Siler, Alvis 84
   Benjamin 77, 78
   Elisha 83
   Jacob 77
   Jno. 62, 69
   John M. 74
   Joseph 80
   Lucinda 54
   Margaret 55
   Marilda 81
   Matilda 83
   Nancy 61, 67, 83
   Sarah 87
   Silattia 88
   Wilena 49
Simmons, Enoch C. 32
   James 23

Simmons (cont.)
   John 36
   Wesley 39
   Winny 10
Simpkins, William 55
Sims, Elizabeth 21
Singleton, James 32
   Jeremiah 3
   Mary A. 31
   Richard 7
Skaggs, Susan 40
Skeen, James R. 92
Skiliner, Ann 77
Skinner, Malinda 82
Skoans, Sarah 62, 69
Slatten (?), Polly 4
Slatton, John 23
   Milly 88
Slaven (?), Ony (?) 11
   Rebecca 78
Slone, James 24
Slotton, Ally 12
Smiddy, Calvin 62, 69
   Elizabeth 84
   Isaac 51
   James 84
   Reubin 62, 68
Smiley, Jacob 18
Smith, (?) 33
   A. D. 56
   Andrew 87
   Andrew B. 31
   Arch. 89
   Berrill (?) 29
   Caswell 83
   Catharin 17
   Catharine 64, 70, 87
   Catherine 58
   Cintha 2
   Constatin (?) 30
   David 72
   Diecy M. 61, 67
   E. 71
   Edward 51
   Eleana (?) 20
   Eliza 59, 65
   Elizabeth 52, 55, 60,
     61, 63, 66, 68, 69,
     82, 85
   Emaline 13
   Ewel 77
   F. E. 76
   Fanny 16
   Franklin M. 11
   Frederick 72
   G. W. 3, 64, 70
   George 80
   Hannah 80
   Harvey 20
   J. E. 92
   J. W. 36
   James 73
   James A. 28
   Jane 51, 53
   Jesse 50
   Jirriael (?) 17
   John 54, 58, 77, 78
   John E. 91
   Joseph 53
   Joseph M. 88
   Josiah 82
   Judy Ann 86
   Julia Ann 64, 70
   Lety 39
   Levi 47
   Love 84
   Mahaly 91
   Manervy 14

Smith (cont.)
   Manirvy (?) 3
   Margaret 7, 88
   Martha 53
   Mary 35, 56, 83, 87
   Mary A. 13
   Mary Ann 55
   Mary Jane 84
   Milly Ann 86
   Moses 37
   Nancy 64, 70, 77, 80,
     86
   Pascal 56
   Polley 49, 58
   Polly 7, 8, 72
   Rachael 9
   Ransom 52
   Rebecca 88, 89
   Richard 47, 49
   Rider 77
   Robt. H. 79
   Rufus K. 86
   Sally 53
   Samuel 87
   Sarah 27, 57, 75
   Sterlin 83
   Sterling 86
   Thomas 85
   Timpa (?) 16
   William 85
   William H. 81
   Wm. 61, 67
Snavely, James 23
   Jonas 43
   Rachel 17
   Sophia 8
Snodderly, Anna 72
   John 72
   Polly 75
Snotherly, Elizabeth 76
Snow, Nancy 30
Snuffer, Charity 18
   Elizabeth 7
Snyder, Minerva S. 90
Soaps, Minerva 85
   Nancy 73
Solomon, Ibba 82
   Wm. 82
Southerland, Joel 11
Southern, Garrett 43
   Isaac 16
   Joseph 40
   Loucy 7
   Mary 9
   Nancy 4
   Robert 38
   Sarah 9
   Stephen 5
Sowder, Cathrine 40
   Daniel F. 29
   Elizabeth 2, 34
   Henry M. 32
   Jacob 34
   Michael 16
   Peruda 37
   Richd. 7
   Wm. 26
Sowders, Nancy 48
Sparks, Pheobe 34
   Preston 37
Speer (?), Arthur 11
Spiers, Elejiceia (?) 22
Spillars, Daniel 42
Spillers, James 31
Spradling, William 44
Sproles, John 17
Spurlock, Nancy 44
Stahdsbery, William A. 27

Turnbull (cont.)
  Nancy (?) 19
Turner, Elihu 79, 82
  James 74
  Joel 24
  P. B. 81
  Valentine 61, 67
Turpin, Samuel B. 78
Tussey (?), Amanda J. 17
Tuttle, Peter 55
Tye, Lucinda 90
  Margaret 50
  Nancy 90
Upton, Nancy J. 43
  Wm. 38
Valentine, Henry 75
Vanbebber, A. 34
  Eliza 43
  Isaac 5
  James 7
  John M. 14
  Marlena 15
  Martha 21
Vanbedder, Nancy Malinda 28
Vance, Agga 3
  Pricila 24
  Prior L. 41
Vancy, Permdy 1
Vandergriff, Winney 40
Vanderpoll, Catherine 62
Vanderpool, Catherine 68
  John 14, 63, 69, 75
  Samuel 78
  Sarah 38
  Telitha 40
Vandevarter (?), Larkan 11
Vane, Sarah 19
Vania, Wadrick 87
Vannoy, Timanda 74
  William L. 33
Vanoy, Mary 7
Vatch, Lucy 84
Vaughn, Martha Jane 38
  Susan 30
Veatch, Philip 12
Venable, Elender 40
  James 27
  Mary 31
  Wm. 25
Venany (?), Jeel 21
Vennoy, Angeline 36
Venoy, Levinda 33
  Lucy S. 40
  William L. 40
Vermillion, Elisabeth 34
Vigger (?), Rhoda Burnt 4
Vines, Sarah 56
Vinsant, James 63
Vinzant, Daniel 49
  Henry L. 74
  James 69
  Lemuel P. 84
Wadkins, Joseph 1
Wagby (?), John 43
Waggoner (?), William (?)
    13
Waisman, J. A. 85
Walden, Delila 81
  Elizabeth 49
  Evin 90
  James 88
  Jarilda 64, 70
  Martha 84
  Mellvill 84
  Nancy 89
  William 78
Walker, A. E. 83
  A. H. 88

Walker (cont.)
  Absolum 77
  Celia 87
  Elizabeth 90
  Eveline 75
  Henry 5
  Isaac 34
  Jacob 28
  James 38
  John W. 43
  Jonathan T. (?) 17
  Louise 57
  Malinda 32
  Martha A. 34
  Mary 84
  Minerva J. 77
  Samuel 34
  Sarah 12, 47, 80
  Sarah Ann 91
  Thomas B. 12
  William 77
Wallace, George
    Washington 9
Wallen, China 20
Waller, Ellender 18
  James 17
Wallera (?), Isaac 20
Wallin, John 15
Wallis, Thomas 36
  Wm. H. 19
Wallon, E. V. 29
Walton, G. W. 87
Wamies (?), Mary 27
Wanocott, Emily J. 15
Ward, Amanda M. L. 17
  Elisabeth 34
  Judia 88
  Letty 13
  Mary J. 75
  Rachel 55
Warfield, Henry 74
Warick, Henry 31
Warnacutt, Letta 35
Warnicutt, William 13
Warrin (?), Thomas 20
Waters, C. 47
  Champ 59, 66
  Melinda 81
  Samuel 82
Watson, William 49
Weaver, A. P. 89
  Aleey 89
  Malinda 88
Webb, Elizabeth 33
  George 91
  Iredele 8
  Larkin 4
  Milly 29
  Polly 3
Weever (?), Sarah 27
Weir, Margaret 16
  Matilda (?) 7
  Polly 13
Welbourn, Claborne 6
Welch, J. M. 26
  John H. 7
  Martha 1
  Mary 2
  Polly 43
  S. 26
  Sarah 37
  William 5, 14
Wells, Eliza 23
  Elizabeth 36
  Wm. 59, 65
Wereman (?), Hiram C. 18
Wesley, Solomon (?) 40
West, Chesley 8

West (cont.)
  James H. 64, 71
  Joseph Anderson 33
  (?), Mastin (?) H. 26
  Winney 75
Western, Polly 29
Wetherford, David 27
Wheeler, Ann Eliza 81
  Henry 54
  Penelope 87
  Thomas J. 6
Wheelus, Wm. 4
Whicker (?), Zachariah 38
Whitaker, Emily L. 41
  Malinda 86
  Nancy N. 33
  Timothy 9
White, Anna 20
  Elizabeth 16
  Hugh G. 44
  Isaac 73
  John 33
  John M. 28
  Lee (?) 12
  Malvina 31
  Mary 28
  (?), S. (?) 15
  Wm. 10
Whiteaker, Mary 15
  Matthew 15
  Melvina 15
Whitecar, Elizabeth 14
Whited (?), Cementha 5
Whiteted, William 35
  (?), Wm. 12
Whitman, Kesiah 53
Wien (?), Nancey (?) 37
Wier, Rebecca 73
Wilbern, William 14
Wilborne, Dicey 23
  Henry 44
  William 27
Wilbourne, Martha 43
Wilburn (?), Susanah 18
Wild, John 86
Wiles, Lear 48
Wiley, Sarah Ann 49
Wilhite, Ben 64, 70
  Jesse 74
  Lucretia 89
  Martha 71
  Orlena 63, 70
  Polly 47
  S. D. 82
  Sarah 48
  Starn 59, 65
  Tabitha 89
Willhite, Ezekiel 88
Williams, Alfred 87
  Andrew 27
  David 35
  Elgina 48
  Elizabet (?) 9
  Gowel 55
  Honer 33
  James 25, 71
  Lena 62, 68
  Mary Ann 6
  Mary E. 12
  Nancy 12
  Polly 6, 8
  Rachael 3
  Russell 48
  Sarah 6, 20, 92
  Silas 14, 58
  William 23, 74, 78
  Wm. H. 54
Williamson, Albert 54

111

Williamson (cont.)
  Charles 83
  Charlie 47
  Morgan 51
  Sally 74
Willis, David 48
  E. D. 21
  Elizabeth 43
  Flemon 40
  Levisa (?) 14
  *Louisa Marie* 37
  Mary 10
  Milley 13
  Nancy 29
  Patrick 24
  Polly 28
  Thersa Ann 39
  (?), William C. 10
Willoby, John 62, 68
Willoughby, Joseph 76
Wills, Martha 20
Willson, (?) 20
  John E. 80
  Norciss 18
  Owen 27
Wilson, Andrew 80
  C. 89
  C. C. 90
  Catharin 9
  Ceny 91
  Cristiniy (?) 10
  Daniel E. 82
  Dolly 56
  Edward 55, 57
  Elisabeth 38
  Elizabeth 51
  Emily 18, 47
  Flora 76
  George W. 41
  Hamilton 83
  Henry 66
  *Henry S.* 78
  James 51, 85
  Jesse 75
  John 74, 90
  Jones 55
  Joshua 56
  Lewis 54
  Lorancy 48
  Lorany 86
  Mahaly 79
  Malilda 84
  Manda 72
  Mariah 64, 71
  Mary 48, 61, 67
  Mary Ann 49
  Melissa 80
  Nancy 63, 69
  Rachel S. 22
  Sampson 90
  Shampson 47
  T. N. 31
  Thompson 80
  William 54, 64, 71
  Wm. 6
Winegar (?), David 17
Winn, E. 26
*Winter (?), Jefferson* 5
Winton, J. C. 91
Wircick, Margret 32
Wirich, Catharine 5
Wise, Washington 49
Withers, Bushood 71
Witt, Edmund 63, 70
  G. W. 84
  John 75, 88
Woattan (?), Nancy 16
Wolfenbarger, E. 24

Wolfenbarger (cont.)
  Peter 44
Wolfingbargor, Jacob 23
Woodall, Bluford (?) 21
Woodard, Alexander 10
  Ledia 30
  Louisa 89
Woods, Henry 61, 67
  Jas. 26
  John 22, 84
  Margaret 55
  Martha 55
  Nathaniel 86
  Pleasant W. 76
  Sarah 89
  *Silas D.* 8
Woodson, Elizabeth Jane 34
  John 34
  Morgan J. 39
  Robert C. 39
  Sarah 32
  Wm. 61
Woodward, Calvin C. 12
  Nancy 41
  Wm. 67
Woolven, Lelitha 10
Woord, Lucinda 56
Woosley, Sarah 47
Word, George R. 33
Worley, Margaret 12
Worrick, Elizabeth Ann 14
Wright, Cenia 60, 66
  David 89
  Judy Ann 7
  Wm. 84
Write, Nancy 19
Wyatt, John 13
  Josiah 38
  Milton 59, 66
  William 28
Yaden, Benjamin A. 14
  *Rebecco* 14
Yancy (see also Yauncy)
  Elisabeth (?) 24
  Elizabeth 63, 70
Yauncy (see also Yancy)
  Elisabeth (?) 24
Year (?), Martha (?) 23
Yearry, Mary 17
Yeary, James W. 3
Yoakum, Ewing 21
  William W. 44
York, Amelia 38
  Catharine 88
  Joseph 55
  Nancy 90
  Thomas 59, 65
  William 64, 71
Young, B. F. 15
  Jane 71
  Nancy 73
  Thomas 90
  Vicey 52
  William 5
Zachary, Mary Ann 48
Zeck, Elisa 3
Zicks, Cathrine 34
  Thos. 37

www.ingramcontent.com/pod-product-compliance
Lightning Source LLC
Chambersburg PA
CBHW071136280326
41935CB00010B/1255